Skin Health Information for Teens

Second Edition

TEEN HEALTH SERIES

Second Edition

Skin Health Information for Teens

Health Tips about Dermatological Concerns and Skin Cancer Risks

Including Facts about Acne, Warts, Allergies, and Other Conditions and Lifestyle Choices, Such as Tanning, Tattooing, and Piercing, That Affect the Skin, Nails, Scalp, and Hair

◆

Edited by Kim Wohlenhaus

Omnigraphics

P.O. Box 31-1640, Detroit, MI 48231

Bibliographic Note

Because this page cannot legibly accommodate all the copyright notices, the Bibliographic Note portion of the Preface constitutes an extension of the copyright notice.

Edited by Kim Wohlenhaus

Teen Health Series

Karen Bellenir, *Managing Editor*
David A. Cooke, M.D., *Medical Consultant*
Elizabeth Collins, *Research and Permissions Coordinator*
Cherry Edwards, *Permissions Assistant*
EdIndex, Services for Publishers, *Indexers*

* * *

Omnigraphics, Inc.

Matthew P. Barbour, *Senior Vice President*
Kevin M. Hayes, *Operations Manager*

* * *

Peter E. Ruffner, *Publisher*

Copyright © 2009 Omnigraphics, Inc.

ISBN 978-0-7808-1042-6

Library of Congress Cataloging-in-Publication Data

Skin health information for teens : health tips about dermatological concerns and skin cancer risks including facts about acne, warts, allergies, and other conditions and lifestyle choices, such as tanning, tattooing, and piercing, that affect the skin, nails, scalp, and hair / edited by Kim Wohlenhaus. -- 2nd ed.
   p. cm.
Includes bibliographical references and index.
  Summary: "Provides basic consumer health information for teens about care of the skin, nails, scalp, and hair, along with facts about related conditions and skin cancer prevention. Includes index, resource information and recommendations for further reading"-- Provided by publisher.
  ISBN 978-0-7808-1042-6 (hardcover : alk. paper) 1. Teenagers--Health and hygiene. 2. Skin--Care and hygiene. 3. Beauty, Personal. I. Wohlenhaus, Kim.
  RA777.S546 2009
  646.7'208352--dc22

2009022833

Table of Contents

Part Three: Acne

Part Four: Understanding And Preventing Skin Cancer

Part Five: Other Diseases And Conditions That Affect The Skin And Scalp

Part Six: Caring For Injuries To The Skin

Part Seven: If You Need More Information

Preface

About This Book

The skin is the body's biggest and most visible organ. It serves as a first-line of defense against microorganisms, and it provides a sensory interface between the body and the environment. Teens often turn it into a canvas for self-expression, modifying its appearance with cosmetics, tanning, piercing, and tattooing. Because it is so exposed and manipulated, however, the skin is also susceptible to a host of injuries, infections, irritations, and even life-threatening cancers. In addition, because it is so visible, problems that affect the skin's appearance can lead to embarrassment and emotional turmoil.

Skin Health Information for Teens, Second Edition provides updated information about the skin, hair, and nails. It explains how the skin and its related structures grow and how to keep them healthy. Common ailments, including acne, eczema, impetigo, psoriasis, vitiligo, and warts are explained, and a section on skin cancer provides information about cancer risks, prevention strategies, warning signs, and treatments. The care of skin injuries, including cuts, scrapes, burns, bites, and stings, is also discussed, and the book concludes with suggestions for further reading and a directory of additional resources.

How To Use This Book

This book is divided into parts and chapters. Parts focus on broad areas of interest; chapters are devoted to single topics within a part.

Part One: Skin Basics provides information about skin anatomy and the ways hereditary and hormonal factors can affect the skin's appearance. It explains why some people's skin develops brown spots, freckles, or birthmarks, and it discusses other concerns related to how the skin looks, including stretch marks and scars.

Part Two: Caring For Skin, Hair, And Nails describes hygiene and lifestyle choices that affect the skin and its ability to function properly. It discusses the use of skin care products and cosmetic procedures, and it offers safety guidelines for teens who are considering piercings or tattoos. Chapters that talk about hair and nail concerns are also included.

Part Three: Acne looks at the biological processes that lead to the development of acne and account for its widespread occurrence during the teen years. It describes over-the-counter and prescription medications and discusses options for treating acne scars, including dermabrasion and chemical peels.

Part Four: Understanding And Preventing Skin Cancer explains the development, symptoms, diagnosis, and treatments for the most common types of skin cancer, including basal cell carcinoma and melanoma. Although skin cancer often does not appear during the teen years, it is estimated that between 50% and 80% of the damage that leads to such cancers occurs during childhood and adolescence as a result of intermittent, unprotected sun exposure. This part includes chapters that explain how to protect the skin for lifelong well being.

Part Five: Other Diseases And Conditions That Affect The Skin And Scalp describes common viral, bacterial, fungal, allergic, and inherited diseases and conditions that may affect the skin. These include cellulitis, eczema, fever blisters and cold sores, psoriasis, rosacea, scabies, scleroderma, swimmer's itch, athlete's foot, jock itch, vitiligo, warts, head lice, and others.

Part Six: Caring For Injuries To The Skin discusses prevention, first aid, and treatment for cuts, scrapes, bruises, corns, calluses, burns, stings, and bites. Special concerns related to diseases that can be transmitted through bites from ticks and mosquitoes are also addressed.

Part Seven: If You Need More Information includes suggestions for further reading about skin-related topics and a directory of additional resources.

Bibliographic Note

This volume contains documents and excerpts from publications issued by the following government agencies: Centers for Disease Control and Prevention; Genetics Home Reference, a service of the U.S. National Library of Medicine; National Cancer Institute; National Institute of Allergy and Infectious Diseases; National Institute of Arthritis and Musculoskeletal and Skin Diseases; National Institute of Dental and Craniofacial Research; and the U.S. Food and Drug Administration.

In addition, this volume contains copyrighted documents and articles produced by the following organizations: A.D.A.M., Inc.; American Academy of Dermatology; American Academy of Facial Plastic and Reconstructive Surgery; American Academy of Family Physicians; American College of Foot and Ankle Orthopedics and Medicine; Cleveland Clinic Foundation; International Hyperhidrosis Society; Louisiana State University School of Veterinary Medicine; Merck & Co., Inc.; National Psoriasis Foundation; Nemours Foundation; New Zealand Dermatological Society; Palo Alto Medical Foundation; Self Care Decisions, LLC; Smith & Nephew; and the Wisconsin Department of Health and Family Services.

The photograph on the front cover is from Creatas Images via Jupiter Images.

Full citation information is provided on the first page of each chapter. Every effort has been made to secure all necessary rights to reprint the copyrighted material. If any omissions have been made, please contact Omnigraphics to make corrections for future editions.

Acknowledgements

In addition to the organizations listed above, special thanks are due to the *Teen Health Series* research and permissions coordinator, Elizabeth Collins, and to its managing editor, Karen Bellenir.

About the *Teen Health Series*

At the request of librarians serving today's young adults, the *Teen Health Series* was developed as a specially focused set of volumes within Omnigraphics'

Health Reference Series. Each volume deals comprehensively with a topic selected according to the needs and interests of people in middle school and high school.

Teens seeking preventive guidance, information about disease warning signs, medical statistics, and risk factors for health problems will find answers to their questions in the *Teen Health Series*. The *Series*, however, is not intended to serve as a tool for diagnosing illness, in prescribing treatments, or as a substitute for the physician/patient relationship. All people concerned about medical symptoms or the possibility of disease are encouraged to seek professional care from an appropriate health care provider.

If there is a topic you would like to see addressed in a future volume of the *Teen Health Series*, please write to:

Editor
Teen Health Series
Omnigraphics, Inc.
P.O. Box 31-1640
Detroit, MI 48231

A Note about Spelling and Style

Teen Health Series editors use *Stedman's Medical Dictionary* as an authority for questions related to the spelling of medical terms and the *Chicago Manual of Style* for questions related to grammatical structures, punctuation, and other editorial concerns. Consistent adherence is not always possible, however, because the individual volumes within the *Series* include many documents from a wide variety of different producers and copyright holders, and the editor's primary goal is to present material from each source as accurately as is possible following the terms specified by each document's producer. This sometimes means that information in different chapters or sections may follow other guidelines and alternate spelling authorities. For example, occasionally a copyright holder may require that eponymous terms be shown in possessive forms (Crohn's disease *vs.* Crohn disease) or that British spelling norms be retained (leukaemia *vs.* leukemia).

Locating Information within the *Teen Health Series*

The *Teen Health Series* contains a wealth of information about a wide variety of medical topics. As the *Series* continues to grow in size and scope, locating the precise information needed by a specific student may become more challenging. To address this concern, information about books within the *Teen Health Series* is included in *A Contents Guide to the Health Reference Series*. The *Contents Guide* presents an extensive list of more than 15,000 diseases, treatments, and other topics of general interest compiled from the Tables of Contents and major index headings from the books of the *Teen Health Series* and *Health Reference Series*. To access *A Contents Guide to the Health Reference Series*, visit www.healthreferenceseries.com.

Our Advisory Board

We would like to thank the following advisory board members for providing guidance to the development of this *Series*:

Dr. Lynda Baker, Associate Professor of Library and Information Science, Wayne State University, Detroit, MI

Nancy Bulgarelli, William Beaumont Hospital Library, Royal Oak, MI

Karen Imarisio, Bloomfield Township Public Library, Bloomfield Township, MI

Karen Morgan, Mardigian Library, University of Michigan-Dearborn, Dearborn, MI

Rosemary Orlando, St. Clair Shores Public Library, St. Clair Shores, MI

Medical Consultant

Medical consultation services are provided to the *Teen Health Series* editors by David A. Cooke, M.D. Dr. Cooke is a graduate of Brandeis University, and he received his M.D. degree from the University of Michigan. He completed residency training at the University of Wisconsin Hospital and Clinics. He is board-certified in internal medicine. Dr. Cooke currently works as part of the University of Michigan Health System and practices in Ann Arbor, MI. In his free time, he enjoys writing, science fiction, and spending time with his family.

Part One
Skin Basics

Chapter 1

What Is Skin?

Quick! What's the biggest organ in your body?

You might be surprised to find out it's the skin, which you might not think of as an organ. No matter how you think of it, your skin is very important. It covers and protects everything inside your body. Without skin, people's muscles, bones, and organs would be hanging out all over the place. Skin holds everything together. It also:

- protects our bodies;

- helps keep our bodies at just the right temperature;

- allows us to have the sense of touch.

Don't Miss Your Epidermis

The skin is made up of three layers, each with its own important parts. The layer on the outside is called the epidermis (say: eh-pih-dur-mis). The epidermis is the part of your skin you can see.

About This Chapter: Text in this chapter is from "Your Skin," March 2007, reprinted with permission from www.kidshealth.org. Copyright © 2007 The Nemours Foundation. This information was provided by KidsHealth, one of the largest resources online for medically reviewed health information written for parents, kids, and teens. For more articles like this one, visit www.KidsHealth.org, or www.TeensHealth.org.

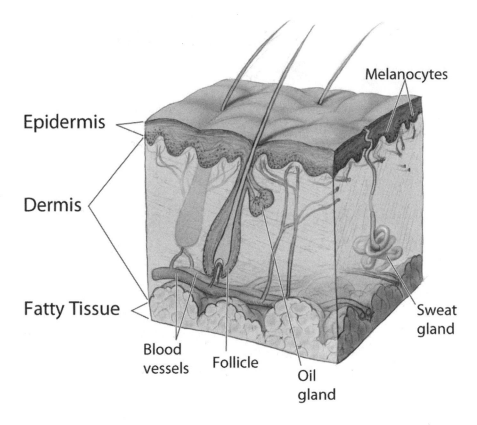

Figure 1.1. The basic structure of the skin (Source: National Cancer Institute, VisualsOnline: "Anatomy: The Skin," 2005).

Look down at your hands for a minute. Even though you can't see anything happening, your epidermis is hard at work. At the bottom of the epidermis, new skin cells are forming.

When the cells are ready, they start moving toward the top of your epidermis. This trip takes about two weeks to a month. As newer cells continue to move up, older cells near the top die and rise to the surface of your skin. What you see on your hands (and everywhere else on your body) are really dead skin cells.

These old cells are tough and strong, just right for covering your body and protecting it. But they only stick around for a little while. Soon, they'll flake off. Though you can't see it happening, every minute of the day we lose about 30,000 to 40,000 dead skin cells off the surface of our skin.

So just in the time it took you to read this far, you've probably lost about 40,000 cells. That's almost nine pounds (four kilograms) of cells every year. But don't think your skin might wear out someday. Your epidermis is always making new skin cells that rise to the top to replace the old ones. Most of the cells in your epidermis (95 percent) work to make new skin cells.

And what about the other 5 percent? They make a substance called melanin (say: mel-uh-nun). Melanin gives skin its color. The darker your skin is, the more melanin you have. When you go out into the sun, these cells make extra melanin to protect you from getting burned by the sun's ultraviolet, or UV, rays.

That's why your skin gets tan if you spend a lot of time in the sun. But even though melanin is mighty, it can't shield you all by itself. You'll want to wear sunscreen and protective clothing, such as a hat, to prevent painful sunburns. Protecting your skin now also can help prevent skin cancer when you get older.

The Dermis Is Under The Epidermis

The next layer down is the dermis (say: dur-mis). You can't see your dermis because it's hidden under your epidermis. The dermis contains nerve endings, blood vessels, oil glands, and sweat glands. It also contains collagen and elastin, which are tough and stretchy.

The nerve endings in your dermis tell you how things feel when you touch them. They work with your brain and nervous system, so that your brain gets the message about what you're touching. Is it the soft fur of a cat or the rough surface of your skateboard?

Sometimes what you feel is dangerous, so the nerve endings work with your muscles to keep you from getting hurt. If you touch something hot, the nerve endings in your dermis respond right away: "Ouch! That's hot!" The nerves quickly send this message to the brain or spinal cord, which then immediately commands the muscles to take your hand away. This all happens in a split second, without you ever thinking about it.

Your dermis is also full of tiny blood vessels. These keep your skin cells healthy by bringing them the oxygen and nutrients they need and by taking away waste. These blood vessels are hard to see in kids, but you might get a better look if you check out your grandparents' skin. As the dermis gets older, it gets thinner and easier to see through.

The dermis is home to the oil glands, too. These are also called sebaceous (say: sih-bay-shus) glands, and they are always producing sebum (say: see-bum). Sebum is your skin's own natural oil. It rises to the surface of your epidermis to keep your skin lubricated and protected. It also makes your skin waterproof—as long as sebum's on the scene, your skin won't absorb water and get soggy.

You also have sweat glands on your epidermis. Even though you can't feel it, you actually sweat a tiny bit all the time. The sweat comes up through pores (say: pors), tiny holes in the skin that allow it to escape. When the sebum meets the sweat, they form a protective film that's a bit sticky.

An easy way to see this film in action is to pick up a pin with your fingers. Then wash your hands well with soap and water and dry them off completely. Now try to pick up that pin again. It won't be so easy because your sticky layer is gone. Don't worry—it will be back soon, as your sebaceous and sweat glands create more sticky stuff.

✎ What's It Mean?

Dermis: The layer under the epidermis that contains nerve endings, blood vessels, oil glands, and sweat glands. It also contains collagen and elastin, which are tough and stretchy.

Epidermis: The part of your skin you can see.

Follicle: A tiny tube in the skin that each hair on your body grows out of.

Hypothalamus: The brain's inner thermometer that signals blood vessels to release some of your body's heat.

Melanin: The substance that gives skin its color.

Pores: Tiny holes in the skin that allow sweat to escape.

Sebaceous Gland: Small gland in the skin that produces an oil called sebum.

Sebum: The skin's own natural oil that keeps the skin lubricated, protected, and waterproof.

Subcutaneous Tissue: The bottom layer of the skin that is made mostly of fat, helps your body stay warm, and absorb shocks.

—KW

The Third Layer Is Subcutaneous Fat

The third and bottom layer of the skin is called the subcutaneous (say: sub-kyoo-tay-nee-us) layer. It is made mostly of fat and helps your body stay warm and absorb shocks, like if you bang into something or fall down. The subcutaneous layer also helps hold your skin to all the tissues underneath it.

This layer is where you'll find the start of hair, too. Each hair on your body grows out of a tiny tube in the skin called a follicle (say: fah-lih-kul). Every follicle has its roots way down in the subcutaneous layer and continues up through the dermis.

You have hair follicles all over your body, except on your lips, the palms of your hands, and the soles of your feet. And you have more hair follicles in some places than in others—there are more than 100,000 follicles on your head alone.

Your hair follicles rely on your sebaceous glands to bring on the shine. Connected to each follicle in the dermis layer is a tiny sebaceous gland that releases sebum onto the hair. This lightly coats the hair with oil, giving it some shine and a little waterproofing.

Skin Can Warm And Cool You

Your skin can help if you're feeling too hot or too cold. Your blood vessels, hair, and sweat glands cooperate to keep your body at just the right temperature. If you were to run around in the heat, you could get overheated. If you play outside when it's cold, your inner temperature could drop. Either way, your skin can help.

Your body is pretty smart. It knows how to keep your temperature right around 98.6° F (37° C) to keep you and your cells healthy. Your skin can respond to messages sent out by your hypothalamus (say: hy-po-thal-uh-mus), the brain's inner thermometer. If you've been running around on a hot day, your blood vessels get the signal from the hypothalamus to release some of your body's heat. They do this by bringing warm blood closer to the surface of your skin. That's why you sometimes get a red face when you run around.

To cool you down, sweat glands also swing into action by making lots of sweat to release body heat into the air. The hotter you are, the more sweat your glands make. Once the sweat hits the air, it evaporates (this means that it changes from a liquid to a vapor) off your skin, and you cool down.

What about when you're ice-skating or sledding? When you're cold, your blood vessels keep your body from losing heat by narrowing as much as possible and keeping the warm blood away from the skin's surface. You might notice tiny bumps on your skin. Most kids call these goosebumps, but the fancy name for them is the pilomotor (say: py-lo-mo-ter) reflex. The reflex makes special tiny muscles called the erector pili (say: ee-rek-tur pie-lie) muscles pull on your hairs so they stand up very straight.

✔ **Quick Tip**
Keep It Clean!

Unlike other organs (like your lungs, heart, and brain), your skin likes a good washing. When you wash your skin, use water and a mild soap. And don't forget to cover scrapes and cuts with gauze or a bandage. This keeps the dirt out and helps prevent infections. It's just one way to be kind to the skin you're in.

Chapter 2

Skin Types: Oily And Dry

Seborrhea

Seborrhea is the name given to excessively oily skin. It is due to over-active sebaceous glands and can affect both males and females. The oil produced by the skin is called *sebum*.

Although most people with seborrhea have no other health problems, it is sometimes a sign of underlying Parkinson's disease or acromegaly. The skin feels unpleasant, and seems to get dirty quickly. The face appears shiny. Make-up may run off or cake.

Seborrhea can also result in acne or seborrheic dermatitis.

Management

- Wash the face with a mild soap and water twice daily
- Topical retinoids
- Antiandrogens (hormone therapy for females)
- Low-dose isotretinoin may be recommended for severe cases

About This Chapter: This chapter begins with a section titled "Seborrhea." This information is reprinted with permission from DermNet, the web site of the New Zealand Dermatological Society. Visit www.dermnetnz.org for patient information on numerous skin conditions and their treatment. © 2008 New Zealand Dermatological Society. Additional information about dry skin is cited separately within the chapter.

✎ What's It Mean?

<u>Acne:</u> The common type of acne is called *acne vulgaris*. It is a condition that mainly affects adolescents but may persist or even become more severe in adulthood. Most, but not all, acne patients have oily skin (seborrhea).

<u>Acromegaly:</u> A disorder marked by progressive enlargement of peripheral parts of the body, especially the head, face, hands, and feet, due to excessive secretion of somatotropin; organomegaly and metabolic disorders occur; diabetes mellitus may develop.

<u>Seborrheic Dermatitis:</u> Seborrheic dermatitis is a common, harmless, scaling rash affecting the face, scalp and other areas. It is most likely to occur where the skin is oily.

<u>Sebum:</u> The oil produced by the skin.

<u>Topical Retinoids:</u> The group of medicines known as retinoids are derived from Vitamin A. Creams containing the retinoids retinol and retinaldehyde can be obtained over the counter at pharmacies and supermarkets. Other topical retinoids containing tretinoin or isotretinoin require a doctor's prescription. Adapalene is a related prescription medicine.

Source: New Zealand Dermatological Society, 2008.

Dry Skin

From "Dry Skin," © 2009 A.D.A.M., Inc. Reprinted with permission.

Dry skin is most common in your lower legs, arms, flanks (sides of the abdomen), and thighs. The symptoms most often associated with dry skin include:

- scaling;
- itching;
- cracks in the skin.

Causes

Dry skin is common. It happens more often in the winter when cold air outside and heated air inside cause low humidity. Forced-air furnaces make skin even drier.

The skin loses moisture and may crack and peel, or become irritated and inflamed. Bathing too frequently, especially with harsh soaps, may contribute to dry skin. Eczema may cause dry skin.

Home Care

It may help to change your bathing habits:

- Keep baths or showers short

- Use warm (not hot) water

- Use as little soap as possible. Limit its use to face, armpits, and genitals if you can. Try mild cleansers like Aveeno or Cetaphil or mild soaps like Neutrogena or Dove.

- Dry your skin thoroughly but gently—pat, don't rub

- Take baths or showers less often

  Also, increase skin and body moisture:

- Use bath oils and moisturizers at least daily. Thick, greasy moisturizers work best. Avoid products with alcohol. Apply just after a bath or shower, when your skin is still damp.

- Use a humidifier if the air is dry

- Drink plenty of water throughout the day

Apply cool compresses to itchy areas, and try over-the-counter cortisone creams or lotions if your skin is inflamed. If this is not enough, talk to your doctor about possible prescription lotions.

What To Expect At Your Office Visit

Your doctor will perform a physical examination with careful attention to all parts of your skin. To better understand the cause of the dry skin, your doctor may ask:

- When did your dry skin develop or has it always been dry?

- Are all parts of your body affected? If not, what are the specific locations involved?

- What seems to make the dryness worse?

- Does anything make it feel better?

- What are your bathing habits?

- Do you have any other symptoms?

✔ Quick Tip
**When To Contact
A Medical Professional**

Call your doctor if:

- you feel itchy without a visible rash;

- dryness and itching are preventing you from sleeping;

- you have any open cuts or sores from scratching;

- home care measures do not relieve your dryness and itching.

Source: © 2009 A.D.A.M., Inc.

Chapter 3

Brown Spots And Freckles

Freckles

Freckles are small flat brown marks arising on the face and other sun exposed areas. They are most often seen in fair-skinned people, especially those with red hair, but they are an inherited characteristic that sometimes affects darker skin types as well.

The medical term for this type of freckle is "ephelis" (plural "ephelides"). The color is due to pigment accumulating in the skin cells (keratinocytes).

Skin pigment (melanin) is made by cells called melanocytes. They don't produce much melanin during the winter months, but produce more when exposed to the sun. The melanin is diffused into the surrounding skin cells, called keratinocytes. The color of ephelides is due to localized accumulation of melanin in keratinocytes.

Ephelides are more prominent in summer but fade considerably or disappear in winter as the keratinocytes are replaced by new cells.

About This Chapter: This information is reprinted with permission from DermNet, the web site of the New Zealand Dermatological Society. Visit www.dermnetnz.org for patient information on numerous skin conditions and their treatment. © 2008 New Zealand Dermatological Society.

As the person ages this type of freckle generally becomes less noticeable. Apart from sun protection, no particular treatment is necessary.

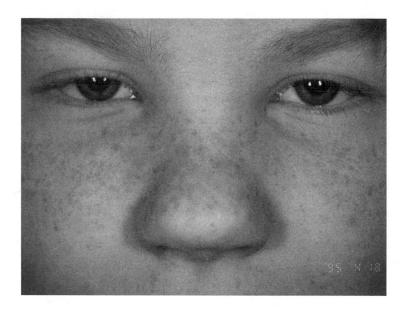

Figure 3.1. Freckles (Source: © 2008 New Zealand Dermatological Society).

Lentigines

Larger flat brown spots on the face and hands arising in middle age also result from sun damage exposure. Unlike freckles they tend to persist for long periods and don't disappear in the winter (though they may fade). Commonly known as age spots or liver spots, the correct term for a single lesion is "solar lentigo" (plural "lentigines").

Lentigines are common in those with fair skin but are also frequently seen in those who tan easily or have naturally dark skin. Lentigines are due to localized proliferation of melanocytes.

It is important to distinguish the harmless solar lentigo from an early malignant melanoma, the "lentigo maligna." If the freckle has arisen recently, is made up of more than one color or has irregular borders, or if you have any doubts, see your dermatologist for advice.

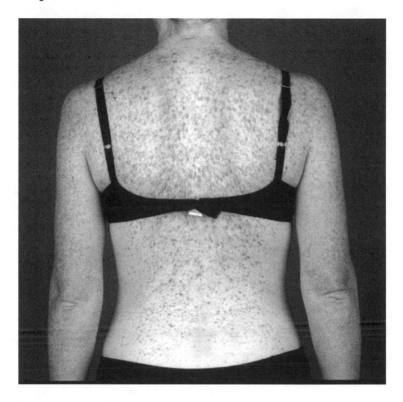

Figure 3.2. Lentigines (Source: © 2008 New Zealand Dermatological Society).

Other Brown Marks

If the brown marks are scaly, they may be solar keratoses (sun damage) or seborrheic keratoses (senile warts). In this case there is a proliferation of keratinocytes.

Treatment Of Brown Marks

Brown marks may fade with careful sun protection, broad spectrum sunscreen applied daily for nine months of the year. Regular applications of anti-aging or "fading" creams may also help. These may contain hydroquinone, or antioxidants such as:

- alpha hydroxy acids;
- vitamin C;

- retinoids;

- azelaic acid.

However, brown marks may be removed more rapidly and effectively by chemical peels, cryotherapy or certain pigment lasers that target melanin in the skin. Multiple treatments may be necessary.

Suitable green-light devices include:

- flashlamp-pulsed tunable dye laser;

- frequency doubled Q-switched Nd:YAG laser (neodynium:yttrium-aluminium-garnet);

- KTP laser;

- krypton laser;

- copper bromide laser.

Suitable red light devices include:

- Q-switched alexandrite;

- Q-switched ruby.

☞ **Remember!!**

Follow-Up: If there is any doubt whether a brown mark may be a cancer, your doctor may choose to observe the lesion (e.g. with mole mapping or photography) or excise it for pathological examination.

Intense pulsed light has a similar effect. Carbon dioxide and erbium:YAG lasers vaporize the surface skin thus removing the pigmented lesions. A fractional laser may also be effective.

Results are variable but sometimes very impressive with minimal risk of scarring.

With superficial resurfacing techniques, there is minimal discomfort and no down-time but several treatments are often necessary. Unfortunately the treatment occasionally makes the pigmentation worse. Continued careful sun protection is essential, because the pigmentation is likely to recur next summer.

Chapter 4

Birthmarks

About Birthmarks

There are two main categories of birthmarks—red birthmarks and pigmented birthmarks. Red birthmarks are a vascular type of birthmark. Pigmented birthmarks are areas in which the color of the birthmark is different from the color of the rest of the skin.

What are red birthmarks?

Red birthmarks are colored, vascular (blood vessel) skin markings that develop before or shortly after birth.

What are the types of red birthmarks?

One common kind of vascular birthmark is the hemangioma. It usually is painless and harmless and its cause is not known. Color from the birthmark comes from the extensive development of blood vessels at the site.

Strawberry hemangiomas (strawberry mark, nevus vascularis, capillary hemangioma, hemangioma simplex) might appear anywhere on the body, but are most common on the face, scalp, back, or chest. They consist of small, closely packed blood vessels. They might be absent at birth, and develop after several weeks. They usually grow rapidly, remain a fixed size, and then subside. In most cases, strawberry hemangiomas disappear by the time a child is nine years old. Some slight discoloration or puckering of the skin might remain at the site of the hemangioma.

Cavernous hemangiomas (angioma cavernosum, cavernoma) are similar to strawberry hemangiomas but are more deeply situated. They might appear as a red-blue spongy mass of tissue filled with blood. Some of these lesions disappear on their own; usually as a child approaches school age.

Port-wine stains are flat purple-to-red birthmarks made of dilated blood capillaries. These birthmarks occur most often on the face and might vary in size. Port-wine stains often are permanent (unless treated) and might result in emotional distress.

> ♣ **It's A Fact!!**
>
> ## What are the symptoms of red birthmarks?
>
> Symptoms of red birthmarks include:
>
> - skin markings that develop before or shortly after birth;
> - red skin patches or lesions;
> - skin markings that resemble blood vessels;
> - possible bleeding;
> - skin that might break open.

Salmon patches (also called stork bites) appear on 30 percent to 50 percent of newborn babies. These marks are small blood vessels (capillaries) that are visible through the skin. They are most common on the forehead, eyelids, upper lip, between the eyebrows, and the back of the neck. Often, these marks fade as the infant grows.

How are red birthmarks diagnosed?

In most cases, a health care professional can diagnose a red birthmark based on the appearance of the skin. Deeper birthmarks can be confirmed with tests such as MRI, ultrasound, CT scans, or biopsies.

What is the treatment for red birthmarks?

Many capillary birthmarks such as salmon patches and strawberry he-mangiomas are temporary and require no treatment. For permanent lesions, concealing cosmetics such as Covermark might be helpful. Cortisone (oral or injected) can reduce the size of a hemangioma that is growing rapidly and obstructing vision or vital structures.

Port wine stains on the face can be treated at a young age with a yellow-pulsed dye laser for best results. Treatment of the birthmarks might help prevent psychosocial problems that can result in individuals who have port wine stains.

Permanent red birthmarks might be treated with methods including:

- cryotherapy (freezing);
- laser surgery;
- surgical removal.

In some cases, birthmarks are not treated until a child reaches school age. However, birthmarks are treated earlier if they cause unwanted symptoms or compromise vital functions such as vision or breathing.

Can red birthmarks be prevented?

Currently, there is no known way to prevent red birthmarks.

What are pigmented birthmarks?

Pigmented birthmarks are skin markings that are present at birth. The marks might range from brown or black to bluish, or blue-gray in color.

What are the types of pigmented birthmarks?

Mongolian spots usually are bluish and appear as bruises. They often appear on the buttocks and/or lower back, but they sometimes also appear on the trunk or arms. The spots are seen most often in people who have darker skin.

Pigmented nevi (moles) are growths on the skin that usually are flesh-colored, brown, or black. Moles can appear anywhere on the skin, alone or in groups.

Congenital nevi are moles that are present at birth. These birthmarks have a slightly increased risk of becoming skin cancer depending on their size. Larger congenital nevi have a greater risk of developing skin cancer than do smaller congenital nevi. All congenital nevi should be examined by a health care provider, and any change in the birthmark should be reported.

Cafe-au-lait spots are light tan or light brown spots that are usually oval in shape. They usually appear at birth but might develop in the first few years of a child's life.

♣ It's A Fact!!
What are the symptoms of pigmented birthmarks?

Symptoms of pigmented birthmarks include skin that is abnormally dark or light, or bluish, brown, black or blue-gray in color. Discolorations of the skin might vary in size and be smooth, flat, raised, or wrinkled. Pigmented birthmarks might increase in size, change colors, become itchy, and might occasionally bleed.

What causes pigmented birthmarks?

The cause of pigmented birthmarks is not known. However, the amount and location of melanin (a substance that determines skin color) determines the color of pigmented birthmarks. Cafe-au-lait spots might be a normal type of birthmark, but the presence of several cafe-au-lait spots larger than a quarter might occur in neurofibromatosis (a genetic disorder that causes abnormal cell growth of nerve tissues). Moles occur when cells in the skin grow in a cluster instead of being spread throughout the skin. These cells are called melanocytes, and they make the pigment that gives skin its natural color. Moles might darken after exposure to the sun, during the teen years, and during pregnancy.

How are pigmented birthmarks diagnosed?

In most cases, health care professionals can diagnose birthmarks based on the appearance of the skin. If a mole exhibits potentially cancerous changes, a biopsy might be performed.

How are pigmented birthmarks treated?

In most cases, no treatment is needed for the birthmarks themselves. When birthmarks do require treatment, however, that treatment varies based on the kind of birthmark and its related conditions.

Large or prominent nevi that affect the appearance and self-esteem might be covered with special cosmetics.

Moles might be removed surgically if they affect the appearance or if they have an increased cancer risk.

What are the complications of pigmented birthmarks?

Some complications of pigmented birthmarks can include psychological effects in cases in which the birthmark is prominent. Pigmented birthmarks also can pose an increased skin cancer risk.

A doctor should check any changes that occur in the color size, or texture of a nevus or other skin lesion. See a doctor right away if there is any pain, bleeding, itching, inflammation, or ulceration of a congenital nevus or other skin lesion.

Can pigmented birthmarks be prevented?

There is no known way to prevent birthmarks. People with birthmarks should use a good quality sunscreen when outdoors in order to prevent complications.

Chapter 5

Concerns About Skin Appearance: Cellulite And Stretch Marks

Cellulite

What is cellulite?

Cellulite is the lumpy substance resembling cottage cheese that is commonly found on the thighs, stomach, and butt. Cellulite is actually a fancy name for collections of fat that push against the connective tissue beneath a person's skin, which causes the surface of the skin to dimple or pucker and look lumpy.

You can check to see if you have cellulite by pinching the skin around your upper thigh. If it looks a bit lumpy, you probably have it. And if you do have cellulite, you're definitely not alone: Most girls and women—and some men—have cellulite.

About This Chapter: This chapter begins with information from "What Is Cellulite?" September 2006, reprinted with permission from www.kidshealth.org. Copyright © 2006 The Nemours Foundation. This information was provided by KidsHealth, one of the largest resources online for medically reviewed health information written for parents, kids, and teens. For more articles like this one, visit www.KidsHealth.org, or www.TeensHealth.org. Additional information about stretch marks is cited separately within the chapter.

Several factors influence whether a person has cellulite and how much they have. Your genes, your gender, the amount of fat on your body, your age, and the thickness of your skin are all associated with the amount of cellulite you have or how visible it is.

Treatments like liposuction (surgery to remove fat) and mesotherapy (injection of drugs into cellulite) are either expensive or may produce only temporary improvement. Many doctors even warn that liposuction is not an effective treatment for cellulite because liposuction is designed to remove deep fat instead of cellulite, which is close to the skin.

If you have cellulite, chances are you won't like it. It's important to remember, though, that almost everyone wishes that something about their body was a bit different. This is particularly true for teens whose bodies are going through all sorts of changes caused by puberty.

If you decide that you want to try to reduce the amount of cellulite you have, the best thing to do is to decrease excess body fat. If you and your doctor think that you are overweight, eat fewer calories and exercise more. Experts agree that an exercise routine that combines aerobic exercise with strength training is the best weapon against cellulite. In the meantime, if you want to conceal your cellulite, try using a self-tanning product. Cellulite tends to be a little bit less noticeable on darker skin.

Remember!!

Whatever the cause of cellulite, it's important to know that there aren't any miracle products, treatments, or medicines that can make it go away. For example, some fancy salon treatments that promise to get rid of cellulite simply cause your skin to puff up through deep massaging, temporarily reducing the appearance of cellulite.

Source: Nemours Foundation, 2006.

Stretch Marks (Striae)

This information is reprinted with permission from DermNet, the web site of the New Zealand Dermatological Society. Visit www.dermnetnz.org for patient information on numerous skin conditions and their treatment. © 2008 New Zealand Dermatological Society.

What are stretch marks?

Stretch marks are fine lines on the body that occur from tissue under your skin tearing from rapid growth or over-stretching. It is a common condition that does not cause any significant medical problems but can be of cosmetic concern for some people. Other names for stretch marks are striae distensae, striae atrophicans, striae rubra (which are red) and striae alba (white).

Who gets stretch marks?

Stretch marks occur in certain areas of the body where skin is subjected to continuous and progressive stretching. These include:

- abdomen and breast in pregnant women;
- adolescents undergoing growth spurts (thighs, buttocks, breasts);
- shoulders in body-builders;
- obese or overweight people.

Stretch marks can also occur from prolonged use of oral or topical corticosteroids. They are also a feature of the disease Cushing's syndrome, where increased adrenal cortical activity (i.e. excessive circulating cortisol) is implicated in their development.

What do stretch marks look like?

An early sign of stretch marks developing is when an area of skin becomes flattened and thin with a pink color. This may also occasionally be itchy. Soon reddish or purplish lines develop (striae rubra). Over time these lighten to become whitish or flesh-colored and much less conspicuous. Stretch marks are usually several centimeters long and 1–10 mm wide. Those caused by corticosteroid use or Cushing's syndrome are often larger and wider and may involve other regions, including the face.

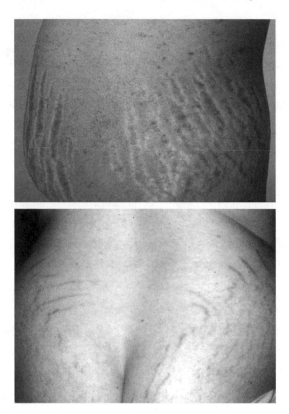

Figure 5.1. Stretch marks (Source: New Zealand Dermatological Society).

What treatment is available?

Stretch marks usually are only a cosmetic problem, but rarely, if extensive they may ulcerate or tear easily in an accident. Stretch marks occurring in adolescents become less visible over time and generally require no treatment. In other cases, if stretch marks are a cause of concern then the following treatments may be tried, but have not been proven to be effective:

- Topical retinoid therapy
- Chemical peels
- Pulse dye laser therapy

Chapter 6

Scars

Scar Facts

There are lots of different causes of scarring—accidents, surgery, skin disease, burns, acne, infection, and crime—but not all scars are the same. Below are some of the different types of scars that occur.

Flat, Pale Scars

These are the most common type of scar and are a result of the body's natural healing process. Initially, they may be red or dark and raised after the wound has healed but will become paler and flatter naturally over time, resulting in a flat, pale scar. This process can take up to two years and there will always be some visible evidence of the original wound.

Hypertrophic Scars (Red Or Dark And Raised)

When a normal wound heals, the body produces new collagen fibers at a rate which balances the breakdown of old collagen. Hypertrophic scars are red and thick and may be itchy or painful. They do not extend beyond the boundary of the original wound but may continue to thicken for up to six months. They usually improve over the next one to two years but may cause distress due to their appearance or the intensity of the itching, also restricting movement if they are located close to a joint.

Hypertrophic scars are more common in the young and people with darker skin. Some people have an inherited tendency to this type of scarring. It is not possible to completely prevent hypertrophic scars, so anyone who has suffered one should inform their doctor or surgeon if they need to have surgery. Scar therapies are available which may speed up the process of change from a hypertrophic scar to a flatter, paler one.

Keloid Scars (Red Or Dark And Raised)

Like hypertrophic scars, keloids are the result of an imbalance in the production of collagen in a healing wound. Unlike hypertrophic scars, keloids grow beyond the boundary of the original wound. They can continue to grow indefinitely. They may be itchy or painful and may not improve in appearance over time.

What's It Mean?

Keloid (pronounced KEY-loyd): A thick, irregular scar caused by excessive tissue growth at the site of an incision or wound.

Source: National Cancer Institute: Dictionary of Cancer Terms.

Keloid scars can result from any type of injury to the skin, including scratches, injections, insect bites and tattoos. Anybody can get a keloid scar and they can occur anywhere on the body. However, the young and people with darker skin are more prone to this type of scarring and they are more common on certain parts of the body, e.g. ears, chest, shoulders and back.

As with hypertrophic scarring, people who have developed one keloid scar are likely to be prone to this condition in the future and should alert their doctor or surgeon if they are likely to need injections or to have any form of surgery.

Sunken Scars

Sunken scars are recessed into the skin. They may be due to the skin being attached to deeper structures (such as muscles) or to loss of underlying fat. They are usually the result of an injury.

Acne And Chicken Pox Scars

A common cause of sunken scarring is acne or chicken pox which can result in a pitted appearance. However, it is important to note that acne scarring is not always sunken in appearance and can even become keloid.

Stretched Scars

Stretched scars occur when the skin around a healing wound is put under tension during the healing process. This type of scarring may follow injury or surgery. Initially, the scar may appear normal but can widen and thin over a period of weeks or months. This can occur where the skin is close to a joint and is stretched during movement or may be due to poor healing due to general ill health or malnutrition.

Stretch Marks

Stretch marks develop when the skin is stretched rapidly, for example during pregnancy or the adolescent growth spurt. Initially, stretch marks appear red but become paler over a number of years.

Facial Scar Revision

"Facial Scar Revision" reprinted with permission from the American Academy of Facial Plastic and Reconstructive Surgery (www.aafprs.org), © 2008.

Surgery Of Facial Scars

When the skin is in the process of recovering from an injury, whether the result of an accident, surgery, a burn, or acne, scarring will occur wherever multiple layers of the skin have been affected. Once a scar forms, it is permanent but may be made less visible or relocated surgically.

With very few exceptions most people are self-conscious about facial scars. Some people may also experience diminished functioning of the eyes, mouth, or nose due to scarring. If you've wondered how facial scar revision could improve your appearance, your self-confidence, or your level of facial functioning, you need to know how scar revision works and what you can expect from this procedure. This chapter address many of your questions and provides you with the information to begin considering facial scar revision surgery.

Successful facial plastic surgery is a result of good rapport between patient and surgeon. Trust, based on realistic expectations and exacting medical expertise, develops in the consulting stages before surgery is performed. Your surgeon can answer specific questions about your specific needs.

Is Facial Scar Treatment For You?

The most basic requirement for all surgery is good health. Other requirements are more subtle and should be carefully considered in discussion with your surgeon. Expectations of the surgery and of the surgeon must be realistic. A person considering facial scar revision must understand that there is no way to remove scars completely. The goal is to improve the appearance of the scar either by disguising it, relocating it, or minimizing its prominence. Skin color and type, age, and the type of scarring, are all important factors that must be part of the discussion prior to surgery.

Different types of scars respond to different plastic surgery techniques. Timing of surgery is another important choice. Some surgeons advise against any scar revision in cases of injury for a period that might extend up to a year after the injury. This interval allows the body enough time to heal fully.

Making The Decision For Scar Treatment

Whether the surgery is desired for functional or cosmetic reasons, your choice of a facial plastic surgeon is of paramount importance. Your surgeon will examine the scar in order to decide upon the proper treatment and inform you of outcomes that can be expected from facial scar revision surgery.

Different scars require different treatments. For example, severe burns that destroy large sections of skin cause the skin to heal in a puckered way. As the skin heals, muscles and tendons may be affected in this "contracting" movement. Keloid scars are a result of the skin's overproduction of collagen after a wound has healed. These scars generally appear as growths in the scar site. Hypertrophic scars, unlike keloids, do not grow out of the boundaries of the scar area, but because of their thick, raised texture, can be unsightly and may also restrict the natural movement of muscles and tendons.

Some facial scars are unattractive simply because of where they appear on the face, while others affect facial expressions. All surgical possibilities will be discussed in the initial consultation along with risks involved for each type of scarring. The agreement between you and your surgeon on how to proceed is a prerequisite for successful surgery. After you both decide to proceed with scar revision, your surgeon will inform you about the anesthesia, the surgical facility, any supportive surgery options, and costs.

👉 Remember!!

Because scars are highly individualistic and the patient's attitude toward scars is so personal, maximum improvement in facial scars may require more than one procedure, and more than one technique may be employed.

Source: American Academy of Facial Plastic and Reconstructive Surgery, 2008.

Understanding The Surgery

When a scar is of the contracture type, surgery generally involves removing the scar tissue entirely. Skin flaps, composed of adjacent healthy, unscarred skin, are then lifted and moved to form a new incision line. Where a flap is not possible, a skin graft may be used. A graft involves taking a section of skin tissue from one area and attaching it to another, and time must be allowed following surgery for new blood vessels and soft tissue to form. Z-plasty is a method to move a scar from one area to another, usually into a natural fold or crease in the skin to minimize its visibility. While Z-plasty does not remove all signs of a scar, it does make it less noticeable.

Dermabrasion and laser resurfacing are methods a surgeon uses to make "rough or elevated" scars less prominent, by removing part of the upper layers of skin with an abrading tool or laser light. Clearly, the scar will remain, but it will be smoother and less visible.

Keloid or hypertrophic scars are often treated first with injections of steroids to reduce size. If this is not satisfactory, the scars can be removed surgically, and the incisions closed with fine stitches, often resulting in less prominent scars.

What To Expect After The Surgery

You can expect to feel some discomfort after facial scar revision surgery. Some swelling, bruising, and redness are generally unavoidable. It is important for you to follow your surgeon's after care recommendations to the letter. Though the sutures will be removed within days after the surgery, your skin needs time to heal. Surgeons generally insist on decreased activity after surgery and instruct the patient to keep the head elevated when lying down, to use cold compresses to reduce swelling, and to avoid any activity that places undue stress on the area of the incision. Depending on the surgery performed and the site of the scar, the facial plastic surgeon will explain the types of activities to avoid. No medication should be taken without first consulting the surgeon. It is important to remember that scar tissues require a year or more to fully heal and achieve maximum improved appearance.

Facial plastic surgery makes it possible to correct facial flaws that can undermine self-confidence. Changing how your scar looks can help change how you feel about yourself.

> **☞ Remember!!**
>
> Insurance does not generally cover surgery that is purely for cosmetic reasons. Surgery to correct or improve scars caused by injury may be reimbursable in whole or in part. It is the patient's responsibility to check with the insurance carrier for information on the degree of coverage.
>
> Source: American Academy of Facial Plastic and Reconstructive Surgery, 2008.

Part Two

Caring For Skin, Hair, And Nails

Chapter 7

Protecting And Taking Care Of Your Skin

Do you have healthy habits? For instance, do you properly cleanse your skin? If you're a woman who wears makeup, be sure to remove all traces of make-up at the end of the day. No matter what your gender is, you should drink plenty of water, providing your skin with vital moisture from the inside. When you're out in the sun, be sure to wear sunscreen. Even though you won't see immediate results, those little steps add up over time to make a big difference in the overall appearance of your skin.

Start Early

It's never too late to integrate a proper skin care routine. If you're a teenager or you have a teenager at home, start now to develop healthy habits. If you're an older adult, lead by example. You can't replace the skin you're in, but you can still nourish and pamper it to protect it for the future. With the proper care, your skin can stay fresh as you age.

Skin Problem?

Skin's not going to be perfect. It can be dry or oily; it can develop rashes and acne, among a million other issues. But don't back down: address the problem with a dermatologist.

Sun Protection

Protecting your skin from the sun is important because the sun emits ultraviolet (UV) radiation. Over time, exposure to UV radiation causes many changes in the skin, including wrinkles, discoloration, freckles or age spots, benign (non-cancerous) growths such as moles, and pre-cancerous or cancerous growths such as basal cell carcinoma, squamous cell carcinoma, and melanoma. In fact, most skin cancers are related to sun exposure.

> ✔ **Quick Tip**
>
> **Age Spots:** Years of sun exposure can cause flat, brown spots called "liver" or age spots to appear on your face, hands, arms, back, and feet. They are not harmful. But if the look of age spots bothers you, ask your doctor about skin-lightening creams, laser therapy, and cryotherapy (freezing). Use sunscreen to prevent more age spots.
>
> Source: From "Skin and Hair Health," *The Healthy Woman: A Complete Guide for All Ages*, National Women's Health Information Center, 2008.

There are two main types of UV radiation: UVB and UVA. UVB sun rays cause sunburns and UVA rays cause tanning. UVA rays are believed to be responsible for photoaging, the damage that occurs to the skin from many years of exposure to the sun. Both UVB and UVA light contribute to the risk of developing skin cancer.

Most sunscreen products available in the past were developed to prevent sunburns by blocking UVB rays. Newer sunscreen products have been developed to more effectively block UVA rays and contain ingredients such as avobenzone, ecamsule, and Helioplex™.

Facial Skin Care For Acne Prone Skin

It may have started in your teen years, that time when age and hormones meet to cause those awful breakouts. Or, did you begin experiencing acne breakouts in your adult years? Even if you had clear skin in your teenage years, hormones, stress, or other factors may conspire in your adult years to cause acne breakouts. If you are prone to acne, choose a cleanser specially formulated for acne. These products often contain salicylic acid or benzoyl peroxide, which help to clear acne sores.

Clean your face gently, as trauma to the acne breakouts may worsen the acne or cause scarring. When washing your face, use your hands, or a soft washcloth.

When you sleep at night, make sure you are sleeping on a clean pillowcase and that you are the only person using your pillowcase. That seemingly harmless item absorbs traces of oil during the night, making it a prime suspect for aggravating breakouts if not changed regularly.

If you have longer hair, you should make sure to pull it back when you sleep at night. The oil in your hair can aggravate your skin as well.

If you need to use a moisturizer, use only light, non-comedogenic moisturizers, which do not aggravate acne. There are oil-free moisturizers on the market that contain anti-bacterial agents for acne-prone skin. This type of product may be your best option. Also, women should

☞ Remember!!

Sun protection recommendations emphasize certain behaviors, as well as the use of sunscreens. The recommendations include:

- avoiding midday sun between 10 a.m. and 3 p.m.;

- wearing wide-brimmed hats, long sleeved shirts, and pants;

- using a generous amount of sunscreen and reapplying it frequently (every two to three hours). One ounce (30 ml, or a shot glass) is required to cover the entire exposed skin surface.

- using sunscreens that have a sun protection factor (SPF) greater than 15, and that have both UVA and UVB coverage;

- avoiding tanning beds;

- using lip balms containing sunscreen.

Source: The Cleveland Clinic Foundation, 2007.

use an oil-free foundation, as heavy makeup or other cosmetic products that block pores may cause a flare-up of acne.

Facial Skin Care For Mature Skin

As people age, they may notice increased roughness, wrinkling, irregular pigmentation (coloration), or inelasticity. They may have enlarged sebaceous (oil) glands. Sometimes, precancerous and cancerous lesions can occur with aged and photoaged skin. Sunscreens and sun protection are important to prevent further progression of photoaging.

You should be aware that your skin requires different care as you age. Skin doesn't produce new cells at the same pace, and environmental and

✔ Quick Tip
Caring For Your Skin And Hair

Good skin and hair care involves:
- eating a variety of healthy foods rich in vitamins and nutrients;
- keeping physically active;
- managing stress;
- practicing sun safety;
- limiting alcohol;
- not using tobacco and other recreational drugs;
- drinking plenty of water.

Unhealthy behaviors can take a toll on skin and hair. For instance, habits like smoking and sunbathing dry out skin and cause wrinkles.

Source: From "Skin and Hair Health," *The Healthy Woman: A Complete Guide for All Ages*, National Women's Health Information Center, 2008.

✎ What's It Mean?

There are different types of dermatitis that may cause dry, itchy, and flaking skin. They include:

Allergic Contact Dermatitis: This type occurs when the skin comes into contact with a substance that causes an immune reaction, such as poison ivy. Allergic contact dermatitis of the hands often causes scaling on the fingers.

Athlete's Foot: In many cases, athlete's foot, a fungal infection, shows up as dry flaking on the soles of the feet.

Atopic Dermatitis: This is a long-lasting type of dermatitis (eczema) that often runs in families. It also may cause excessively dry, itchy skin.

Seborrheic Dermatitis: This type involves a red, scaly, itchy rash on various areas of the body, particularly those areas that contain many oil glands. Seborrheic dermatitis can occur as scaling on the scalp (dandruff), eyebrows, outer ear canals, and sides of the nose.

Source: The Cleveland Clinic Foundation, 2007.

biological factors greatly impact how we age. Products that allow for cell management (creams, for instance), would be your best bet. You want to seek out those products that contain ingredients like retinol, tretinoin (found in the prescriptions Retin-A® and Renova®), or glycolic acid.

What are your habits? If you smoke, that's working directly against your skin. Smoking has been shown to accelerate aging of skin, so quitting now is important for good skin health. In addition, a well-balanced diet—with or without a multivitamin—helps the skin get the nutrition it needs to help repair ongoing damage from the sun and other environmental elements.

There are many topical non-prescription and prescription products currently available that help maintain and protect your skin's health. Ask your dermatologist or skin care specialist which medications are best for you.

Dry Skin

Dry skin is defined as flaking or scaling—which may or may not be itchy—when there is no evidence of dermatitis, or inflammation, of the skin. Flaking, however, may be a sign of underlying dermatitis (which is also called *eczema*).

Dry skin that is not caused by dermatitis most often occurs on the shins, hands, and sides of the abdomen. It is more common during the winter months, when humidity is low. Some people also have a genetic, or hereditary, tendency to develop dry skin. In addition, elderly people tend to have more trouble with dry skin due to the natural changes in skin that occur with age.

Treatment of dry skin is important because extensively dry skin can lead to eczema or other forms of dermatitis. Dry skin may be prevented or treated by:

- taking lukewarm baths or showers;
- limiting baths and showers to five to 10 minutes;
- applying a moisturizer right after drying off from a shower or washing your hands;
- using a moisturizing body soap and hand soap;
- using heavier creams or ointments during the winter months and lighter lotions in the summer.

Chapter 8

Skin Care Products And Your Skin

Cosmetics and skin care products are part of most people's daily grooming habits. The average adult uses at least seven different skin care products each day. These include fragrances, astringents, moisturizers, sunscreens, skin cleansers, hair care items, deodorants or antiperspirants, colored cosmetics, hair cosmetics, and nail cosmetics.

The majority of people experience few problems from these products, however, problems can arise either with the first few applications, or after years of use. People usually know which product is causing the problem, but severe, chronic reactions may require the skills of a dermatologist.

What are the possible problems associated with the use of cosmetics and skin care products?

Reactions to skin care products can be simple irritations, depending on the condition of the skin, or a true allergy involving the immune system. Irritant contact dermatitis is the most common problem seen with cosmetics and skin care products.

What is irritant contact dermatitis?

Uninjured skin is an excellent barrier to most substances found in cosmetics and skin care products. If skin is very dry or injured, openings make that barrier less protective. Burning, stinging, itching, and redness may be signs that a product is irritating the skin. Bath soaps, detergents, antiperspirants, eye cosmetics, moisturizers, permanent hair-waving solutions and shampoos are the most common skin irritants. Even water can irritate very dry skin.

What is allergic contact dermatitis?

Some people are allergic to a specific ingredient or ingredients in a product. They react whenever they are exposed to the ingredient, although it can take up to several days for the symptoms to appear. Signs include redness, swelling, itching, and fluid-filled blisters.

What are some of the ingredients that cause allergic reactions?

Fragrances and preservatives, ingredients commonly found in skin care products and cosmetics, are the most common cause of cosmetic allergic reactions.

Fragrances: Fragrances cause more allergic contact dermatitis than any other ingredient. More than 5,000 different fragrances are used in cosmetics and skin care products. Less "allergenic" fragrances have been developed to minimize the problem.

Preservatives: Preservatives in cosmetics and skin care products are the second most common cause of skin reactions. Preservatives prevent the growth of fungus and bacteria that can cause skin infections, and protect products from oxygen and light damage. Cosmetics that contain water must include some type of preservative.

☞ Remember!!

A product labeled "unscented" may really contain a fragrance which masks other chemical odors. A product must be marked "fragrance-free" or "without perfume" to indicate nothing has been added to make it smell good. Some fragrance reactions occur only when the skin is exposed to sunlight.

What are skin care products?

Skin care products are designed to maintain healthy skin. They include astringents, moisturizers, and sunscreens.

Astringents: Astringents remove oils and soap residue from the skin. They are generally drying and may contain water, alcohol, propylene glycol, witch hazel, or salicylic acid. These may cause itching, burning, or tingling in people with dry, sensitive, or irritated skin.

Moisturizers: Moisturizers prevent water loss by layering an oily substance over the skin to keep water in, or by attracting water to the outer skin layer from the inner skin layer. Dry skin causes cracks and fine wrinkles, losing its effectiveness as a barrier, and causing pain and itching. Substances that stop water loss include petrolatum, mineral oil, lanolin, and silicone. Substances that attract water to the skin include glycerin, propylene glycol, proteins, and some vitamins. These ingredients may cause an allergic reaction.

Sunscreens: Sunscreens contain chemicals that absorb, reflect, or scatter light. Light-absorbing chemicals include the PABA esters, avobenzone, and the cinnamates, that can cause an allergic reaction. Physical sunscreens contain fine powders of zinc oxide or titanium dioxide that reflect or scatter light. There are no known allergies to physical sunscreens.

What are personal care products?

Personal care products that help keep skin and hair clean and fresh smelling include skin cleansers, shampoos, conditioners, and deodorants or antiperspirants.

☞ Remember!!

Consumers who react to one preservative will not necessarily react to others. Examples of preservatives include:

- paraben;
- imidazolidinyl urea;
- Quaternium-15;
- DMDM hydantoin;
- phenoxyethanol;
- methylchloroisothiazolinone;
- formaldehyde.

These preservatives should be listed as ingredients on product labels.

Skin Cleansers: Soaps, detergents, bath and shower gels, and bubble baths remove dirt, body oils, and bacteria. They prevent odor and infection, but heavy use of these products can over dry the skin causing flaking, itching, and irritation. People with dry skin should choose a mild cleanser, bathe and/or shower with cool water, minimize water contact, and apply a moisturizer immediately after bathing while the skin is slightly wet.

There are several different varieties of soaps. Deodorant soaps have an antibacterial agent to eliminate odors. Beauty-bar soaps are generally less drying and irritating.

Shampoos: Shampoos remove dirt and oils from the scalp and leave the hair soft and shiny. Allergic reactions to shampoos are uncommon since their contact with the skin is brief, but they can irritate and dry the skin when rinsed over the body.

There are several types of shampoos: mild baby shampoos do not irritate the eyes; conditioning shampoos cleanse lightly and leave hair soft; shampoos for oily hair remove oil; and shampoos for damaged hair are pH-adjusted to prevent more damage.

Conditioners: Conditioners are applied after shampooing to make hair shiny, easier to comb and style, and more manageable. They are not a common source of skin reactions themselves; they can have fragrance and preservatives.

Deodorants And Antiperspirants: Deodorants kill bacteria and leave a pleasant smell. Antiperspirants prevent sweating. The fragrance in deodorants and the aluminum salts in antiperspirants rarely cause problems. Skin irritation can occur if these products are used on already irritated skin, immediately after shaving, or if spread too widely around the armpit.

What are colored cosmetics?

Colored cosmetics are applied to the face, eyes, and lips to beautify and adorn the body.

Facial Cosmetics: Facial cosmetics, or "make-up," are used to color the face. It is important to select make-up carefully since it remains in contact with the skin for a long time. Ideally, make-up should be hypoallergenic, non-comedogenic, and non-acnegenic—meaning it produces fewer allergies and will not plug pores or cause acne. Look for cosmetics with sunscreen, which will help prevent skin cancer and wrinkles.

Eye Cosmetics: Eyelids are the most sensitive skin on the body. Eye cosmetics include eye shadow, eyeliner, and mascara. Lighter colored, matte-finish powdered eye shadows are less irritating. Water-based (soluble or washable) eye cosmetics are easier to remove. This is important because scrubbing or vigorous rubbing to remove eye cosmetics may cause irritation. Often irritating and allergenic substances can be introduced to the eye area by the fingers.

✔ Quick Tip

Eye cosmetics should never be shared and should be replaced every three to four months because of possible bacterial contamination.

Lip Cosmetics: Lip cosmetics include lipsticks and lip balms. They moisturize dry, cracked lips, and provide sun protection. Some long-wearing lip stains have been linked to allergic contact dermatitis. Saliva is a common cause of irritant contact dermatitis.

What are hair cosmetics?

The appearance of hair can be altered by changing its color through dyeing, or its shape by permanent waving.

Dyes: Temporary hair dyes wash out after one shampoo. Gradual hair dyes produce a color change over a two to three week period. These dyes generally do not cause problems. Semipermanent hair dyes that wash out after four to six shampoos and permanent hair dyes that do not wash out can cause allergic reactions. These products should be tested on a small area of skin behind the ear or inside the elbow for 24 hours before using.

Permanent hair dyes make hair lighter or darker. Ammonium persulfate, sometimes used to lighten hair, can cause contact dermatitis. It can also cause an immediate allergic reaction like hives and wheezing.

Permanent Waving: "Permanents" make straight hair curly. A perm solution breaks the chemical bonds in straight hair to reform them in a curled position. This process can damage the hair. Hair should not be permed more often than every three months. If the perming solution is left on too long, is too strong or is applied to hair already damaged by dyes, bleaches, or recent permanents, the hair could break. Scalp irritation may also occur.

What are nail cosmetics?

Nail cosmetics are used to color nails, increase nail strength, or to artificially add nail length.

Polishes: Nail polish can cause allergic contact dermatitis. A person allergic to nail polish may develop a rash on the fingers, eyelids, face, and neck—places the nail polish or fumes may have touched while it was drying. Formaldehyde is a common ingredient that causes allergies. People with nail polish allergies can try hypoallergenic polishes that are formaldehyde free. Red polishes may cause a harmless yellow discoloration of the nail.

> ✔ **Quick Tip**
> Cuticles prevent infection and protect the nail-forming cells and should not be cut or removed.

Artificial Nails: The illusion of long nails can be created with plastic nails that cover the entire nail or nail tips. These artificial nails are attached with glue that may contain methacrylate, a common allergen. Methacrylate-free glues may cause the underlying nail to peel and crack. Nail repair kits also use these glues.

Sculptured Nails: Long-term use of sculptured nails, custom-made to fit permanently over natural nails, can cause severe and painful reactions, including infection of the skin around the nail, loosening or loss of nails, and dermatitis.

Women who have worn artificial or sculptured nails for a long time may notice their real nails are thin, dull, and brittle. Dermatologists recommend that regular artificial nail users take them off every three months to allow natural nails to rest.

What are cosmeceuticals?

Cosmeceuticals are skin care products designed to go beyond strictly coloring and adorning the skin. These products may improve the functioning of the skin and be helpful in preventing premature aging. Examples are alpha hydroxy acids such as glycolic acid, and beta hydroxy acid such as salicylic acid. These hydroxy acids increase skin exfoliation (the removal of dead skin cells) making aging skin appear smoother and feel softer. Some vitamins, such as vitamin A (retinol), may improve the appearance of aging skin by making the skin function better, but they may be drying or irritating and must be used appropriately. Dermatologists know how to use cosmeceutical ingredients and can advise their patients about the best ways to achieve healthy looking skin. Sunblocks prevent photo-aging and photo-carcinogenesis (cancer from the sun) and should be the cornerstone of any skin care regimen.

What The Dermatologist Does

Cosmetics and skin care products are part of grooming and daily hygiene. If a problem is suspected, a dermatologist can diagnose and treat the problem. Patch testing may be used to determine if there is an allergy to specific ingredients in these products. Dermatologists can tell you what should be avoided and personalize a skin care regime for you. They can also answer your questions and provide additional information about the safe use of cosmetics and skin care products.

Chapter 9

Using Cosmetics Safely

Cosmetics

People use cosmetics to enhance their beauty. These products range from lipstick and foundation to deodorant, toothpaste, and hairspray. In 1938, Congress passed the U.S. Food, Drug, and Cosmetics Act. In the 70 years since the law was passed, the federal government has worked with industry to keep cosmetics safe. Together they have made many changes to protect consumers. Here are some important things to know.

What Is FDA's Authority Over Cosmetics?

It is important to understand that Congress passes the laws that govern the United States. To put those laws into effect, Congress authorizes certain government agencies, including FDA, to create and enforce regulations, but only as authorized under the law. A change in FDA's statutory authority over cosmetics would require Congress to change the law.

FDA's legal authority over cosmetics is different from other products regulated by the agency, such as drugs, biologics, and medical devices. Cosmetic products and ingredients are not subject to FDA premarket approval

About This Chapter: Information in this chapter is excerpted from "Cosmetics," 2008, "What is the shelf life of cosmetics?" 2002, and "What is FDA's authority over cosmetics?" 2006, U.S. Food and Drug Administration (www.fda.gov).

authority, with the exception of color additives. However, FDA may take regulatory action if it has information to support that a cosmetic is adulterated or misbranded. The agency can pursue action through the Department of Justice in the federal court system to remove adulterated and misbranded cosmetics from the market. To prevent further shipment of an adulterated or misbranded product, the agency may request a federal district court to issue a restraining order against the manufacturer or distributor of the violative cosmetic. Violative cosmetics may be subject to seizure. FDA also may initiate criminal action against a person violating the law.

How Does The Law Protect You?

By law, cosmetics are required to meet the following standards:

- Must be made and packaged in clean factories

- Cannot contain poison, rotten, or harmful ingredients

- May only use color additives that are FDA-approved

- Must have a clear, truthful label

✎ What's It Mean?

Cosmetic: (1) articles intended to be rubbed, poured, sprinkled, or sprayed on, introduced into, or otherwise applied to the human body or any part thereof for cleansing, beautifying, promoting attractiveness, or altering the appearance, and (2) articles intended for use as a component of any such articles; except that such term shall not include soap.

Source: Federal Food, Drug, and Cosmetic Act, Sec. 201 (i).

Read The Label

The law says a label must include the following information:

- What the product is

- A list of what is in the product and how to use it safely

- How much of the product the package contains by weight

- The name of the company that makes or sells the product

Does The U.S. Food And Drug Administration Test Cosmetics Before They Are Sold?

The U.S. Food and Drug Administration (FDA) does not test cosmetics before they are sold in stores. Companies must make sure their products and ingredients are safe before they sell them. FDA can take action against companies who break the law.

Safety Tips For Beauty

- Follow all directions on the label, including "Cautions" and "Warnings"

- Keep makeup containers clean and closed tight when not in use

- Wash your hands before you put on makeup

- Do not share makeup

- Do not add saliva or water to makeup

- Throw away makeup if the color or smell changes.

- Don't store your makeup above 85° F (29° C)

- Stop using a product if you get a rash or have a problem

- Do not use spray cans while you are smoking or near an open flame. It could start a fire.

- Do not put on makeup while you are driving

Special Tips For Your Eyes

- Do not keep mascara too long. Some companies say three months is long enough.

- Do not use eye makeup if you have an eye infection. Throw away eye makeup you were using.

- Do not use cosmetics near your eyes unless they are meant for your eyes. For example, don't use a lip liner as an eyeliner. You may spread germs from your mouth to your eyes.

Will My Cosmetics Expire?

- There is no law that cosmetics must have an expiration date.

- Expiration dates are just guidelines. A product may go bad sooner if you store it the wrong way.

What Is The Shelf Life Of Cosmetics?

There are no regulations or requirements under current U.S. law that require cosmetic manufacturers to print expiration dates on the labels of cosmetic products. Manufacturers have the responsibility to determine shelf life for products, as part of their responsibility to substantiate product safety. FDA believes that failure to do so may cause a product to be adulterated or misbranded.

Voluntary shelf-life guidelines developed by the cosmetic industry vary, depending on the product and its intended use.

Consumers should be aware that expiration dates are simply "rules of thumb," and that a product's safety may expire long before the expiration date if the product has not been properly stored.

☞ Remember!! Cosmetic Practices

Makeup: Good skin care is the foundation of beauty. But many women enjoy using makeup (cosmetics), too. If you use makeup, follow these tips:

- Read the labels for product content and safety information

- Wash your hands before applying makeup

- Throw out products if the color changes or they get an odor

- Throw out mascara after three months

- Keep product containers tightly closed when not in use

- Don't share your makeup

- Call your doctor if a product causes skin changes like itching and rash—you may be having an allergic reaction

Source: From "Skin and Hair Health," *The Healthy Woman: A Complete Guide for All Ages*, National Women's Health Information Center, 2008.

Sharing makeup increases the risk of contamination. "Testers" commonly found at department store cosmetic counters are even more likely to become contaminated than the same products in an individual's home. If you feel you must test a cosmetic before purchasing it, apply it with a new, unused applicator, such as a fresh cotton swab.

✔ **Quick Tip**
Beauty Tips To Live By

Skin or hair care products claiming to reduce wrinkles or enhance shine are tempting to try. But keep in mind, the best beauty tips are free and up to you to follow. Living a healthy lifestyle and practicing sun safety can have you radiating beauty from both outside and within.

Source: From "Skin and Hair Health," *The Healthy Woman: A Complete Guide for All Ages*, National Women's Health Information Center, 2008.

Are "Testers" At Makeup Counters Safe?

• Testers can have lots of germs because so many people use them.

• When you test a product at the counter, use a new sponge or cotton swab.

Could I Be Allergic To Something In A Cosmetic?

• Some people may react to something in a product. For example, they may have itching, redness, rash, sneezing, or wheezing.

• Allergies may happen the first time you use a product or after you have used it more than once.

What Should I Do If I Have A Bad Reaction To A Cosmetic?

- Stop using the product

- Call your doctor to find out how to take care of the problem

- Call FDA's Center for Food Safety and Applied Nutrition (CFSAN) at (301) 436-2405 or send an e-mail to CAERS@cfsan.fda.gov

- Call the company that makes the product

Chapter 10

Surgical And Nonsurgical Cosmetic Procedures

A smaller nose. Bigger breasts. Slimmer thighs. Plumper lips. Less hair on the body. More hair on the head. Whether we're looking to tighten our tummies or lighten our laugh lines, America's fascination with youth and beauty has long fueled the development of medical products for cosmetic purposes. And if such "vanity drugs" can be shown to be safe and effective, the Food and Drug Administration just may approve.

The ongoing fight to delay or reverse the aging process has dermatologists and cosmetic plastic surgeons responding with products like Restylane (hyaluronic acid), one of a handful of soft tissue fillers recently approved by the FDA to treat facial wrinkles. Restylane is an injectable gel that acts as a filler to remove the wrinkle, producing instantaneous results. Such products are not as invasive as facelifts, eyelid surgery, and other reconstructive procedures. And they are more effective and last longer than creams, lotions and other topical products, whether over-the-counter or prescription. In addition, the fact that the treatments result in little or no downtime makes them more attractive to those seeking a quick fix. Without making a single incision, doctors can erase wrinkles, acne scars and sun damage in a matter of minutes.

About This Chapter: Information in this chapter is excerpted from "Science Meets Beauty: Using Medicine to Improve Appearances," U.S. Food and Drug Administration, 2004.

"This is a huge industry," says Jonathan K. Wilkin, M.D., a medical officer in the FDA's Division of Dermatologic and Dental Drug Products. "The way people try to move the clock back is through the skin." Basically, he says, through various products and procedures, "they are addressing the effects of gravity on the skin over time."

Aging Skin 101

An increased understanding of the structure and function of the skin is helping to drive the development of products that reduce the visible signs of facial aging, according to the American Academy of Dermatology (AAD).

With aging, all skin cells begin to produce excess amounts of free radicals—unstable oxygen molecules that, under ideal circumstances, are removed by naturally occurring antioxidants within the skin's cells. In aging skin cells, antioxidants are in short supply. The free radicals generated are left unchecked and cause damage to cell membranes, proteins, and DNA. These free radicals eventually break down a protein substance in connective tissue (collagen) and release chemicals that cause inflammation in the skin. It is a combination of these cellular and molecular events that leads to skin aging and the formation of wrinkles, the AAD says.

As we get older, two components of our skin—collagen and elastin—degenerate, setting the stage for the appearance of wrinkles, creases, folds, and furrows. The breakdown of these components, accelerated by sun exposure and gravity, results in the sagging skin of old age.

Considerable research has been done to understand the aging process, and studies now show that products containing bioactive ingredients (those that interact with living tissues or systems) can benefit sun-damaged, discolored, and aging skin, giving consumers new choices for restoring their overall appearance. But why is the FDA reviewing products that simply make people look and feel good when typically the agency evaluates disease-fighting treatments?

"If something that is being implanted into the body could have health consequences, we're concerned about it," says Stephen P. Rhodes, M.S., chief of the FDA's Plastic and Reconstructive Surgery Devices Branch. "Wrinkle fillers affect the structure of the face and could have such health consequences."

Facing Facts

Under the Federal Food, Drug and Cosmetic Act, the FDA legally defines products by their intended uses. Drugs are defined as products intended for treating or preventing disease and affecting the structure or any function of the body. A medical device is a product that also is intended to affect the structure or function of the body, but which does not achieve its primary intended purposes through the chemical action of a drug—nor is it dependent on being metabolized.

The hyaluronic acid in Restylane, although biosynthetically produced (formed of chemical compounds by the enzyme action of living organisms), is almost identical to that in all living organisms. Hyaluronic acid is a structural component of skin that creates volume and shape. Concentrations of hyaluronic acid throughout the body decline with age, causing undesirable changes in the skin. Restylane binds to water and provides volume to easily fill in larger folds of skin left by tissue loss around the mouth and cheeks. "This makes it a structural action," says Rhodes, "much like a chin implant."

In contrast, cosmetics are defined as substances that cleanse, beautify, promote attractiveness, or alter the appearance, without affecting the body's structure or function. This definition includes skin-care products such as creams, lotions, powders and sprays; perfume; lipstick; fingernail polish; and more.

Different laws and regulations apply to each type of product. Some products must comply with the requirements for both cosmetics and drugs. This happens when a product has two intended uses, such as an antidandruff shampoo. A shampoo is a cosmetic because it is intended to clean hair. An antidandruff shampoo is a cosmetic and a drug because it is intended to treat dandruff (which affects the follicles where the hair is formed) and clean hair.

Warning letters issued by the FDA to firms that marketed hair care products with claims such as restoration of hair growth and hair loss prevention illustrate an important distinction between the legal definitions of cosmetics and drugs. Warning letters officially inform companies that they may be engaged in illegal activities, and instruct manufacturers on how to bring their products into compliance with the law. Hair growers and hair loss prevention products, because of their mechanism of action, are considered drugs, not cosmetics, and these firms were not meeting the legal requirements for marketing a drug.

Unlike drugs and medical devices, neither cosmetic products nor cosmetic ingredients are reviewed or approved by the FDA before they are sold to the public. The agency only acts against cosmetic products found to cause harm after they are on the market.

Cosmetics Or Drugs?

Much confusion exists about the status of cosmetic products having medicinal or drug-like benefits, says Linda Katz, M.D., M.P.H., director of the FDA's Office of Cosmetics and Colors. Although the FDA does not consider the term *cosmeceutical* to be a valid product class, Katz says it is used throughout the cosmetic industry to describe products that are marketed as cosmetics but that have drug-like effects. Tretinoin (retinoic acid), the biologically active form of vitamin A, for example, is not prohibited from use in cosmetics. However, when it is used topically for treating mild to moderate acne, sun-damaged skin, and other skin conditions, it is recognized by the FDA as a drug. This is because it acts deep at the skin's cellular level by increasing collagen.

According to the AAD, the answer to whether or not cosmeceuticals really work lies in the ingredients and how they interact with the biological mechanisms that occur in aging skin. The regulatory question the FDA faces when considering such products, Katz says, "is whether or not a manufacturer is making a structure or function claim."

The FDA uses different standards when evaluating the risks and benefits of products used for cosmetic treatments than for therapeutic uses of products. Steven K. Galson, M.D., M.P.H., acting director for the FDA's Center for Drug Evaluation and Research, adds that products like tretinoin and Restylane that are not indicated for serious or life-threatening conditions are subject to close examination by the agency because of the benefit-to-risk ratio.

"Because these products are for cosmetic purposes, they must be extraordinarily safe," Galson says. This means that the FDA may allow someone to incur a greater risk from products that treat medical conditions, rather than from those that are intended for cosmetic purposes. "We generally won't tolerate much risk for a drug whose primary use is cosmetic," he says.

Welcome Side Effects

Many cosmetic treatments are the result of common disease therapies whose unexpected side effects were pleasant surprises. Vaniqa (eflornithine hydrochloride), the first prescription drug for removing unwanted hair, is a topically applied version of a drug that was originally developed to treat African sleeping sickness. Similarly, minoxidil originally had been prescribed as an oral tablet to treat high blood pressure. As a result of side effects that included hair growth and reversal of male baldness, Rogaine (two percent minoxidil) was the first drug approved by the FDA for the treatment of hair loss (androgenetic alopecia).

"There's a lot of serendipity in drug development," says the FDA's Wilkin. A pill to help smokers quit, for example, evolved out of the unexpected observation that a drug intended to treat depression also seemed to take away the desire to smoke. Bupropion was first marketed in 1989 by GlaxoSmithKline as an antidepressant under the name Wellbutrin. After doctors noticed that patients being treated with Wellbutrin gave up smoking spontaneously, studies were done to show that the product could help smokers quit, as well. As a result, the slow-release form of bupropion, marketed as Zyban, was approved by the FDA in 1997 as an aid to smoking cessation treatment.

Some pharmaceutical companies, however, apparently aren't ready to enter the vanity drugs arena. Patrick Davish, the global product communications spokesman for Merck & Co. Inc., says that the drug company has no "cosmetic" drugs in its product pipeline at this time.

"The fact that we don't participate in that market right now—I'm not sure that's reflective of any particular deliberation or decision," he says. "That's just not where the science has taken us."

☞ Remember!!
Before Electing To Have A Cosmetic Procedure

- Discuss it with a physician who can refer you to a specialist in the fields of dermatology and aesthetic plastic surgery

- Begin with a consultation to find the right doctor, and select one who is qualified to do the procedure you want

- Make sure the doctor you choose is certified by an appropriate medical board

- Have realistic expectations about the benefits you want to achieve

- Compare fees—insurance does not usually cover elective procedures.

Source: "Science Meets Beauty: Using Medicine to Improve Appearances," U.S. Food and Drug Administration, 2004.

Table 10.1. Top 5 Cosmetic Nonsurgical Procedures (2002)

Procedure	Number Of Procedures
Botulinum toxin injection (Botox®, Myobloc®)	1,658,667
Microdermabrasion	1,032,417
Collagen injection	783,120
Laser hair removal	736,458
Chemical peel	495,415

Source: American Society for Aesthetic Plastic Surgery, 2002.

Saving Face

According to the American Society for Aesthetic Plastic Surgery (ASAPS), nearly seven million Americans underwent surgical and nonsurgical cosmetic procedures in 2002. Laura Bradbard was one of them.

Despite the sudden explosion of such "lunchtime" techniques as Restylane for erasing wrinkles, and Botox (botulinum toxin type A) for smoothing out frown lines, Bradbard, of Gaithersburg, Maryland, opted for a longer-lasting reconstructive facelift that included a chin implant, eyelid surgery, and surprisingly, only a few days of pain-free recovery.

"None of this was medically necessary," admits Bradbard, a 48-year-old FDA press officer, "but I had been feeling worn out and tired. What I saw in the mirror was sad." Bradbard says she didn't get a facelift to look younger; she only wanted her face to look more balanced. In the end, she says, "My doctor gave me a chin that geometrically fit my face," and a look that she says makes her feel better about herself.

Table 10.2. Top 5 Cosmetic Surgical Procedures (2002)

Procedure	Number Of Procedures
Lipoplasty (liposuction)	372,831
Breast augmentation	249,641
Eyelid surgery	229,092
Rhinoplasty (nose reshaping)	156,973
Breast reduction	125,614

Source: American Society for Aesthetic Plastic Surgery, 2002.

Like Bradbard, others are spending a lot of money to look good. "With patients living 90-plus years, today's anti-aging modalities offer people noninvasive procedures that mimic true facelifts," says Craig R. Dufresne, M.D., a plastic and reconstructive surgeon in Chevy Chase, Maryland, who performed Bradbard's surgery. However, Dufresne says he suggested reconstructive surgery for Bradbard because "she wanted to deal with structural changes to restore facial balance," which was more than the chemical action of a drug could produce. "And skin product application (such as wrinkle fillers) following a facelift," adds Dufresne, "will actually allow the facelift or any other reconstructive procedure to last longer and make a great result even better."

Seeking Professional Advice

Since it is often difficult for people to determine the validity of claims made about topical products and to decide among the overwhelming number of anti-aging procedures, how do people know what's right for them?

"A good place to start is with a dermatologist," says Arielle N.B.

> ✔ **Quick Tip**
> **Cosmetic Procedures And Surgery**
>
> Some women choose to have cosmetic procedures to improve appearance and self-esteem. But the decision to have a cosmetic procedure should not be made lightly. If you are thinking about having a cosmetic procedure, ask your doctor:
>
> • How is the procedure done?
>
> • Am I good candidate for the procedure?
>
> • How does my health history affect my risk of problems?
>
> • What results and side effects can I expect?
>
> • What are the risks?
>
> • When can I restart normal activities?
>
> • How much will the procedure cost? (Cosmetic procedures usually are not covered by insurance.)
>
> • What is your training and experience?
>
> • Can you provide references from patients you have treated?
>
> Source: From "Skin and Hair Health," *The Healthy Woman: A Complete Guide for All Ages*, National Women's Health Information Center, 2008.

Kauvar, M.D., clinical associate professor of dermatology at the New York University School of Medicine. "Dermatologists are trained in the health, function and disease state of the skin, and people could save time, money, and confusion by seeking the advice of a dermatologist rather than guessing what might work for them."

Kauvar says a dermatologist's recommendations can help consumers make informed decisions. "People shouldn't hunt and peck for products," she adds. "Not knowing what type of skin you have is why so many people try unnecessary products that can often do more harm than good."

An expert in laser procedures, Kauvar says that, in the past, techniques for improving aging skin required invasive laser or surgical procedures, which produced open wounds and required long recovery times. Today, she says, people can choose from a variety of non-ablative (non-wounding) laser treatments that are designed to reverse, improve, or erase the early signs of aging, take very little time to perform, and have a minimal, if any, recovery time.

While Bradbard wasn't interested in removing wrinkles at the time of her facelift, given what she knows about new technologies and drug delivery systems today, she says, "I would consider both non-invasive procedures and another facelift down the road, depending on how much my skin changes. I would ask my doctor what would give me the best results with the longest-lasting effects."

Buyer Beware

Anti-aging products that promise to diminish wrinkles and fine lines are found on many store shelves. However, dermatologists recommend that people consider only those procedures and products that have proven, over time, to be most effective at reversing the aging process. Most doctors agree that the leading product to prevent premature wrinkles and sun damage is sunscreen. A broad-spectrum sunscreen that protects the skin from both UVA and UVB rays, with a sun protection factor (SPF) of 15 or higher, can prevent the skin from looking older than it is.

According to the American Society for Aesthetic Plastic Surgery, it's important to realize that although certain products and procedures are effective, they are also limited by the skin's normal aging process. A product that has been deemed effective for erasing wrinkles doesn't necessarily erase wrinkles—there are lots of variables that determine its effectiveness.

For example, the active ingredient in a drug must be delivered to the skin at a therapeutic concentration and remain in the skin long enough to have an effect. Also, because the composition of a man's body differs from a woman's, products or procedures can have different effects. The facial area in men contains hair, for example, and their skin is thicker. This means the blood supply is greater—and so is the risk of bleeding—but it also could mean better healing.

And cosmetic procedures come with risks. If a procedure is performed poorly, the physical and emotional scars could be carried for life. Understand the risks and side effects that may be involved.

Chapter 11

Body Piercing: A Guide For Teens

Body art has become so popular in the past few years that it's hard to walk down the street, go to the mall, or watch TV without seeing someone with a piercing or a tattoo. Whether it's ears, lips, nostrils, eyebrows, belly buttons, tongues, or even cheeks, you've probably seen piercings—maybe multiple piercings—on lots of people.

Perhaps you think body piercings look cool and you've thought about getting one. But are they safe? Are they a good idea? And what should you be aware of if you do decide to get one?

What Is A Body Piercing And What Can You Expect?

A body piercing is exactly that—a piercing or puncture made in your body by a needle. After that, a piece of jewelry is inserted into the puncture. The most popular pierced body parts seem to be the ears, the nostrils, and the belly button.

If the person performing the piercing provides a safe, clean, and professional environment, this is what you should expect from getting a body part pierced:

About This Chapter: From "Body Piercing," November 2008, reprinted with permission from www.kidshealth.org. Copyright © 2008 The Nemours Foundation. This information was provided by KidsHealth, one of the largest resources online for medically reviewed health information written for parents, kids, and teens. For more articles like this one, visit www.KidsHealth.org, or www.TeensHealth.org.

- The area you've chosen to be pierced (except for the tongue) is cleaned with a germicidal soap (a soap that kills disease-causing bacteria and microorganisms).

- Your skin is then punctured with a very sharp, clean needle.

- The piece of jewelry, which has already been sterilized, is attached to the area.

- The person performing the piercing disposes of the needle in a special container so that there is no risk of the needle or blood touching someone else.

- The pierced area is cleaned.

- The person performing the piercing checks and adjusts the jewelry.

- The person performing the piercing gives you instructions on how to make sure your new piercing heals correctly and what to do if there is a problem.

Before You Pierce That Part

If you're thinking about getting pierced, do your research first. If you're under 18, some places won't allow you to get a piercing without a parent's consent. It's a good idea to find out what risks are involved and how best to protect yourself from infections and other complications.

Certain sites on the body can cause more problems than others—infection is a common complication of mouth and nose piercings because of the millions of bacteria that live in those areas. Tongue piercings can damage teeth over time. And tongue, cheek, and lip piercings can cause gum problems.

Studies have shown that people with certain types of heart disease might have a higher risk of developing a heart infection after body piercing. If you have a medical problem such as allergies, diabetes, skin disorders, a condition that affects your immune system, or infections—or if you are pregnant—ask your doctor if there are any special concerns you should have or precautions you should take beforehand. Also, it's not a good idea to get a body piercing if you're prone to getting keloids (an overgrowth of scar tissue in the area of the wound).

☞ **Remember!!**

If You Decide To Get A Body Piercing

- Make sure you're up to date with your immunizations (especially hepatitis B and tetanus).

- Plan where you will get medical care if your piercing becomes infected (signs of infection include excessive redness or tenderness around the piercing site, prolonged bleeding, pus, and change in your skin color around the piercing area).

- If you plan to get a tongue or mouth piercing, make sure your teeth and gums are healthy.

Making Sure The Piercing Shop Is Safe And Sanitary

Body piercing is regulated in some states but not others. Although most piercing shops try to provide a clean and healthy environment, some might not take proper precautions against infections or other health hazards.

If you decide to get a body piercing, do a little investigative work about a shop's procedures and find out whether it provides a clean and safe environment for its customers. Every shop should have an autoclave (a sterilizing machine) and should keep instruments in sealed packets until they are used. Ask questions and make sure:

- the shop is clean;

- the person doing the piercing washes his or her hands with a germicidal soap;

- the person doing the piercing wears fresh disposable gloves (like those worn at a doctor's office);

- the person doing the piercing uses sterilized instruments or instruments that are thrown away after use;

- the person doing the piercing does not use a piercing gun (they're not sterile);

- the needle being used is new and is being used for the first time;

- the needle is disposed of in a special sealed container after the piercing;

- there are procedures for the proper handling and disposal of waste (like needles or gauze with blood on them).

It's also a good idea to ask about the types of jewelry the shop offers because some people have allergic reactions to certain types of metals. Before you get a piercing, make sure you know if you're allergic to any metals.

If you think the shop isn't clean enough, if all your questions aren't answered, or if you feel in any way uncomfortable, go somewhere else to get your piercing.

Some Health Risks

If all goes well, you should be fine after a body piercing except for some temporary symptoms, including some pain, swelling at the pierced area, and in the case of a tongue piercing, increased saliva. But be aware that several things, including the following, can go wrong in some cases:

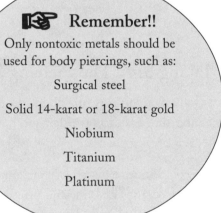

Remember!!

Only nontoxic metals should be used for body piercings, such as:

Surgical steel

Solid 14-karat or 18-karat gold

Niobium

Titanium

Platinum

- Chronic infection

- Uncontrollable or prolonged bleeding

- Scarring

- Hepatitis B and C

- Tetanus

- Skin allergies to the jewelry that's used

- Abscesses or boils (collections of pus that can form under your skin at the site of the piercing)

- Inflammation or nerve damage

Depending on the body part, healing times can take anywhere from a few weeks to more than a year. If you do get a piercing, make sure you take good care of it afterward—don't pick or tug at it, keep the area clean with soap (not alcohol), and don't touch it without washing your hands first. Never use hydrogen peroxide because it can break down newly formed tissue. If you have a mouth piercing, use an alcohol-free, antibacterial mouthwash after eating.

If you're thinking of donating blood, be aware that some organizations won't accept blood donations from anyone who has had a body piercing or tattoo within the last year because both procedures can transmit blood-borne diseases you may not realize were passed on to you at the time of the piercing.

If your piercing doesn't heal correctly or you feel something might be wrong, it's important to get medical attention. Most important, don't pierce yourself or have a friend do it—make sure it's done by a professional in a safe and clean environment.

Chapter 12

Tattoos And Permanent Makeup

Tattoos And Permanent Makeup

The U.S. Food and Drug Administration (FDA) considers the inks used in intradermal tattoos, including permanent makeup, to be cosmetics and considers the pigments used in the inks to be color additives requiring premarket approval under the Federal Food, Drug, and Cosmetic Act. However, because of other public health priorities and a previous lack of evidence of safety concerns, FDA traditionally has not exercised its regulatory authority over tattoo inks or the pigments used in them. The actual practice of tattooing is regulated by local jurisdictions. FDA is aware of more than 150 reports of adverse reactions in consumers to certain permanent makeup ink shades, and it is possible that the actual number of women affected was greater. In addition, concerns raised by the scientific community regarding the pigments used in these inks have prompted FDA to investigate the safe use of tattoo inks. FDA continues to evaluate the extent and severity of adverse events associated with tattooing and is conducting research on inks. As new information is assessed, the agency will consider whether additional actions are necessary to protect public health.

About This Chapter: Excerpted from "Tattoos And Permanent Makeup," CFSAN/ Office of Cosmetics and Colors, U.S. Food and Drug Administration, June 2008; and "Temporary Tattoos and Henna/Mehndi," CFSAN/Office of Cosmetics and Colors, U.S. Food and Drug Administration, September 2006.

In addition to the reported adverse reactions, areas of concern include tattoo removal, infections that result from tattooing, and the increasing variety of pigments and diluents being used in tattooing. More than fifty different pigments and shades are in use, and the list continues to grow. Although a number of color additives are approved for use in cosmetics, none is approved for injection into the skin. Using an unapproved color additive in a tattoo ink makes the ink adulterated. Many pigments used in tattoo inks are not approved for skin contact at all. Some are industrial grade colors that are suitable for printers' ink or automobile paint.

Nevertheless, many individuals choose to undergo tattooing in its various forms. For some, it is an aesthetic choice or an initiation rite. Some choose permanent makeup as a time saver or because they have physical difficulty applying regular, temporary makeup. For others, tattooing is an adjunct to reconstructive surgery, particularly of the face or breast, to simulate natural pigmentation. People who have lost their eyebrows due to alopecia (a form of hair loss) may choose to have "eyebrows" tattooed on, while people with vitiligo (a lack of pigmentation in areas of the skin) may try tattooing to help camouflage the condition.

Whatever their reason, consumers should be aware of the risks involved in order to make an informed decision.

What Risks Are Involved In Tattooing?

The following are the primary complications that can result from tattooing:

- **Infection:** Unsterile tattooing equipment and needles can transmit infectious diseases, such as hepatitis and skin infections caused by *Staphylococcus aureus* ("staph") bacteria. Tattoos received at facilities not regulated by your state or at facilities that use unsterile equipment (or re-use ink) may prevent you from being accepted as a blood or plasma donor for twelve months.

- **Removal Problems:** Despite advances in laser technology, removing a tattoo is a painstaking process, usually involving several treatments and considerable expense. Complete removal without scarring may be impossible.

- **Allergic Reactions:** Although FDA has received reports of numerous adverse reactions associated with certain shades of ink in permanent makeup, marketed by a particular manufacturer, reports of allergic reactions to tattoo pigments have been rare. However, when they happen they may be particularly troublesome because the pigments can be hard to remove. Occasionally, people may develop an allergic reaction to tattoos they have had for years.

- **Granulomas:** These are nodules that may form around material that the body perceives as foreign, such as particles of tattoo pigment.

- **Keloid Formation:** If you are prone to developing keloids—scars that grow beyond normal boundaries—you are at risk of keloid formation from a tattoo. Keloids may form any time you injure or traumatize your skin.

- **MRI Complications:** There have been reports of people with tattoos or permanent makeup who experienced swelling or burning in the affected areas when they underwent magnetic resonance imaging (MRI). This seems to occur only rarely and apparently without lasting effects.

✔ Quick Tip
Reporting Adverse Reactions

FDA urges consumers and healthcare providers to report adverse reactions to tattoos and permanent makeup, problems with removal, or adverse reactions to temporary tattoos. Consumers and healthcare providers can register complaints by contacting their FDA district office (see the blue pages of your local phone directory) or by contacting FDA's Center for Food Safety and Applied Nutrition (CFSAN) Adverse Events Reporting System (CAERS) by phone at (301) 436-2405 or by e-mail at CAERS@cfsan.fda.gov.

Source: FDA, June 23, 2008.

There also have been reports of tattoo pigments interfering with the quality of the image. This seems to occur mainly when a person with permanent eyeliner undergoes MRI of the eyes. Mascara may produce a similar effect. The difference is that mascara is easily removable.

The cause of these complications is uncertain. Some have theorized that they result from an interaction with the metallic components of some pigments.

However, the risks of avoiding an MRI when your doctor has recommended one are likely to be much greater than the risks of complications from an interaction between the MRI and tattoo or permanent makeup. Instead of avoiding an MRI, individuals who have tattoos or permanent makeup should inform the radiologist or technician of this fact in order to take appropriate precautions and avoid complications.

A Common Problem: Dissatisfaction

A common problem that may develop with tattoos is the desire to remove them. Removing tattoos and permanent makeup can be very difficult.

Although tattoos may be satisfactory at first, they sometimes fade. Also, if the tattooist injects the pigments too deeply into the skin, the pigments may migrate beyond the original sites, resulting in a blurred appearance.

Another cause of dissatisfaction is that the human body changes over time, and styles change with the season. The permanent makeup that may have looked flattering when first injected may later clash with changing skin tones and facial or body contours. People who plan to have facial cosmetic surgery are advised that the appearance of their permanent makeup may become distorted. The tattoo that seemed stylish at first may become dated and embarrassing. And changing tattoos or permanent makeup is not as easy as changing your mind.

Consult your health care provider about the best removal techniques for you.

Temporary Tattoos And Henna/Mehndi

FDA has received reports of adverse reactions to some temporary skin-staining products. The following information is intended to respond to questions about the safety and legality of such products.

♣ It's A Fact!!
What About "Decal"-Type
Temporary Tattoos?

Temporary tattoos, such as those applied to the skin with a moistened wad of cotton, fade several days after application. Many contain color additives approved for cosmetic use on the skin. However, FDA has received reports of allergic reactions to some temporary tattoos.

An import alert is in effect for several foreign-made temporary tattoos. According to Consumer Safety officer Allen Halper of FDA's Office of Cosmetics and Colors, the temporary tattoos subject to the import alert are not allowed into the United States because they don't have the required ingredient declaration on the label or they contain colors not permitted for use in cosmetics applied to the skin.

Source: FDA, September 2006.

What About Henna, Or Mehndi?

Henna, a coloring made from a plant, is approved only for use as a hair dye, not for direct application to the skin, as in the body-decorating process known as mehndi. This unapproved use of a color additive makes these products adulterated and therefore illegal. An import alert is in effect for henna intended for use on the skin. FDA has received reports of injuries to the skin from products marketed as henna.

Since henna typically produces a brown, orange-brown, or reddish-brown tint, other ingredients must be added to produce other colors, such as those marketed as "black henna" and "blue henna." So-called "black henna" may contain the "coal tar" color p-phenylenediamine, also known as PPD. This ingredient may cause allergic reactions in some individuals. The only legal use of PPD in cosmetics is as a hair dye. It is not approved for direct application to the skin. Even brown shades of products marketed as henna may contain other ingredients intended to make them darker or make the stain last longer.

In addition to color additives, these skin-decorating products may contain other ingredients, such as solvents.

How Do I Know What's In A Temporary Tattoo Or Henna/Mehndi Product?

Cosmetics, including temporary skin-staining products, that are sold on a retail basis to consumers must have their ingredients listed on the label. Without such an ingredient declaration, they are considered misbranded and are illegal in interstate commerce. FDA requires the ingredient declaration under the authority of the Fair Packaging and Labeling Act (FPLA).

Because the FPLA does not apply to cosmetic samples and products used exclusively by professionals—for example, for application at a salon, or a booth at a fair or boardwalk—the requirement for an ingredient declaration does not apply to these products.

Does FDA Approve Color Additives?

By law, except for coal tar colors used in hair dyes, color additives used in cosmetics must be approved by FDA for their intended uses. Some may not be used unless FDA has certified in its own labs that the composition of each batch meets the regulatory requirements. Cosmetics—including temporary tattoo products—that do not comply with restrictions on color additives are considered adulterated and are illegal in interstate commerce.

Does FDA Approve Other Cosmetic Ingredients?

Except for color additives, FDA does not have the authority to approve cosmetic products or ingredients, although the use of several substances in cosmetics is prohibited or restricted due to safety concerns. However, if the safety of the product or its ingredients has not been substantiated, the product is misbranded—and therefore illegal in interstate commerce—if it does not have this warning on the label: "Warning: The safety of this product has not been determined."

Chapter 13

Removing Unwanted Hair

As you browse the aisles of your local drugstore, you may feel a little dizzy. Next to the dozens of products devoted to making the hair on your head thicker or shinier, you'll see dozens more promising to get rid of unwanted hair. So which hair removal methods work best? And do you need any of them?

Different Types Of Hair

Before removing hair, it helps to know about the different types of hair on our bodies. All hair is made of keratin, a hard protein that's also found in your fingernails and toenails. Hair growth begins beneath the surface of your skin at a hair root inside a hair follicle, a small tube in the skin.

You have two types of hair on your body. Vellus hair is soft, fine, and short. Most women have vellus hair on their chest, back, and face. It can be darker and more noticeable in some women than others, especially those with darker complexions. Vellus hair helps the body maintain a steady temperature by providing some insulation.

About This Chapter: From "Hair Removal," January 2008, reprinted with permission from www.kidshealth.org. Copyright © 2008 The Nemours Foundation. This information was provided by KidsHealth, one of the largest resources online for medically reviewed health information written for parents, kids, and teens. For more articles like this one, visit www.KidsHealth.org, or www.TeensHealth.org.

Terminal hair is coarser, darker, and longer than vellus hair. It's the type of hair that grows on your head. Around puberty, terminal hair starts to grow in the armpits and pubic region. On guys, terminal hair begins to grow on the face and other parts of the body such as the chest, legs, and back. Terminal hair is there to provide cushioning and protection.

In some cases, excess hair growth, called hirsutism (pronounced: hur-soo-tih-zum), may be the result of certain medical conditions. In girls, polycystic ovary syndrome and other hormonal disorders can cause dark, coarse hair to grow on the face, especially the upper lip and chin, as well as on the chest, belly, and back. Some medications, like anabolic steroids, also can cause hirsutism.

Getting Rid Of Hair

Shaving

How It Works: Using a razor, a person removes the tip of the hair shaft that has grown out through the skin. Some razors are completely disposable, some have a disposable blade, and some are electric. Guys often shave their faces, and women often shave their underarms, legs, and bikini areas.

How Long It Lasts: One to three days.

Pros: Shaving is fairly inexpensive, and you can do it yourself. All you need is some warm water, a razor, and if you choose, shaving gel or cream.

Cons: Razor burn, bumps, nicks, cuts, and ingrown hairs are side effects of shaving. Ingrown hairs can happen with close, frequent shaving. When the hair begins to grow, it grows within the surrounding tissue rather than growing out of the follicle. The hair curls around and starts growing into the skin, irritating it.

Tips: You'll get a closer shave if you shave in the shower after your skin has been softened by warm water. Go slowly, pulling looser areas of skin taut before running the razor over them. Change razors often to avoid nicks. Using shaving cream may also help protect sensitive skin, like the skin around the genitals. If you're nervous about cutting yourself, you can try an electric razor instead.

Although most people shave in the opposite direction from the hair growth, if you want to avoid ingrown hairs it can help to shave in the direction the hair grows.

Plucking

How It Works: Using tweezers, a person stretches the skin tightly, grips the hair close to the root, and pulls it out.

How Long It Lasts: Three to eight weeks.

Pros: Plucking is inexpensive because all you need are tweezers. But it can be time-consuming because you can only remove one hair at a time. Devices called epilators, which cost around $25 to $70, can pull out multiple hairs at once.

Cons: Plucking can be painful. If the hair breaks off below the skin, a person may get an ingrown hair. After plucking, you may notice temporary red bumps because the hair follicle is swollen and irritated. Epilators aren't a good idea for use on areas like eyebrows because they pull out a bunch of hairs at once and don't give you precise control.

Tips: Make sure you sterilize your tweezers or other plucking devices with rubbing alcohol before and after use to reduce the chance of infection.

✔ **Quick Tip**

Dealing With Ingrown Hairs

If you have an ingrown hair, try exfoliating (removing dead skin cells using an exfoliating wash in the shower) and moisturizing the area. You can apply an antiseptic to help prevent infection, but if you notice redness or swelling, or have pain in the area, see a doctor. Avoid ingrown hairs by shaving in the direction of hair growth.

Depilatories

How They Work: A depilatory is a cream or liquid that removes hair from the skin's surface. They work by reacting with the protein structure of the hair, so the hair dissolves and can be washed or wiped away.

How Long They Last: Several days to two weeks.

Pros: Depilatories work quickly, are readily available at drugstores and grocery stores, and are inexpensive. They're best on the leg, underarm, and bikini areas; special formulations may be used on the face and chin.

Cons: Applying depilatories can be messy and many people dislike the odor. If you have sensitive skin, you might have an allergic reaction to the chemicals in the depilatory, which may cause a rash or inflammation. Depilatories may not be as effective on people with coarse hair.

Tips: Read product directions carefully and be sure to apply the product only for the recommended amount of time for best results. Before using a depilatory on pubic hair, read product labels to find one that says it's safe to use on the "bikini" area or genitals.

Waxing

How It Works: A sticky wax is spread on the area of skin where the unwanted hair is growing. A cloth strip is then applied over the wax and quickly pulled off, taking the hair root and dead skin cells with it. The wax can be warmed or may be applied cold. Waxing can be done at a salon or at home.

How Long It Lasts: Three to six weeks.

Pros: Waxing leaves the area smooth and is long lasting. Waxing kits are readily available in drugstores and grocery stores. Hair regrowth looks lighter and less noticeable than it is after other methods of hair removal, such as shaving.

Cons: Many people say the biggest drawback to waxing is the discomfort: Because the treatment works by pulling hair out at the roots, it can sting a bit as the hair comes off—luckily that part is fast. People may notice temporary redness, inflammation, and bumps after waxing.

Professional waxing is more expensive than other hair removal methods. However, it can help to get a first waxing treatment done in a salon to watch how the professionals do it (because salon staff are used to waxing all parts of the male and female body there's no need to feel embarrassed).

Teens who use acne medications such as tretinoin and isotretinoin may want to skip waxing because those medicines make the skin more sensitive. People with moles or skin irritation from sunburn should also avoid waxing.

Tips: For waxing to work, hair should be at least ¼ inch (about 6 milli-meters) long. So skip shaving for a few weeks before waxing. Waxing works well on the legs, bikini area, and eyebrows.

Electrolysis

How It Works: Over a series of several appointments, a professional elec-trologist inserts a needle into the follicle and sends an electric current through the hair root, killing it. A small area such as the upper lip may take a total of four to 10 hours and a larger area such as the bikini line may take eight to 16 hours.

How Long It Lasts: Intended to be permanent, but some people have regrowth of hair.

Pros: Some people have permanent hair removal.

Cons: Electrolysis takes big bucks and lots of time, so it's usually only used on smaller areas such as the upper lip, eyebrows, and underarms. Many people describe the process as painful, and dry skin, scabs, scarring, and in-flammation may result after treatment. Infection may be a risk if the needles and other instruments aren't properly sterilized.

Tips: Talk to your doctor if you're interested in this method. He or she may be able to recommend an electrologist with the proper credentials.

Laser Hair Removal

How It Works: A laser is directed through the skin to the hair follicle, where it stops growth. It works best on light-skinned people with dark hair because the melanin (colored pigment) in the hair absorbs more of the light, making treatment more effective.

How Long It Lasts: Intended to be permanent, but people often need to return every six months to a year for maintenance.

Pros: This type of hair removal is long lasting and large areas of skin can be treated at the same time.

Cons: A treatment session may cost $400 or more. Side effects of the treatment may include inflammation and redness.

Tips: Using cold packs may help diminish any inflammation after treatment. Avoiding the sun before a treatment may make results more effective.

Prescription Treatments

A cream called eflornithine is available by prescription to treat facial hair growth in women. The cream is applied twice a day until the hair becomes softer and lighter—more like vellus hair. Side effects may include skin irritation and acne. Talk to your doctor or dermatologist if you are concerned about hair growth and removal.

Antiandrogen medications are another method that doctors prescribe to reduce the appearance of unwanted hair. Because androgen hormones can be responsible for hair growth in unwanted areas, these medications can reduce hair growth by blocking androgen production. Doctors often prescribe oral contraceptives in conjunction with these medications to enhance their effect, avoid pregnancy (since antiandrogens can be harmful to a developing fetus) and help regularize the menstrual cycle in girls who need it.

Deciding to remove body hair is a personal choice. Getting rid of body hair doesn't make a person healthier, and you shouldn't feel pressured to do so if you don't want to. Some cultures view body hair as beautiful and natural, so do what feels right to you.

Chapter 14

Taking Care Of Your Hair

We have about 100,000 hairs on our heads. Each hair shaft has three layers, with the cuticle, or outside layer, protecting the two inner layers.

Shiny hair is a sign of health because the layers of the cuticle lie flat and reflect light. When the scales of the cuticle lie flat they overlap tightly, so the inner layers are well protected from heat, sun, chlorine, and all the other hazards that can come from living in our environment. When hair is damaged, though, the scales may separate and hair can become dry. Because the scales on dry hair don't protect the inner two layers as well, hair can break and look dull.

The type of hair a person has—whether it's straight or curly—can also affect how shiny it is. Sebum, which is the natural oil on the hair, covers straight hair better than curly hair, which is why straight hair can appear shinier.

Depending how long a person's hair is or how fast it grows, the end of each hair shaft can be a couple of years old. So the hair at the end of the shaft could have survived a few summers of scorching sun and saltwater and winters of cold, dry air. How well you care for your hair from the time it emerges from the root plays a role in how healthy it looks.

Caring For Hair

How you take care of your hair depends on the type of hair you have, your lifestyle, and how you style your hair.

♣ It's A Fact!!

Hair Disorders

Living with a hair disorder can be hard, especially in a culture that views hair as a feature of beauty. To cope, try to value yourself for who you are—not by how you look. Also, play up your best features, which can boost self-esteem. Many women with hair disorders also find that talking to others with the same problem is helpful.

Hair Loss: It's normal to shed about 100 hairs each day as old hairs are replaced by new ones. But some women have hair loss—called alopecia (AL-uh-PEE-shuh). Hair loss can happen for many reasons:

- Female pattern baldness causes hair to thin, but rarely leads to total baldness. It tends to run in families.

- Alopecia areata (AR-ee-AYT-uh) is an autoimmune disease that causes patchy hair loss on the scalp, face, or other areas of your body.

- Hormone changes during and after pregnancy.

- Underlying health problems, such as polycystic ovary syndrome (PCOS) or thyroid disease.

- Certain medicines, such as birth control pills or those to treat cancer, arthritis, depression, or heart problems.

- Extreme stress, such as from a major illness.

- Hairstyles that twist or pull hair.

Your Hair Type

People with dry, curly hair have different hair care needs than people with straight, fine hair. But all hair needs to be treated gently, especially when it's wet. Wet hair can stretch, making it more vulnerable to breakage or cuticle damage. That's why using a hot blow-dryer (or other heat styling products) on very wet hair can damage it.

Whether or not hair will grow back depends on the cause of hair loss. Some medicines can help speed up the growth of new hair. If hair loss is permanent, you can try hair weaving or changing your hairstyle. Or talk with your doctor about other options, such as a hair transplant.

Hirsutism: When dark, thick hair grows on a woman's face, chest, belly, or back, the condition is called hirsutism (HUR-suh-TIZ-uhm). Health problems and family genes can cause high levels of male hormones, which can result in hirsutism. If you are overweight, try losing weight, which reduces male hormone levels. Consider methods for removal of unwanted hair. Also, ask your doctor about medicines to slow or reduce hair growth.

Polycystic Ovary Syndrome (PCOS): Women with polycystic ovary syndrome (PCOS) make too many male hormones. This can cause male pattern balding or thinning hair and/or hirsutism.

Trichotillomania: People with trichotillomania (TRIH-koh-TIL-uh-MAY-nee-uh) have a strong urge to pull out their hair, which leads to visible hair loss. Some people with this hair-pulling disorder also pluck their eyebrows, eyelashes, and body hair. Hair pulling gives people with this disorder a sense of relief or pleasure. But it also is a source of distress and shame. Behavioral therapy and medicines can help a person stop hair pulling.

Source: From "Skin and Hair Health," *The Healthy Woman: A Complete Guide for All Ages*, National Women's Health Information Center, 2008.

Some people find that their hair gets oily in their teen years. That's because the hair follicles contain sebaceous glands that make sebum, which moisturizes the hair and skin. During adolescence, the sebaceous glands may become overactive, producing more oil than needed. As with acne, oily hair is usually a temporary part of puberty.

Many teens care for oily hair by washing it once a day—or more if they're active. As long as you treat your hair gently when it's wet, frequent washing shouldn't harm it. If you have acne, it's a good idea to keep the hair around your face clean so hair oils don't clog your pores.

If you're washing your hair every day or more, it may be better to choose a mild shampoo instead of a shampoo designed for oily hair. For some people—especially people with fine, fragile, or combination hair (hair that's oily at the crown but dry on the ends)—shampoos for oily hair can be too harsh. If you have oily hair and want to use a conditioner, choose one that's made for oily hair.

If your hair is dry, it's a good idea to wash it less frequently. Some people only need to wash their hair once a week—and that's fine. Many people who have curly hair also have dry hair. Curly and dry hair types are usually more fragile than straight hair, so you'll need to be especially careful about using heat styling products. Shampoos made for dry hair and hair conditioners can help.

Your Activity Level And Interests

Do you play sports or spend a lot of time at the beach? These kinds of things can affect your hair. For example, if you're an athlete with oily hair, you may want to wash your hair after working up a sweat during practice and games. But if you're a lifeguard or a swimmer, sun and saltwater (or the chlorine in pool water) can dry your hair out, no matter what your hair type. If you're exposed to sun, wind, or other elements, you may want to use a shampoo designed for dry hair or use a conditioner. It's also a good idea to wear a hat to protect your hair when you're outdoors.

Your Hairstyle

Heat styling products like curling and straightening irons can dry out even oily hair if they're used too much. Follow the instructions carefully, and don't use them on wet hair or high settings, and give your hair a vacation from styling once in a while. Ask your hair stylist or dermatologist for advice on using heat styling products.

Chemical treatments can also harm hair if they're not used properly. If you decide you want a chemical treatment to color, straighten, or curl your hair, it's best to trust the job to professionals. Stylists who are trained in applying chemicals to hair will be able to evaluate your hair type and decide which chemicals will work best for you.

Here are some things to be aware of when getting chemical treatments:

- **Relaxers:** Relaxers (straighteners) work by breaking chemical bonds in curly hair. Relaxers containing lye can cause skin irritation and hair breakage. Although "no lye" relaxers may cause less irritation, both types of relaxers can cause problems if they are used in the wrong way (for example, if they're mixed incorrectly or left on the hair for too long). Scratching, brushing, or combing your hair right before a chemical relaxing treatment can increase these risks. And don't use relaxers—or any hair treatment—if your scalp is irritated.

  If you decide to keep straightening your hair, you'll need to wait at least six weeks before your next treatment to protect your hair. Relaxers can cause hair breakage when used over a period of time, even when they're used properly. Using blow-dryers, curling or straightening irons, or color on chemically relaxed hair can also increase the risk of damage.

- **Perms:** Perms take straight hair and make it curly. The risks are similar to those associated with relaxers.

- **Color:** There are two types of color: permanent (which means the color stays in your hair until it grows out) and semi-permanent (the color washes out after a while). Some semi-permanent coloring treatments, like henna, are fairly safe and easy to use at home. Some people get a condition called contact dermatitis (an allergic reaction with a rash) from henna and other "natural" products, so be sure to test a small area first.

  Other color treatments—especially permanent treatments—can cause hair loss, burning, redness, and irritation. A few types of coloring treatments can cause allergic reactions in certain people, and in rare cases these can be very serious. So talk to your stylist if you are worried that you may be sensitive to the products. Also, talk to your stylist about doing a patch test before using a product. And never use hair dyes on your eyelashes or eyebrows.

Regular haircuts are one of the best ways to help keep hair healthy. Even if you have long hair or you're trying to grow your hair, a haircut can help protect the ends of your hair from splitting and damage. In fact, cutting may actually help your hair grow better because it's healthy and not breaking off.

Dealing With Hair Problems

Here are some common hair problems—and tips on how to deal with them.

Dandruff

Dandruff—or flakes of dead skin—can be noticeable in a person's hair and on clothing. No one really knows what causes dandruff, although recent studies seem to show that it may be caused by a type of fungus.

♣ It's A Fact!!

So do blondes have more fun? No—but they do have more hair. People with blond hair have more hairs on their heads than people with brown or red hair.

Source: Nemours Foundation, 2008.

Dandruff isn't contagious or dangerous. Over-the-counter shampoos containing salicylic acid, zinc, tars, or selenium sulfide can reduce dandruff flakes. When shampooing, massage your scalp (but don't scratch) for at least five minutes, loosening the flakes with your fingers. Rinse your hair well after washing. If your dandruff doesn't improve, see your doctor. He or she may prescribe a prescription shampoo and possibly a lotion or liquid to rub into your scalp.

Hair Breakage

Hair can break when points in the hair thicken or weaken. Sometimes this happens near the scalp so a person's hair never grows very long. When hairs break at the ends, they're called "split ends," and the splits can travel up the hair shaft.

A major cause of hair breakage is improper use of chemical hair treatments, like the treatments described above. But brushing or combing hair too frequently or in the wrong way (such as using a fine-toothed comb on very thick, curly hair or teasing hair) can lead to breakage. Hair extensions and braids can also cause breakage. Leaving them in too long or pulling them out without professional help can cause hair and scalp damage or even hair loss.

Sometimes hair breakage and dry, brittle hair are signs of a medical problem, such as hypothyroidism or an eating disorder. If your hair is breaking even though you don't treat it with chemicals or other styling products, see a doctor.

Hair Loss (Alopecia)

It's normal for everyone to lose some hair. In fact, we lose about 100 hairs each day as old hairs fall out and are replaced with new ones. With hair loss, though, hair thins at a rate that can't be replaced. When hair falls out and isn't replaced by new hair, a person can become bald or have bald patches. Hair loss can be temporary or permanent, depending on the cause. If changing your hairstyle or other treatment doesn't help, see a doctor. He or she may prescribe a drug to slow or stop hair loss and to help hair grow.

As with the rest of our bodies, hair is healthiest when we eat right, exercise, and protect it from too much sun.

Chapter 15

New Warning About Ceramic Flat Irons

Dermatologists Warn Ceramic Flat Irons Could Damage Hair And Lead To Hair Breakage

Straight Hair Enthusiasts Urged To Give Their Hair A Break By Limiting Use And Avoiding Improper Application Of Popular Hair Device

While hairstyles come and go, pin-straight hair favored by A-list celebrities and emulated by scores of loyal fans from coast to coast appears to have real staying power. That's why the use of flat irons, which are used to straighten hair, has increased in popularity in recent years. Now, dermatologists warn that some flat irons can damage hair and cause hair breakage which could put a crimp in this coveted hairstyle.

At the American Academy of Dermatology's Summer Academy Meeting 2008 in Chicago, dermatologist Paradi Mirmirani, MD, FAAD, assistant clinical professor of dermatology, University of California, San Francisco, presented evidence that when ceramic flat irons are used improperly or too frequently, hair breakage can occur.

✔ Quick Tip

Treatment of damaged or broken hair includes avoiding any heat or chemicals, cutting the damaged hair, and minimizing friction to the hair. Because it does not affect normal hair growth, most hair loss from breakage is temporary.

Once hair is sufficiently damaged, it may take up to two years to be fully repaired. For successful diagnosis and treatment of hair damage, including hair loss, see your dermatologist.

"The newer flat irons that have a ceramic coating instead of a metal one are marketed as providing more rapid and uniform heat transmission. While this allows for quicker straightening of the hair with less damage, it is really a classic case of buyer beware," said Dr. Mirmirani. "We're seeing that when these ceramic flat irons are used at the highest heat settings and on a daily basis to achieve straight hair, they can really take a toll on the structure of the hair and cause very noticeable problems that can be hard to repair."

Temporary hair straightening using a flat iron is achieved by applying heated tongs to the length of the hair. This heat breaks and then reforms the hydrogen bonds in the inner core of the hair fiber. Dr. Mirmirani noted that while the goal of straightening is to alter the inner substance of the hair, the unwanted consequence may be damage to the outer protective cuticle, causing weathering, damage and eventual hair breakage.

Hair weathering or damage is usually characterized by dry ends or flyaway hair. However, if breakage occurs, it can happen anywhere along the length of the hair and cause a shaggy or skimpy appearance to the hair. When this occurs, flat iron users may use the device even more frequently to try to tame the broken or uneven appearance of their hair—which can lead to more damage.

Today, many ceramic flat irons on the market have variable heat settings with maximum temperatures of up to 410 degrees Fahrenheit (210 degrees

Celsius). Prior studies have shown that temperatures of 347 to 419 degrees Fahrenheit (175 to 215 degrees Celsius) for as little as five minutes are enough to damage most hair. However, Dr. Mirmirani warns this threshold may be even lower if the heat is applied to damp hair or hair that has been chemically treated with color or permanents, as she is seeing patients who fit this scenario more frequently. If women are not willing to give up their flat irons in the quest for straight hair, Dr. Mirmirani advised them to take precautions.

"Proper use of flat irons is extremely important, especially given how quickly hair can be damaged with high heat settings," said Dr. Mirmirani. "Flat irons should only be applied to dry hair, and specialized styling products that act as heat protectors may be applied to the hair prior to pressing to help prevent burning and allow for smoother hair that remains straight longer. If there is a temperature setting on the device, it should be set no higher than 347 degrees Fahrenheit, or 175 degrees Celsius, or on the low/medium setting."

Although how frequently a flat iron should be used depends on an individual's hair type, Dr. Mirmirani recommended that these devices should probably not be used more than two to three times per week. For those who won't leave home without the ultra straight look, Dr. Mirmirani acknowledged that forgoing the daily flat iron routine will take willpower—but the end result will be healthier, stronger hair that is not as prone to breakage and will look better in the long run.

Dr. Mirmirani added that for many women and young girls, flat irons are not the only source of hair damage.

"Improper hair care is a common cause of hair loss, and excessive or improper use of devices, such as flat irons, is only one piece of the puzzle," she said. "In fact, many of the styling products that women routinely use—including hair dyes, perms and relaxers—can all cause hair breakage. Pairing these products with the regular use of a flat iron to straighten hair could exacerbate hair breakage and cause lasting damage if left untreated."

Chapter 16

Nail Care And Nail Problems

Nails—Finger And Toe

What And Why?

Nails are a specialized form of skin. They provide 10 (or 20) little places that you can decorate. But more than that, they protect your sensitive fingers and toes, and they help you pick up small things, scratch itches, and hold on to or manipulate objects. You can also abuse them by biting, peeling, and picking at them.

Nail Care And Grooming

Your nails provide important clues to your overall health. Broken, discolored or misshapen nails can indicate nutritional deficiencies, infections, or skin conditions. Good nail care keeps your hands and feet looking nice and is part of a general program of good health habits. Below are tips for caring for your nails.

About This Chapter: This chapter begins with "Nails—Finger And Toe," reprinted with permission from the Palo Alto Medical Foundation Sports Medicine Department website, http://www.pamf.org/sports. © 2008 Palo Alto Medical Foundation. All rights reserved. Additional information under the heading "Stubborn Nail Problems Can Improve From Proper Diagnosis, Treatment By Dermatologists," is cited separately within the chapter.

✔ **Quick Tip**
Artificial Nails And Manicures

Artificial nails and manicures are very popular and can help your hands look nice. They can also be a source of health problems. Manicure tools and instruments used in salons are used on many different people. If these tools are not properly sterilized, you can get an infection such as HIV, hepatitis B or C, or warts. If you have your nails professionally applied or manicured, you should check to make sure the manicurists sterilize their equipment after each use, or take your own manicure tools for the manicurist to use.

Source: Palo Alto Medical Foundation, © 2008.

• Keep them clean and dry. This helps prevent infection.

• Shape them straight across rather than to a point. Pointed nails are weaker and can break more easily.

• Do not bite or pick them. Bitten nails are more easily infected.

Nail Polish And Removers

Nail polishes and removers are chemical lacquers, hardeners and solvents. FDA-approved nail products are safe to use, but some people have allergic reactions to some of the chemicals. Acetone, a common solvent in nail polish remover, can dry your nails, making them brittle and prone to splitting and breaking. One compound used in some acrylic nails, methacrylate (MMA), has caused allergic reactions so severe that people have lost entire nails, causing it to be banned in many states. If your nail salon uses MMA, ask them if they have an alternative product. It's not worth risking the loss of your nails.

Nail Problems

Because they're right out there on the ends of our hands and feet, nails are subject to a lot of abuse. Some of it, like biting, is self-inflicted. But everyone has experienced broken or ripped nails from catching them on or in something, or cracking and splitting from overexposure to water and chemicals. Minor nail problems usually heal as the nail grows out and require little treatment other than perhaps protecting the finger or toe if it is especially sensitive. In addition to allergic reactions to nail cosmetics and chemicals, there are a few other common problems that can occur with nails.

Abuse: Biting, picking and peeling. When you bite your nails, you are interfering with their ability to protect your sensitive fingers. What's more, you are inviting infection. Your nails can become infected because the surface is broken or removed. You can also be eating all kinds of nasty things that may be under your nails from things you have touched during the day. If you touch your dog, your car, or your school books and then bite your nails, you are ingesting the same kinds of things you would if you licked these objects. Pretty disgusting, huh? In addition, bitten-down nails are not very attractive.

Fungal Infections: Fungal infections are discussed in more detail later in this chapter.

Color Changes: Nails may change in color as a result of injury, some medications, nutritional imbalances and skin conditions. If the color of your nails has changed dramatically, it is a good idea to check with your doctor.

Hangnails: The skin around your nails can become irritated and infected from biting or chewing, minor injuries, or exposure to water and chemicals. Hangnails can cause soreness around your nails, and if an infection develops you should see your doctor.

Ingrown Nails: These can be painful. They are usually caused by improper trimming of the nail or by wearing shoes that are too tight. If you have an ingrown toenail, do not attempt to treat it by cutting or digging at it. Have it treated properly by your doctor.

Stubborn Nail Problems Can Improve From Proper Diagnosis, Treatment by Dermatologists

Brittle Nails, Nail Fungus And Problems From Nail Cosmetics Are Among The Most Common Complaints

For many of us, the health of our nails is something we often take for granted. That is until something goes wrong and changes the appearance or texture of the nails. Dermatologists, who are the physician experts in the care of skin, hair, and nails, find that brittle nails, nail fungus, and problems from nail cosmetics are among the most common sources of nail disorders. Help can be found by seeking proper diagnosis and starting a proven treatment regimen, which can include medications and behavioral changes.

At the American Academy of Dermatology's Summer Academy Meeting 2008 in Chicago, dermatologist C. Ralph Daniel, MD, FAAD, clinical professor of dermatology at the University of Mississippi in Jackson, Mississippi, and clinical associate professor of dermatology at the University of Alabama in Birmingham, Alabama, discussed these common nail complaints and how to recognize when a problem requires medical intervention.

Brittle Nails: Brittle nails are a common nail problem frequently seen by dermatologists in their practices. While it is rare for an internal illness or a drug to cause brittle nails, the primary cause is typically environmental. Dr. Daniel explained that there are two types of brittle nails—hard and brittle nails, and soft and brittle nails.

Hard and brittle nails are caused by too little moisture, with older people more prone to this condition. This type of brittle nails can make nails feel dry, and chipping or flaking commonly occurs anywhere on the nail plate. Dry skin also is common in people with brittle nails, and the condition occurs more frequently in the winter from dry heat used to warm the indoors and in very dry climates with little humidity, such as Arizona.

At the other end of the spectrum, soft and brittle nails are thought to be caused by too much moisture and can affect people of any age. However, soft and brittle nails are more common in young people, particularly those who wash their hands frequently—including medical professionals and chefs. While soft and brittle nails don't feel dry, they tend to layer more at the end of the nail plate when they chip.

> "When we treat brittle nails, we always ask patients if their toenails are affected as well—and most will say no," said Dr. Daniel. "This indicates that if the condition was caused by a lack of something in the body, such as a vitamin or mineral, it also would cause brittleness in the toenails. For that reason, dermatologists believe brittle nails are the result of contact with the environment, particularly work environments due to contact with water, or low or high humidity."

Typically, hard and brittle nails are treated by adding moisture to the nails; whereas patients with soft and brittle nails need to reduce the amount of moisture that comes in contact with their hands. For example, Dr. Daniel recommends that people with soft and brittle nails who engage in wet work should wear light cotton gloves under vinyl gloves to keep moisture away from the nails. Latex gloves are not preferred, because latex is more irritating and causes the hands to sweat. In general, he said it is a good idea for patients with either type of brittle nails to wear gloves and avoid irritants.

Nail Fungus: Fungal infections, known as *onychomycosis*, comprise approximately half of all visits to the dermatologist for nail-related problems. Since the infection occurs under the nail plate or in the nail bed, it can be difficult to treat. Fungal infections—which can be white, green, yellow or black in color—often cause the end of the nail to separate from the nail bed, and they may build up under the nail plate and discolor the nail bed. Because the feet are usually confined in a warm, moist environment, toenails are more susceptible to fungal infections.

> "We know that the foot acts as a reservoir for fungus that can spread elsewhere on the body, so it is important for dermatologists to treat the source of an infection and check the toenails and bottom of the foot when a fungus is present," said Dr. Daniel. "Patients who have

had trauma to a nail also are more susceptible to nail fungus, as the trauma can serve as a pre-disposing event."

Dr. Daniel added that psoriasis patients are prone to developing nail fungus. In fact, one study found that the occurrence of nail fungus was 56 percent greater in patients with psoriasis than in non-psoriatic patients. Men with psoriasis also were two-and-a-half times more likely to have nail fungus than women with psoriasis. Dermatologists find that while medications traditionally used to treat nail fungus work for psoriatic patients affected by this infection, these medications will not improve the underlying psoriasis.

> ✔ **Quick Tip**
>
> Nail fungus can be difficult to treat, but most cases improve with the use of available prescription topical medications. Experimental treatments for nail fungus include photodynamic therapy (PDT) and new topical treatments, and studies are currently being done with nanoparticles.
>
> Source: American Academy of Dermatology, © 2008.

Side Effects Of Nail Cosmetics

Nail cosmetics, used to enhance the appearance of nails, also can be a source of potential problems. Though not common, allergic reactions and infections from nail cosmetics used at home or at nail salons pose serious health risks.

For example, Dr. Daniel reported that most of the problems associated with nail salons are from the use of acrylic glues to hold artificial nails in place, which can cause pain, redness, itching or scaling. Although the U.S. Food and Drug Administration (FDA) banned the use of methyl acrylics, there are still instances of these types of nails being used at some salons despite their known health risks.

In addition, some of the ingredients in nail polishes and polish removers can cause allergic reactions. Free formaldehyde, which means it is not bound to another substance, also is banned by the FDA as a nail hardener because it can cause itching, redness or even blisters. Dr. Daniel also advised that consumers use nail polish remover with acetates rather than acetones, which are more drying and irritating.

To decrease the chance of contracting an infection at nail salons, Dr. Daniel recommended these tips:

- Don't use the instruments at nail salons—bring your own instruments with you.

- If you don't own your own instruments, buy a pack of disposable instruments at the nail salon that are only intended for one-time use.

- If you must use the reusable instruments at a nail salon, make sure they are sterilized properly in an autoclave. If not, find another salon.

"To ensure that your nails are strong and healthy, it is important to take care of them properly and not subject them to harsh environmental conditions or unnecessary hazards in an attempt to improve their appearance," said Dr. Daniel. "Oftentimes, changes in our nails can signal a serious underlying health problem. In a sense, dermatologists act as detectives who can diagnose a variety of health problems from clues they observe in the nails. So, see your dermatologist if you notice any abnormalities or have any concerns about the health of your nails."

Part Three

Acne

Chapter 17

Understanding Acne

What Is Acne?

Acne is a disorder resulting from the action of hormones and other substances on the skin's oil glands (sebaceous glands) and hair follicles. These factors lead to plugged pores and outbreaks of lesions commonly called pimples or zits. Acne lesions usually occur on the face, neck, back, chest, and shoulders. Although acne is usually not a serious health threat, it can be a source of significant emotional distress. Severe acne can lead to permanent scarring.

How Does Acne Develop?

Doctors describe acne as a disease of the pilosebaceous units (PSUs). Found over most of the body, PSUs consist of a sebaceous gland connected to a canal, called a follicle, that contains a fine hair (see Figure 17.1.). These units are most numerous on the face, upper back, and chest. The sebaceous glands make an oily substance called sebum that normally empties onto the skin

About This Chapter: This chapter begins with text adapted from "Acne," National Institute of Arthritis and Musculoskeletal and Skin Diseases, January 2006. Brand names included in this chapter are provided as examples only, and their inclusion does not mean that these products are endorsed by the National Institutes of Health or any other government agency. Also, if a particular brand name is not mentioned, this does not mean or imply that the product is unsatisfactory. Additional information under the heading "The Social Impact Of Acne," is cited separately within the chapter.

surface through the opening of the follicle, commonly called a pore. Cells
called keratinocytes line the follicle.

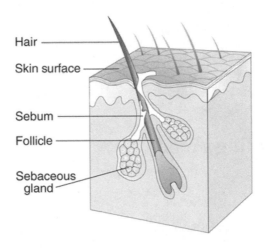

Figure 17.1. Normal Pilosebaceous Unit

The hair, sebum, and keratinocytes that fill the narrow follicle may produce a plug, which is an early sign of acne. The plug prevents sebum from
reaching the surface of the skin through a pore. The mixture of oil and cells
allows bacteria *Propionibacterium acnes* (*P. acnes*) that normally live on the
skin to grow in the plugged follicles. These bacteria produce chemicals and
enzymes and attract white blood cells that cause inflammation. (Inflammation is a characteristic reaction of tissues to disease or injury and is marked
by four signs: swelling, redness, heat, and pain.) When the wall of the plugged
follicle breaks down, it spills everything into the nearby skin—sebum, shed
skin cells, and bacteria—leading to lesions or pimples.

People with acne frequently have a variety of lesions, some of which are
shown in Figure 17.2. The basic acne lesion, called the comedo (KOM-e-
do), is simply an enlarged and plugged hair follicle. If the plugged follicle, or
comedo, stays beneath the skin, it is called a closed comedo and produces a
white bump called a whitehead. A comedo that reaches the surface of the
skin and opens up is called an open comedo or blackhead because it looks
black on the skin's surface. This black discoloration is due to changes in

sebum as it is exposed to air. It is not due to dirt. Both whiteheads and blackheads may stay in the skin for a long time.

Types Of Lesions

Some troublesome acne lesions that can develop include the following:

- **Papules:** Inflamed lesions that usually appear as small, pink bumps on the skin and can be tender to the touch

- **Pustules (Pimples):** Papules topped by white or yellow pus-filled lesions that may be red at the base

- **Nodules:** Large, painful, solid lesions that are lodged deep within the skin

- **Cysts:** Deep, painful, pus-filled lesions that can cause scarring

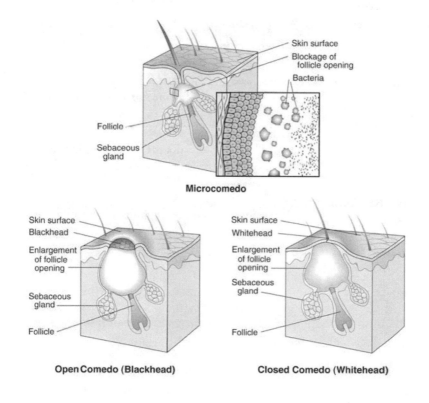

Figure 17.2. Types of Lesions

What Causes Acne?

The exact cause of acne is unknown, but doctors believe it results from several related factors. One important factor is an increase in hormones called androgens (male sex hormones). These increase in both boys and girls during puberty and cause the sebaceous glands to enlarge and make more sebum. Hormonal changes related to pregnancy or starting or stopping birth control pills can also cause acne.

Another factor is heredity or genetics. Researchers believe that the tendency to develop acne can be inherited from parents. For example, studies have shown that many school-age boys with acne have a family history of the disorder. Certain drugs, including androgens and lithium, are known to cause acne. Greasy cosmetics may alter the cells of the follicles and make them stick together, producing a plug.

Factors That Can Make Acne Worse

Factors that can cause an acne flare include the following:

> ## ✤ It's A Fact!!
> ### Myths About The Causes Of Acne
> There are many myths about what causes acne. Chocolate and greasy foods are often blamed, but there is little evidence that foods have much effect on the development and course of acne in most people. Another common myth is that dirty skin causes acne; however, blackheads and other acne lesions are not caused by dirt. Stress doesn't cause acne, but research suggests that for people who have acne, stress can make it worse.
>
> Source: National Institute of Arthritis and Musculoskeletal and Skin Diseases, 2006.

- Changing hormone levels in adolescent girls and adult women two to seven days before their menstrual period starts

- Oil from skin products (moisturizers or cosmetics) or grease encountered in the work environment (for example, a kitchen with fry vats)

- Pressure from sports helmets or equipment, backpacks, tight collars, or tight sports uniforms

- Environmental irritants, such as pollution and high humidity

- Squeezing or picking at blemishes

- Hard scrubbing of the skin

- Stress

Who Gets Acne?

People of all races and ages get acne. It is most common in adolescents and young adults. An estimated 80 percent of all people between the ages of 11 and 30 have acne outbreaks at some point. For most people, acne tends to go away by the time they reach their thirties; however, some people in their forties and fifties continue to have this skin problem.

How Should People With Acne Care For Their Skin?

Clean Skin Gently

If you have acne, you should gently wash your face with a mild cleanser, once in the morning and once in the evening, as well as after heavy exercise. Wash your face from under the jaw to the hairline and be sure to thoroughly rinse your skin.

Ask your doctor or another health professional for advice on the best type of cleanser to use.

Using strong soaps or rough scrub pads is not helpful and can actually make the problem worse. Astringents are not recommended unless the skin is very oily, and then they should be used only on oily spots.

It is also important to shampoo your hair regularly. If you have oily hair, you may want to wash it every day.

Avoid Frequent Handling Of The Skin

Avoid rubbing and touching skin lesions. Squeezing, pinching or picking blemishes can lead to the development of scars or dark blotches.

Shave Carefully

Men who shave and who have acne should test both electric and safety razors to see which is more comfortable. When using a safety razor, make sure the blade is sharp and soften your beard thoroughly with soap and water before applying shaving cream. Shave gently and only when necessary to reduce the risk of nicking blemishes.

Avoid A Sunburn Or Suntan

Many of the medicines used to treat acne can make you more prone to sunburn. A sunburn that reddens the skin or suntan that darkens the skin may make blemishes less visible and make the skin feel drier. However, these benefits are only temporary, and there are known risks of excessive sun exposure, such as more rapid skin aging and a risk of developing skin cancer.

Choose Cosmetics Carefully

While undergoing acne treatment, you may need to change some of the cosmetics you use. All cosmetics, such as foundation, blush, eye shadow, moisturizers, and hair-care products should be oil free. Choose products labeled noncomedogenic (meaning they don't promote the formation of closed pores). In some people, however, even these products may make acne worse.

For the first few weeks of treatment, applying foundation evenly may be difficult because the skin may be red or scaly, particularly with the use of topical tretinoin or benzoyl peroxide.

What Research Is Being Done On Acne?

Medical researchers are working on new drugs to treat acne, particularly topical antibiotics to replace some of those in current use. As with many other types of bacterial infections, doctors are finding that, over time, the bacteria that are associated with acne are becoming resistant to treatment with certain antibiotics, though it is not clear how significant a problem this resistance represents.

Scientists are also trying to better understand the mechanisms involved in acne so that they can develop new treatments that work on those mechanisms.

For example, one group of NIAMS-supported researchers is studying the mechanisms that regulate sebum production in order to identify ways to effectively reduce its production without the side effects of current medicines. Another group is trying to understand how *P. acnes* activates the immune system in order to identify possible immunologic interventions. Other areas of research involve examining the effects of isotretinoin on an area of the brain that might lead to depression and developing a laser system to treat acne and acne-related scars without damaging the outer layers of the skin.

Researchers in Germany, funded by German institutions, have taken *P. acnes* and identified its genetic information (genome). This information may help researchers develop new treatments to target the bacteria.

The Social Impact Of Acne

How Acne Affects People's Lives

"There is no single disease which causes more psychic trauma, more maladjustment between parents and children, more general insecurity and feelings of inferiority and greater sums of psychic suffering than does acne vulgaris."

—Sulzberger & Zaldems, 1948

While known for quite some time, the psychosocial effects of acne have not been fully appreciated until recently. The reasons for this are many. After all, everyone gets acne to one degree or another. In most cases, it goes away on its own. While it's running its course, it is not a serious threat to anyone's overall physical health. In addition, until the last couple of decades, there was very little anyone could do to treat it.

Acne, nonetheless, has a significant impact on a person's outlook on life. Recent studies have detected the following as common among people with acne:

- Social withdrawal
- Decreased self-esteem

- Reduced self-confidence

- Poor body image

- Embarrassment

- Feelings of depression

- Anger

- Preoccupation

- Frustration

- Higher rate of unemployment

The effects listed above are often interrelated, with one effect leading to another and another, only to make the first effect worse. These negative psychosocial effects can have a crippling impact, discouraging patients from pursuing life's opportunities—socially, on the job, or at school.

Chapter 18

How Is Acne Treated?

Acne is often treated by dermatologists (doctors who specialize in skin problems). These doctors treat all kinds of acne, particularly severe cases. Doctors who are general or family practitioners, pediatricians, or internists may treat patients with milder cases of acne.

The goals of treatment are to heal existing lesions, stop new lesions from forming, prevent scarring, and minimize the psychological stress and embarrassment caused by this disease. Drug treatment is aimed at reducing several problems that play a part in causing acne:

- Abnormal clumping of cells in the follicles

- Increased oil production

- Bacteria

- Inflammation

All medicines can have side effects. Some medicines and side effects are mentioned in this chapter. Some side effects may be more severe than others.

About This Chapter: Adapted from "Acne" National Institute of Arthritis and Musculoskeletal and Skin Diseases, January 2006. Brand names included in this chapter are provided as examples only, and their inclusion does not mean that these products are endorsed by the National Institutes of Health or any other government agency. Also, if a particular brand name is not mentioned, this does not mean or imply that the product is unsatisfactory.

You should review the package insert that comes with your medicine and ask your health care provider or pharmacist if you have any questions about the possible side effects.

Depending on the extent of the problem, the doctor may recommend one of several over-the-counter (OTC) medicines and/or prescription medicines. Some of these medicines may be topical (applied to the skin), and others may be oral (taken by mouth). The doctor may suggest using more than one topical medicine or combining oral and topical medicines.

Treatment For Blackheads, Whiteheads, And Mild Inflammatory Acne

Doctors usually recommend an OTC or prescription topical medicine for people with mild signs of acne. Topical medicine is applied directly to the acne lesions or to the entire area of affected skin.

There are several OTC topical medicines used for mild acne. Each works a little differently. The following medicines are the most common:

- **Benzoyl Peroxide:** Destroys *Propionibacterium acnes,* and may also reduce oil production

- **Resorcinol:** Can help break down blackheads and whiteheads

- **Salicylic Acid:** Helps break down blackheads and whiteheads. Also helps cut down the shedding of cells lining the hair follicles

- **Sulfur:** Helps break down blackheads and whiteheads

✤ It's A Fact!!
OTC topical medicines are somewhat effective in treating acne when used regularly; however, it may take up to eight weeks before you see noticeable improvement.

Source: National Institute of Arthritis and Musculoskeletal and Skin Diseases, 2006.

Topical OTC medicines are available in many forms, such as gels, lotions, creams, soaps, or pads. In some people, OTC acne medicines may cause side effects such as skin irritation, burning, or redness, which often get better or go away with continued use of the medicine. If you experience severe or prolonged side effects, you should report them to your doctor.

Treatment For Moderate To Severe Inflammatory Acne

People with moderate to severe inflammatory acne may be treated with prescription topical or oral medicines, alone or in combination.

Prescription Topical Medicines

Several types of prescription topical medicines are used to treat acne, including the following:

- **Antibiotics:** Help stop or slow the growth of bacteria and reduce inflammation

- **Vitamin A Derivatives (Retinoids):** Unplug existing comedones (plural of comedo), allowing other topical medicines, such as antibiotics, to enter the follicles. Some may also help decrease the formation of comedones. These drugs contain an altered form of vitamin A. Some examples are tretinoin (Retin-A2), adapalene (Differin), and tazarotene (Tazorac)

- **Others:** May destroy *P. acnes* and reduce oil production or help stop or slow the growth of bacteria and reduce inflammation. Some examples are prescription strength Benzoyl peroxide, sodium sulfacetamide/sulfur-containing products, or Azelaic acid (Azelex).

Like OTC topical medicines, prescription topical medicines come as creams, lotions, solutions, gels, or pads. Your doctor will consider your skin type when prescribing a product. Creams and lotions provide moisture and tend to be good choices for people with sensitive skin. If you have very oily skin or live in a hot, humid climate, you may prefer an alcohol-based gel or solution, which tends to dry the skin. Your doctor will tell you how to apply the medicine and how often to use it.

For some people, prescription topical medicines cause minor side effects, including stinging, burning, redness, peeling, scaling, or discoloration of the skin. With some medicines, such as tretinoin, these side effects usually decrease or go away after the medicine is used for a period of time. If side effects are severe or don't go away, notify your doctor.

As with OTC medicines, the benefits of prescription topical medicines are not immediate. Your skin may seem worse before it gets better. It may take four to eight weeks to notice improvement.

Prescription Oral Medicines

For patients with moderate to severe acne, doctors often prescribe oral antibiotics. Oral antibiotics are thought to help control acne by curbing the growth of bacteria and reducing inflammation. Prescription oral and topical medicines may be combined. Common antibiotics used to treat acne are tetracycline (Achromycin V), minocycline (Dynacin, Minocin), and doxycycline (Adoxa, Doryx, and Monodox).

Other oral medicines less commonly used are clindamycin (Cleocin), erythromycin, or sulfonamides (Bactrim). Some people taking these antibiotics have side effects, such as an upset stomach, dizziness or lightheadedness, changes in skin color, and increased tendency to sunburn. Because tetracyclines may affect tooth and bone formation in fetuses and young children, these drugs are not given to pregnant women or children under age 14. There is some concern, although it has not been proven, that tetracycline and minocycline may decrease the effectiveness of birth control pills. Therefore, a backup or another form of birth control may be needed. Prolonged treatment with oral antibiotics may be necessary to achieve the desired results.

Treatment For Severe Nodular Or Cystic Acne

People with nodules or cysts should be treated by a dermatologist. For patients with severe inflammatory acne that does not improve with medicines such as those described above, a doctor may prescribe isotretinoin (Accutane), a retinoid (vitamin A derivative). Isotretinoin is an oral drug that is usually taken once or twice a day with food for 15 to 20 weeks. It markedly reduces the size of the oil glands so that much less oil is produced. As a result, the growth of bacteria is decreased.

Advantages Of Isotretinoin (Accutane)

Isotretinoin is a very effective medicine that can help prevent scarring. After 15 to 20 weeks of treatment with isotretinoin, acne completely or almost completely goes away in most patients. In those patients where acne recurs after a course of isotretinoin, the doctor may institute another course of the same treatment or prescribe other medicines.

Disadvantages Of Isotretinoin (Accutane)

Isotretinoin can cause birth defects in the developing fetus of a pregnant woman. It is important that women of childbearing age are not pregnant and do not get pregnant while taking this medicine. Women must use two separate effective forms of birth control at the same time for one month before treatment begins, during the entire course of treatment, and for one full month after stopping the drug. You should ask your doctor when it is safe to get pregnant after you have stopped taking isotretinoin.

Some people with acne become depressed by the changes in the appearance of their skin. Changes in mood may be intensified during treatment or soon after completing a course of medicines like isotretinoin. There have been a number of reported suicides and suicide attempts in people taking isotretinoin; however, the connection between isotretinoin and suicide or depression is not known. Nevertheless, if you or someone you know feels unusually sad or has other symptoms of depression, such as loss of appetite, loss of interest in once-loved activities, or trouble concentrating, it's important to consult your doctor.

Other possible side effects of isotretinoin include dry eyes, mouth, lips, nose, or skin (very common); itching; nosebleeds; muscle aches; sensitivity to the sun; and, sometimes, poor night vision. More serious side effects included changes in the blood, such as an increase in fats in the blood (triglycerides and cholesterol), or a change in liver function. To be able to determine if isotretinoin should be stopped if side effects occur, your doctor may test your blood before you start treatment and periodically during treatment. Side effects usually go away after the medicine is stopped.

Treatments For Hormonally Influenced Acne In Women

In some women, acne is caused by an excess of androgen (male) hormones. Clues that this may be the case include hirsutism (excessive growth of hair on the face or body), premenstrual acne flares, irregular menstrual cycles, and elevated blood levels of certain androgens.

The doctor may prescribe one of several drugs to treat women with this type of acne:

- **Birth Control Pills:** To help suppress the androgen produced by the ovaries

- **Low-Dose Corticosteroid Drugs:** Such as prednisone (Deltasone) or dexamethasone (Decadron, Hexadrol)—to help suppress the androgen produced by the adrenal glands

- **Antiandrogen Drugs:** Such as spironolactone (Aldactone)—to reduce the excessive oil production.

Side effects of antiandrogen drugs may include irregular menstruation, tender breasts, headaches, and fatigue.

Other Treatments For Acne

Doctors may use other types of procedures in addition to drug therapy to treat patients with acne. For example, the doctor may remove the patient's comedones during office visits. Sometimes the doctor will inject corticosteroids directly into lesions to help reduce the size and pain of inflamed cysts and nodules.

Early treatment is the best way to prevent acne scars. Once scarring has occurred, the doctor may suggest a medical or surgical procedure to help reduce the scars. A superficial laser may be used to treat irregular scars. Dermabrasion (or microdermabrasion), which is a form of "sanding down" scars, is sometimes used. Another treatment option for deep scars caused by cystic acne is the transfer of fat from another part of the body to the scar. A doctor may also inject a synthetic filling material under the scar to improve its appearance.

Chapter 19

Safety Information About Isotretinoin

What Is Isotretinoin?

Isotretinoin is used to treat the most severe form of acne (nodular acne) that cannot be cleared up by any other acne treatments, including antibiotics. Isotretinoin is only for patients who understand and agree to carry out all the instructions in the iPLEDGE program, because isotretinoin can cause serious side effects.

What Is The iPLEDGE Program?

The iPLEDGE program, implemented on March 1, 2006, is a strength-ened risk management program to educate women about the risk of becoming pregnant while taking isotretinoin (Accutane and its generics), a drug to treat severe recalcitrant nodular acne. This comprehensive program seeks to reduce the risk of inadvertent pregnancy exposure by tightly linking negative pregnancy testing with dispensing of isotretinoin.

The iPLEDGE program has been developed through a cooperative ef-fort of several manufacturers of isotretinoin, a drug that has been marketed for several decades. Isotretinoin is highly effective in the treatment of severe

About This Chapter: Text in this chapter is excerpted from U.S. Food and Drug Administration's "Patient Information Sheet: Isotretinoin (marketed as Accutane)" (2005); and "iPLEDGE Program Press Release," (2006).

♣ It's A Fact!!

FDA Warning:

Risks Of Buying Accutane (Isotretinoin) Over The Internet

Isotretinoin is a potentially dangerous prescription medicine that should only be taken under the close supervision of your healthcare professional and pharmacist. If you are pregnant or may get pregnant, isotretinoin can cause birth defects, miscarriage, premature births, and death in babies. Buying this product over the internet bypasses important procedures to ensure that patients can take this drug safely. When these procedures are ignored, isotretinoin can cause serious and harmful side effects. Patients taking isotretinoin may experience side effects including bad headaches, blurred vision, dizziness, nausea, vomiting, seizures, stroke, diarrhea, and muscle weakness. Additionally, serious mental health problems, such as depression and suicide, have been reported with isotretinoin use.

- You should *never* buy Accutane (isotretinoin) or any of the generic versions of Accutane without first seeing your healthcare professional.

- You should *never* take Accutane (isotretinoin) or any of the generic versions of Accutane if you are pregnant or trying to get pregnant or could accidentally become pregnant.

- Some websites sell prescription drugs without a prescription. This is illegal and dangerous.

To learn more about FDA's program to warn consumers against buying Accutane and its generic versions online, please see: http://www.fda.gov/bbs/topics/NEWS/2007/NEW01595.html

Source: U.S. Food and Drug Administration, 2007.

recalcitrant nodular acne, but has known serious side effects, particularly its ability to cause birth defects when pregnant women use the drug, and more recent concerns regarding its potential to be associated with severe depression.

The U.S. Food and Drug Administration (FDA) has worked closely with isotretinoin sponsors and their vendor, Covance Inc., to maintain a critical balance between access to the drug by patients who need it and ensuring its safe use.

The iPLEDGE program is aimed at preventing use of the drug during pregnancy. To obtain the drug, in addition to registering with iPLEDGE, patients must comply with a number of key requirements that include completing an informed consent form, obtaining counseling about the risks and requirements for safe use of the drug, and, for women of childbearing age, complying with necessary pregnancy testing.

Prescribers and patients who have questions about the iPLEDGE program should contact the iPLEDGE call center at (866) 495-0654 or online at https://www.ipledgeprogram.com/

See the "iPLEDGE Update" box later in this chapter for updated information regarding the program.

Who Should Not Take Isotretinoin?

Isotretinoin should **not** be used by pregnant women. Do not take isotretinoin if you are:

- pregnant, plan to become pregnant, or become pregnant during isotretinoin treatment;

- breast-feeding;

- allergic to anything in it. Isotretinoin contains parabens, which are used as preservatives in the gelatin capsule.

What Are The Risks?

Some of the risks of taking isotretinoin include birth defects (deformed babies), loss of baby before birth (miscarriage), death of baby, and early (premature) births. Female patients who are pregnant or who plan to become pregnant must not take isotretinoin. Female patients must not get pregnant:

- for one month before starting isotretinoin;

- while taking isotretinoin;

- for one month after stopping isotretinoin.

☞ Remember!!

If you get pregnant while taking isotretinoin, stop taking it right away and call your doctor.

Source: U.S. Food and Drug Administration, 2005.

Serious Mental Health Problems

Isotretinoin may cause the following mental health problems:

- Depression

- Psychosis (seeing or hearing things that are not real)

- Suicidal thoughts or actions

- Aggressive and violent behavior

Stop taking isotretinoin and call your doctor right away if you experience any of the following:

- Start to feel sad or have crying spells

- Lose interest in activities you once enjoyed

- Sleep too much or have trouble sleeping

- Become more irritable, angry, or aggressive than usual

- Have a change in your appetite or body weight

- Have trouble concentrating

- Withdraw from your family or friends

- Feel like you have no energy

- Have feelings of worthlessness or wrong guilt

- Start having thoughts about hurting yourself or taking your own life (suicidal thoughts)

- Start acting on dangerous impulses

- Start seeing or hearing things that are not real

Serious Brain Problems: Isotretinoin may increase the pressure in your brain, possibly leading to permanent loss of eyesight, or in rare cases, death. Stop taking isotretinoin and call your doctor right away if you get any signs of increased brain pressure such as bad headaches, blurred vision, dizziness, nausea or vomiting, seizures (convulsions) or stroke.

Stomach Area (Abdomen) Problems: Certain symptoms may mean that your internal organs are being damaged. These organs include the liver, pancreas, bowel (intestines), and esophagus (connection between mouth and stomach). Stop taking isotretinoin and call your doctor if you get severe stomach, chest or bowel pain, trouble swallowing or painful swallowing, new or worsening heartburn, diarrhea, rectal bleeding, yellowing of your skin or eyes, or dark urine.

♣ It's A Fact!!

Suicidal Thoughts Or Actions

In addition to the strengthened risk management program for pregnancy, the U.S. Food and Drug Administration, continues to assess reports of suicide or suicide attempts associated with the use of isotretinoin. All patients treated with isotretinoin should be observed closely for symptoms of depression or suicidal thoughts, such as sad mood, irritability, acting on dangerous impulses, anger, loss of pleasure or interest in social or sports activities, sleeping too much or too little, changes in weight or appetite, school or work performance going down, or trouble concentrating, or for mood disturbance, psychosis, or aggression. Patients should stop isotretinoin and they or their caregiver should contact their healthcare professional right away if the patient has any of the previously mentioned symptoms. Discontinuation of treatment may be insufficient and further evaluation may be necessary.

Source: U.S. Food and Drug Administration, 2005.

Bone And Muscle Problems: Tell your doctor if you plan any vigorous physical activity during treatment with isotretinoin. Tell your doctor if you get muscle weakness, back pain, joint pain, or a broken bone.

Hearing Problems: Stop taking isotretinoin and call your doctor if your hearing gets worse or if you have ringing in the ears.

Vision Problems: Isotretinoin may affect your ability to see in the dark. Stop taking isotretinoin and call your doctor right away if you have any problems with your vision or dryness of the eyes that is painful or constant. If you wear contact lenses, you may have trouble wearing them while taking isotretinoin and after treatment.

Lipid (Fats And Cholesterol In Blood) Problems: Isotretinoin can raise the level of fats and cholesterol in your blood.

Allergic Reactions: Stop taking isotretinoin and get emergency care right away if you develop hives, a swollen face or mouth, or have trouble breathing. Stop taking isotretinoin and call your doctor if you get a fever, rash, or red patches or bruises on your legs.

Blood Sugar Problems: Tell your doctor if you are very thirsty or urinate a lot.

Decreased Red And White Blood Cells: Call your doctor if you have trouble breathing, faint, or feel weak.

Others: The common, less serious side effects of isotretinoin are dry skin, chapped lips, dry eyes, and dry nose that may lead to nosebleeds.

What Should I Do Before Taking Isotretinoin?

Tell your healthcare professional if you or someone in your family has had any kind of mental problems, asthma, liver disease, diabetes, heart disease, osteoporosis (bone loss), weak bones, an eating problem called anorexia nervosa (where people eat too little), or any food or medicine allergies.

As of March 1, 2006, all patients must be registered and activated by their doctors in iPLEDGE to get isotretinoin and only prescriptions from iPLEDGE doctors will be filled by iPLEDGE pharmacies. You must sign the patient information/informed consent form.

You must agree to follow all the instructions in the iPLEDGE program.

☞ **Remember!!**

If you have sex any time without using two forms of effective birth control, get pregnant, or miss your expected period, stop using isotretinoin and call your doctor right away.

Source: U.S. Food and Drug Administration, 2005.

Females who can become pregnant must follow these instructions:

- Agree to use two separate forms of effective birth control at the same time one month before, while taking, and for one month after stopping isotretinoin. You must also call and enter your two types of birth control each month into the iPLEDGE system by telephone or the internet.

- Have negative results from two pregnancy tests before receiving the initial isotretinoin prescription.

- Have a negative pregnancy test before each refill.

- Sign an additional patient information/informed consent form that contains warnings about the risk of potential birth defects if the fetus is exposed to isotretinoin.

Are There Any Interactions With Drugs Or Foods?

Tell your healthcare professional about all the medicines you take, including prescription and nonprescription medicines, vitamins, and herbal supplements. Isotretinoin and other medicines may affect each other, sometimes causing serious side effects. Especially tell your healthcare professional if you take any of the following:

- Progestin-only containing birth control pills ("minipills")

- Vitamin A supplements

- Tetracycline medicines

- Dilantin (phenytoin)

- Corticosteroid medicines

- St. John's Wort

✦ It's A Fact!!

iPLEDGE Update

The U.S. Food and Drug Administration (FDA) is providing an update about iPLEDGE, a risk management program to reduce the risk of fetal exposure to isotretinoin (a drug to treat severe recalcitrant nodular acne). In October 2007, FDA approved several changes to the program, including elimination of the 23-day lockout for females of childbearing potential, with the exception of the first prescription to be filled. In October 2006, the 23-day lockout for males and females of non-childbearing potential was removed. Previously, all patients prescribed isotretinoin had to fill their prescription within seven days of their office visit. Patients who missed this window of opportunity and attempted to fill their prescription after seven days had elapsed could not receive isotretinoin for another 23 days.

Other changes to the program that were approved today include linkage of the 7-day prescription window for females of childbearing potential to the date of pregnancy testing rather than the date of the office visit, and extension of the prescription window from seven days to 30 days for males and females not of childbearing potential.

Changes approved to iPLEDGE were discussed at a joint meeting of the Dermatologic and Ophthalmic Drugs and the Drug Safety and Risk Management Advisory Committees held on August 1, 2007. The joint committee recommended unanimously to accept the changes proposed. Additional information can be viewed at:

http://www.fda.gov/ohrms/dockets/ac/07/briefing/2007-4311b1-00-index.htm

Source: U.S. Food and Drug Administration, October 2007.

Is There Anything Else I Need to Know?

Do not give blood while you take isotretinoin and for one month after stopping isotretinoin. If someone who is pregnant gets your donated blood, her baby may be exposed to isotretinoin and may be born with birth defects.

Do not drive at night until you know if isotretinoin has affected your vision. Do not have cosmetic procedures to smooth your skin, including waxing, dermabrasion, or laser procedures, while you are using isotretinoin and for at least six months after you stop. Isotretinoin can increase your chance of scarring from these procedures.

Avoid sunlight and ultraviolet lights as much as possible. Tanning machines use ultraviolet lights.

Do not share isotretinoin with other people. It can cause serious birth defects and other serious health problems.

You will only be able to get up to a 30-day supply of isotretinoin at one time. Refills will require you to get a new prescription from your doctor.

You should receive an isotretinoin "Medication Guide" each time you receive isotretinoin. This is required by law.

Chapter 20

Acne Scarring

Scars from acne can seem like double punishment—first you had to deal with the pimples, now you have marks as a reminder. Is there anything you can do?

To understand scars, you need to understand acne. Acne refers to lesions or pimples caused when the hair follicles (or "pores") on the skin become plugged with oil and dead skin cells. A plugged follicle is the perfect place for bacteria to grow and create the red bumps and pus-filled red bumps known as pimples. (The usual bacteria that causes acne is called *Propionibacterium acnes*.) Hormonal changes during the teen years often cause increased oil production that contributes to the problem.

Acne Comes In Different Forms

- Mild acne, which refers to the whiteheads or blackheads that most of us get at various times

- Moderately severe acne, which includes red inflamed pimples called papules and red pimples with white centers called pustules

About This Chapter: Text in this chapter is from "Can Acne Scars Be Removed?" April 2007, reprinted with permission from www.kidshealth.org. Copyright © 2007 The Nemours Foundation. This information was provided by KidsHealth, one of the largest resources online for medically reviewed health information written for parents, kids, and teens. For more articles like this one, visit www.KidsHealth.org, or www.TeensHealth.org.

• Severe acne, which causes nodules—painful, pus-filled cysts or lumps—
to appear under the skin

If you have serious scarring from previous bouts with acne, there are some
things you can do. One form of treatment is laser resurfacing, which can be
done in the doctor's or dermatologist's office. The laser removes the damaged top layer of skin and tightens the middle layer, leaving skin smoother.
This can take anywhere from a few minutes to an hour. The doctor will try
to lessen any pain by first numbing the skin with local anesthesia. It usually
takes between three and 10 days for the skin to heal completely.

♣ It's A Fact!!

Most serious scarring is caused by the more severe forms
of acne, with nodules more likely to leave permanent scars than
other types of acne. The best way to deal with acne is to get treatment
soon after the acne appears to prevent further severe acne and
more scarring. If you have nodules, see your doctor or
dermatologist for treatment.

Another method for treating acne scarring is dermabrasion, which uses a
rotating wire brush or spinning diamond instrument to wear down the surface of the skin. As the skin heals, a new, smoother layer replaces the abraded
skin. It may take a bit longer for skin to heal using dermabrasion—usually
between 10 days and three weeks.

The newest form of treatment for acne scarring is called fractional laser
therapy. This type of treatment works at a deeper level than laser resurfacing
or dermabrasion. Because fractional laser therapy doesn't wound the top layer
of tissue, healing time is shorter. Fractional laser therapy is quite costly, and
it's not usually covered by insurance.

A person's acne will need to be under control before having any of these
treatments.

✔ **Quick Tip**

One thing you shouldn't do to deal with acne scars is load up your face with masks or fancy lotions—these won't help and may irritate your skin further, making the scars red and even more noticeable.

Depending on the severity of the acne scars, the doctor or dermatologist may also suggest a chemical peel or microdermabrasion to help improve the appearance of scarred areas. These milder treatments can be done right in the office.

Sometimes doctors inject material under the scar to raise it to the level of normal skin. Finally, in some cases, a doctor may recommend surgery to remove deeply indented scars.

If you have a red or brownish mark on your face that you got from a bad zit, have no fear—it will eventually fade, just like the scars you had on your knees after you fell off your bike when you were a kid. However, it may take 12 months or longer—so your best bet is to avoid these kinds of marks by not squeezing or popping your zits, no matter how tempting it may seem.

Chapter 21

Dermabrasion

Dermabrasion is a skin resurfacing technique that is used to treat facial scarring. When it was first developed in the early 1950s it was used predominantly to improve acne scars, chicken pox marks, and scars resulting from accidents or disease. Nowadays, dermabrasion is also used to treat deep facial lines and wrinkles, severe sun damage, pigmentation disorders and certain types of skin lesions.

Dermabrasion Equipment

Dermabrasion is a surgical procedure that uses a power-driven handheld tool that looks a bit like a dentist's drill. The tool has an abrasive end piece such as a serrated metal wheel, diamond fraise, or a wire brush. Fraises come in a variety of shapes, sizes, and grades of coarseness. The doctor moves the rapidly spinning wheel gently over the surface of the scar causing the topmost layers of the skin to be worn away.

Preparation For Dermabrasion

Before you can receive dermabrasion, your doctor will take a complete medical history and will carefully examine the skin lesion or defect. The doctor will need to know the following factors:

About This Chapter: This information is reprinted with permission from DermNet, the website of the New Zealand Dermatological Society. Visit www.dermnetnz.org for patient information on numerous skin conditions and their treatment. © 2008 New Zealand Dermatological Society.

Skin Type: Mid-range skin types (III-IV) that tan easily are more likely to show transient hyperpigmentation (dark marks) four to eight weeks after the surgery and hypopigmentation (pale marks) 12 to 18 months post surgery. However, discoloration can be a problem with all skin types.

Tendency To Form Keloids (Deposits Of Fibrous Tissue) Or Hypertrophic Scarring: Patients with a history of keloid formation may need to have a test spot performed first before any full face resurfacing.

Herpes Simplex Lesions (Cold Sores): Active herpes infection usually necessitates postponement of the procedure until the lesions have cleared.

Other Active Facial Skin Diseases Such As Acne, Rosacea, And Dermatitis: These may flare after dermabrasion.

Recent Isotretinoin Therapy: This can delay healing and cause scarring so dermabrasion should be postponed for six to 12 months.

The doctor will tell you about the procedure, possible risks and complications, and what results might realistically be expected. Photographs are usually taken before and after surgery to help evaluate the degree of improvement.

Medical Treatment For Dermabrasion

Dermabrasion can precipitate herpes simplex infection causing unpleasant blistering and possibly permanent scarring so acyclovir, famciclovir or valacyclovir tablets are used to prevent it. Those with a history of cold sores may require larger doses than normal.

📎 What's It Mean?

Fraise: A burr in the shape of a hemispherical button with cutting edges, used to enlarge a trephine opening in the skull or to cut osteoplastic flaps; the smooth convexity of the button prevents injury to the dura. [Fr. strawberry][2]

Hypopigmentation: Pale marks[1]

Hyperpigmentation: Dark marks[1]

Impetigo: A bacterial skin infection most often affecting children. It is quite contagious.[2]

Reepithelialization: New skin growth[1]

Sources: 1. New Zealand Dermatological Society, 2008.

2. Stedman's Online Dictionary, 2009.

Most patients are only prescribed antibiotics if infection occurs after the procedure. The exceptions are immunosuppressed patients or patients with a recent history of impetigo, or who are carriers of *Staphylococcus aureus*, who may be started on antibiotics beforehand.

For two to three weeks prior to dermabrasion, tretinoin cream may be prescribed to apply each night to the area to be treated. Tretinoin appears to decrease the time for reepithelialization (new skin growth).

Dermabrasion may be performed using general anesthetic but local anesthetic may be preferred for small areas. Sedating medications may be used to induce a calming effect prior to and after surgery.

Dermabrasion Procedure

Dermabrasion may require admission to a hospital or it may be done as an outpatient procedure in a doctor's surgical facility. The procedure begins with thoroughly cleaning the area to be 'sanded' with antiseptic cleansing agent. A numbing spray may be applied to freeze and firm the surface that is being treated. The doctor will then carefully maneuver the dermabrasion tool over the area to carefully remove layers of skin until he or she reaches the desired level that will make the scar or wrinkle less visible, aiming to avoid more scarring.

For small areas the procedure should only take a few minutes. For larger areas, the procedure can take one to two hours to perform.

Care After Dermabrasion

Following the procedure the treated skin will be red, swollen, and tender. A compress or special dressing is usually applied to reduce any tingling, burning or stinging sensation and to speed up healing. Instructions will be given on caring for the wound until new skin starts to grow; this usually takes seven to 10 days. The face may itch as the new skin grows and may be slightly swollen, sensitive, and bright pink for several weeks after dermabrasion.

Microdermabrasion

Microdermabrasion was developed in Italy in 1985 and has since become a popular skin resurfacing technique. It has the advantages of low risk and

> ### ☞ Remember!!
>
> The following measures should be taken to ensure rapid healing and prevent any complications.
>
> - Inform your doctor of any yellow crusting or scabs—this may be the start of an infection.
>
> - Swelling and redness should subside after a few days to a month. Persistent redness of an area could be the sign of a scar forming so contact your doctor immediately.
>
> - Continue antiviral medication for several days beyond the new skin forming.
>
> - To avoid pigmentation, once the new skin is healed, keep out of the sun and apply a broad spectrum sunscreen daily for at least three months after dermabrasion. Even the sun through window glass can promote unwanted pigmentation.

rapid recovery compared with other techniques such as standard dermabrasion, chemical peeling and laser resurfacing.

Microdermabrasion is similar to dermabrasion but as its name suggests, it uses tiny crystals to remove the surface skin layers. It is promoted for correcting fine lines and more superficial scars. Advantages include:

- anesthesia is not required;
- it is almost painless;
- facial redness is minimized;
- simple and quick to perform;
- can be repeated at short intervals;
- does not disrupt the patient's life greatly.

The disadvantages of microdermabrasion are that multiple treatments are needed and there may be minimal improvement in appearance.

Microdermabrasion is now possible using home kits that use a vibrating foam applicator to massage a moisturizing cream containing aluminium oxide crystals on the surface of the skin.

Chapter 22

Chemical Peels

A facial peel refers to the application of one or more chemicals to the face which "burn" off damaged cells. Chemical peels are sometimes applied to other sites such as the hands. They may be used to treat damage caused by exposure to the sun (photoaging), to remove pigmentation such as freckles and melasma and fine lines and wrinkles.

A peel removes several layers of sun damaged skin cells, leaving fresh skin which has a more even surface and color. It may stimulate new collagen to be formed, improving skin texture. Peels may result in superficial, moderate depth, or deep skin injury.

A nurse or aesthetician (beauty therapist) may perform superficial peels. A dermatologist or plastic surgeon usually performs deeper peels.

Peels can be repeated as necessary; some people have superficial peels every few weeks. It is wise to wait three to six months before repeating a moderate depth peel.

Glycolic acid, salicylic acid, and Jessner peels result in superficial skin injury and are well tolerated—the 'lunchtime' peel. They remove thin lesions

About This Chapter: This information is reprinted with permission from DermNet, the website of the New Zealand Dermatological Society. Visit www.dermnetnz.org for patient information on numerous skin conditions and their treatment. © 2008 New Zealand Dermatological Society.

on the skin surface, reducing pigment and surface dryness. The result of the first peel may be disappointing, but after repeated peels, significant improvement is usually evident.

Trichloroacetic acid (TCA) is the most common chemical used for a medium depth peel. The results depend on its concentration, usually 20 to 35 percent. The treatment is painful and treated areas are swollen, red and crusted for the next week or so. It can lead to an impressive improvement in skin texture with a reduction in blotchy pigmentation, freckling, and solar keratoses (dry sunspots). Although fine wrinkles and some acne scars are less obvious, the TCA peel has no effect on deep furrows.

Phenol results in deep skin injury. It is rarely used for facial peels nowadays because of the risk of scarring and because of its toxicity. Absorption of phenol through the skin results in potentially fatal heart rhythm disturbances and nerve damage. However, it is very effective at improving both surface wrinkles and deep furrows. After a phenol peel, the treated skin is pale and smooth but it may be waxy and "mask-like."

Before The Peel

Pre-treatment creams are applied to the face at night for several weeks prior to the peel. By exfoliating the skin and reducing pigmentation themselves, they improve the results seen from chemical peeling. They may also reduce the time needed for healing. The creams usually include one or more of the following:

- tretinoin;
- alpha hydroxy acid, for example, glycolic or lactic acid;
- hydroquinone for tanned or dark-skinned patients or those with melasma.

Broad-spectrum SPF 30+ sunscreen should be used during the day.

The Peel

Superficial chemical peels are a minor procedure and no special arrangements are needed. But you may need painkillers, sedation, local anesthetic or even a general anesthetic for deeper peels.

First the face is thoroughly washed to remove surface oil. The peeling agent is then applied for several minutes. It stings—how badly and for how long depends on the chemical, its concentration, whether you've had pre-treatment with aspirin, and individual factors. A fan can help. The peel is then neutralized, and the burning sensation lessens.

Individual treatments may include peels with several agents on the same occasion, with the aim of improving results and reducing risks.

Antibiotics and oral antiviral agents may be recommended after deeper peels.

Afterwards

Superficial peels result in mild facial redness and occasional swelling which usually resolve within 48 hours. The peeling is similar to sunburn. Most people can continue their normal activities. Make-up can be applied a few hours after the procedure.

Moderate depth peels result in intense inflammation and swelling, which resolve within a week. The peeling is more marked. Mild redness can persist for several weeks. Most people take a week off from work after a moderate depth peel.

Complications

Complications are uncommon if the health professional performing the peel is properly trained.

- Comedones (blocked pores) or acne may result from the

✔ Quick Tip
Looking After
The Skin After The Peel

- Keep treated areas cool (use a water spray)

- Do not pick. Picking delays healing and causes scarring.

- Moisturize—use light preparations after a superficial peel, thicker moisturizers after a deeper peel

- Protect from the sun—especially for the first six months

- If advised to do so, continue to use tretinoin, glycolic acid and/or hydroquinone at night long term

peel itself or from thick moisturizers used afterwards; ask your dermatologist for treatment.

- Infection due to bacteria (*Staphylococcus aureus*), yeast (*Candida albicans*),
  or virus (*Herpes simplex*); you may need antibiotics.

- Scarring may result from infection or picking the scabs, and can be
  permanent.

- Blotchy pigmentation is most likely in those with darker skin or who
  had a pigmentation problem before the peel; keep out of the sun and
  use hydroquinone.

- Persistent solar keratoses may require treatment. Your dermatologist
  may choose cryotherapy, 5-fluorouracil cream or biopsy a lesion in case
  it is skin cancer.

General Advice

- Ensure your doctor's instructions are carefully followed

- If you don't understand, ask

- Let your doctor know promptly if there are any problems—complications are easier to deal with early than late

Part Four

Understanding And Preventing Skin Cancer

Chapter 23

Protect Yourself From The Sun

Basic Information

Skin cancer is the most common form of cancer in the United States. The two most common types of skin cancer—basal cell and squamous cell carcinomas—are highly curable. However, melanoma, the third most common skin cancer, is more dangerous, especially among young people. Approximately, 65 to 90 percent of melanomas are caused by exposure to ultraviolet (UV) light or sunlight.

The following statistics refer to new cases of—and deaths from—melanomas of the skin. Non-epithelial skin cancers, which are not reflected below, represent 7 percent of skin cancers that are tracked by central cancer registries. These statistics also do not include data for basal cell and squamous cell carcinomas, which are not tracked by central cancer registries.

About This Chapter: This chapter includes excerpts from "Skin Cancer: Basic Information," January 2009, and "Protect Yourself from the Sun," July 2008, Centers for Disease Control and Prevention (www.cdc.gov). Note: Data in this chapter include the most recent year for which statistics are currently available. Incidence counts cover approximately 96 percent of the U.S. population. Death counts cover 100 percent of the U.S. population. Use caution in comparing incidence and death counts.

Protect Yourself From The Sun

Summer is a great time to have fun outdoors. It's also a time to take precautions to avoid sunburns, which can increase your risk of skin cancer.

Skin cancer is the most common form of cancer in the United States. Exposure to the sun's ultraviolet (UV) rays appears to be the most important environmental factor involved with developing skin cancer. During the summer months, UV radiation tends to be greater.

To help prevent skin cancer while still having fun outdoors, regularly use such sun protective practices as these:

- Seek shade, especially during midday hours (10 a.m.–4 p.m.), when UV rays are strongest and do the most damage.

- Cover up with clothing to protect exposed skin. A long-sleeved shirt and long pants with a tight weave are best.

- Get a hat with a wide brim to shade the face, head, ears, and neck.

- Grab shades that wrap around and block as close to 100 percent of both UVA and UVB rays as possible.

♣ It's A Fact!!

In 2005

- 53,792 people in the United States were diagnosed with melanomas of the skin, 30,544 of them men and 23,248 of them women.

- 50,589 whites, 1,122 Hispanics, 261 blacks, 159 Asian/Pacific Islanders, and 95 American Indian/Alaska Natives in the United States were diagnosed with melanomas of the skin.

That Same Year

- 8,345 people in the United States died of melanomas of the skin, 5,283 of them men and 3,062 of them women.

- 8,146 whites, 168 Hispanics, 124 blacks, 55 Asian/Pacific Islanders, and 20 American Indians/Alaska Natives in the United States died of melanomas of the skin.

Source: "Skin Cancer: Basic Information," CDC, 2009.

- Rub on sunscreen with sun protective factor (SPF) 15 or higher, and both UVA and UVB protection.

It's always wise to choose more than one way to cover up when you're in the sun. Use sunscreen and put on a shirt. Seek shade and grab your sunglasses. Wear a hat, but rub on sunscreen too. Combining these sun protective actions helps protect your skin from the sun's damaging UV rays.

UV rays reach you on cloudy and hazy days, as well as bright and sunny days. UV rays will also reflect off any surface like water, cement, sand, and snow. Additionally, UV rays from artificial sources of light, like tanning beds, cause skin cancer and should be avoided.

Most forms of skin cancer can be cured. However, the best way to avoid skin cancer is to protect your skin from the sun.

Just a few serious sunburns can increase your risk of skin cancer later in life. You don't have to be at the pool, beach, or on vacation to get too much sun. Your skin needs protection from the sun's harmful UV rays whenever you're outdoors.

You need protection from the sun when you're at school, too.

Remember, when in the sun, seek shade, cover up, get a hat, wear sunglasses, and use sunscreen.

♣ It's A Fact!!

Cancer Burden

- 50,039 people were diagnosed with melanomas of the skin in 2004.

- 7,952 people died from melanomas of the skin in 2004.

- Skin cancer is the most common form of cancer in the United States.

Source: U.S. Cancer Statistics Working Group. United States Cancer Statistics: 2004 Incidence and Mortality. Atlanta (GA): Department of Health and Human Services, Centers for Disease Control and Prevention, and National Cancer Institute; 2007.

Chapter 24

Sunscreen: The Burning Facts

The Burning Facts

Although the sun is necessary for life, too much sun exposure can lead to adverse health effects, including skin cancer. More than one million people in the United States are diagnosed with skin cancer each year, making it the most common form of cancer in the country, but it is largely preventable through a broad sun protection program. It is estimated that 90 percent of non-melanoma skin cancers and 65 percent of melanoma skin cancers are associated with exposure to ultraviolet (UV) radiation from the sun.

By themselves, sunscreens might not be effective in protecting you from the most dangerous forms of skin cancer. However, sunscreen use is an important part of your sun protection program. Used properly, certain sunscreens help protect human skin from some of the sun's damaging UV radiation. But according to recent surveys, most people are confused about the proper use and effectiveness of sunscreens. The purpose of this chapter is to educate you about sunscreens and other important sun protection measures so that you can protect yourself from the sun's damaging rays.

About This Chapter: Text in this chapter is from "Sunscreen: The Burning Facts," United States Environmental Protection Agency (EPA), September 2006.

How Does UV Radiation Affect My Skin? What Are The Risks?

UV radiation, a known carcinogen, can have a number of harmful effects on the skin. The two types of UV radiation that can affect the skin—UVA and UVB—have both been linked to skin cancer and a weakening of the immune system. They also contribute to premature aging of the skin and cataracts (a condition that impairs eyesight), and cause skin color changes.

UVA Rays

UVA rays, which are not absorbed by the ozone layer, penetrate deep into the skin and heavily contribute to premature aging. Up to 90 percent of the visible skin changes commonly attributed to aging are caused by sun exposure.

UVB Rays

These powerful rays, which are partially absorbed by the ozone layer, mostly affect the surface of the skin and are the primary cause of sunburn. Because of the thinning of the ozone layer, the effects of UVB radiation will pose an increased threat until the layer is restored in the latter half of the 21st century.

Are Some People Predisposed To Adverse Health Effects?

Everybody, regardless of race or ethnicity, is subject to the potential adverse effects of overexposure to the sun. However, some people are more vulnerable than others to the harmful effects of the sun.

Skin Type

Skin type affects the degree to which some people burn and the time it takes them to burn. The Food and Drug Administration (FDA) classifies skin type on a scale from one to six. Individuals with lower number skin types (one and two) have fair skin and tend to burn rapidly and more severely. Individuals with higher number skin types (five and six), though capable of burning, have darker skin and do not burn as easily.

Table 24.1. How Do I Know What My Skin Type Is?

Skin Type	Skin Color	Skin Color
I	Pale white	Always burns—never tans
II	White to light beige	Burns easily—tans minimally
III	Beige	Burns moderately—tans gradually to light brown
IV	Light brown	Burns minimally—tans well to moderately brown
V	Moderate brown	Rarely burns—tans profusely to dark brown
VI	Dark brown or black	Never burns—tans profusely

Source: "How Do I Know What My Skin Type Is?" U.S. Food and Drug Administration (FDA), Center for Devices and Radiological Health, August 2007.

How Do Sunscreens Work? What Is The Sun Protection Factor (SPF)?

Sunscreens protect your skin by absorbing and/or reflecting UVA and UVB rays. The FDA requires that all sunscreens contain a Sun Protection Factor (SPF) label. The SPF reveals the relative amount of sunburn protection that a sunscreen can provide an average user (tested on skin types one, two, and three) when correctly used.

Sunscreens with an SPF of at least 15 are recommended. You should be aware that an SPF of 30 is not twice as protective as an SPF of 15; rather, when properly used, an SPF of 15 protects the skin from 93 percent of UVB radiation, and an SPF 30 sunscreen provides 97 percent protection.

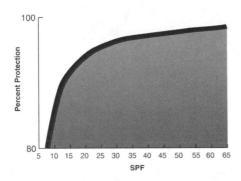

Figure 24.1. SPF Versus UVB Protection

Although the SPF ratings found on sunscreen packages apply mainly to UVB rays, many sunscreen manufacturers include ingredients that protect the skin from some UVA rays as well. These "broad-spectrum" sunscreens are highly recommended.

What Are The Effects Resulting From Sun Exposure?

The same people who are most likely to burn are also most vulnerable to skin cancer. Studies have shown that individuals with large numbers of freckles and moles also have a higher risk of developing skin cancer. Although people with higher-number skin types have a lower incidence of skin cancer, they should still take action to protect their skin and eyes from overexposure to the sun, since cases of skin cancer in people with darker skin are often not detected until later stages when it is more dangerous.

Additional Factors

Certain diseases, such as lupus, can also make a person more sensitive to sun exposure. Some medications, such as antibiotics and antihistamines and even certain herbal remedies, can cause extra sensitivity to the sun's rays. Discuss these issues with your physician.

What Are The Active Ingredients In Sunscreen?

Broad-spectrum sunscreens often contain a number of chemical ingredients that absorb UVA and UVB radiation. Many sunscreens contain UVA-absorbing avobenzone or a benzophenone (such as dioxybenzone, oxybenzone, or sulisobenzone), in addition to UVB-absorbing chemical ingredients (some of which also contribute to UVA protection). In rare cases, chemical ingredients cause skin reactions, including acne, burning, blisters, dryness, itching, rash, redness, stinging, swelling, and tightening of the skin. Consult a physician if these symptoms occur. These reactions are most commonly associated with para-aminobenzoic acid (PABA)-based sunscreens and those containing benzophenones. Some sunscreens also contain alcohol, fragrances, or preservatives, and should be avoided if you have skin allergies.

Physical Ingredients

The physical compounds titanium dioxide and zinc oxide reflect, scatter, and absorb both UVA and UVB rays. These ingredients, produced through chemical processes, do not typically cause allergic reactions. Using new technology, the particle sizes of zinc oxide and titanium dioxide have been reduced, making them more transparent without losing their ability to screen UV.

♣ It's A Fact!!

All of the chemical and physical ingredients mentioned in this chapter have been approved by the FDA.

Source: "Sunscreen: The Burning Facts," EPA, 2006.

How Do I Apply Sunscreen?

Use a broad-spectrum sunscreen with an SPF rating of 15 or higher. Apply sunscreen 20 minutes before going out into the sun (or as directed by the manufacturer) to give it time to absorb into your skin. Apply it generously and regularly—about one ounce every two hours—and more often if you are swimming or perspiring. A small tube containing between three and five ounces of sunscreen might only be enough for one person during a day at the beach.

Do not forget about lips, ears, feet, hands, bald spots, and the back of the neck. In addition, apply sunscreen to areas under bathing suit straps, necklaces, bracelets, and sunglasses. Keep sunscreen until the expiration date or for no more than three years, because the sunscreen ingredients might become less effective over time.

According to the FDA, "water resistant" sunscreens must maintain their SPF after 40 minutes of water immersion, while "very water resistant" sunscreens must maintain their SPF after 80 minutes of water immersion. Either type of water-resistant sunscreen must be reapplied regularly, as heavy perspiration, water, and towel drying remove the sunscreen's protective layer.

♣ **It's A Fact!!**
Can I Get A
Tan Without UV?

Sunless tanners and bronzers are applied to the skin like a cream and can provide a temporary, artificial tan. The only color additive currently approved by FDA for this purpose is dihydroxyacetone (DHA). Application can be difficult, and areas of the skin can react differently, resulting in an uneven appearance.

Bronzers stain the skin temporarily, and they can generally be removed with soap and water. They may streak after application and can stain clothes. Sunless tanners and bronzers might not contain active sunscreen ingredients. Read their labels to find out if they provide any sun protection.

Source: "Sunscreen: The Burning Facts," EPA, 2006.

Chapter 25

Tanning Products

Tanning Lamps, Booths, And Beds

Tanning lamps have become a popular method of maintaining a year-round tan, but their effects can be as dangerous as tanning outdoors.

Like the sun, the lamps used in tanning booths and beds emit UV (ultraviolet) radiation. While most lamps emit both UVA and UVB radiation, some emit only UVA.

Some experts argue that artificial tanning is less dangerous because the intensity of light and the time spent tanning are controlled. There is limited evidence to support these claims. On the other hand, sunlamps may be more dangerous than the sun because they can be used at the same intensity every day of the year—something that is unlikely for the sun because of winter weather and cloud cover. They can also be more dangerous because people can expose their entire bodies at each session, which would be difficult to do outdoors.

Using Tanning Lamps, Booths, Or Beds

If you use indoor tanning equipment, follow these steps to reduce the dangers of UV exposure:

About This Chapter: Text in this chapter is from "Tanning Products," U.S. Food and Drug Administration (FDA), Center for Devices and Radiological Health, July 2007.

- Be sure to wear the goggles provided, making sure they fit snugly and are not cracked.

- Start slowly and use short exposure times to build up a tan over time.

- *Don't* use the maximum exposure time the first time you tan because you could get burned, and burns are thought to be related to melanoma.

- Follow manufacturer-recommended exposure times for your skin type. Check the label for exposure times.

- Stick to your time limit.

- After a tan is developed, tan no more than once a week. Depending on your skin type, you may even be able to maintain your tan with one exposure every two to three weeks.

Because sunburn takes six to 48 hours to develop, you may not realize your skin is burned until it is too late.

FDA has a radiation safety performance standard for sunlamp products. All sunlamp products must have a warning label, an accurate timer, an emergency stop control, and include an exposure schedule and protective goggles.

☞ Remember!!

You should *not* use a tanning bed or lamp if these circumstances apply to you:

- You sunburn easily and do not tan. Skin that does not tan in the sun will probably not tan under a sunlamp.

- You have a family history of melanoma.

- You get frequent cold sores. UV radiation may cause them to appear more frequently due to immune system suppression.

- You are taking medicines that can make you more sensitive to UV rays. Check with your doctor or pharmacist.

✔ **Quick Tip**
Using Sunless Tanners

Before using a sunless tanning booth, ask the tanning salon these questions to make sure you will be protected:

- Will my eyes and the area surrounding them be protected?

- Will my nose, mouth, and ears be protected?

- Will I be protected from inhaling the tanning spray through my nose or mouth?

If the answer to any of these questions is "no," look for another salon. Otherwise you are putting yourself at risk for exposure to chemicals with potentially dangerous effects.

Sunless Tanning Sprays And Lotions

Sunless tanning delivers a faux glow by coating your skin with the chemical dihydroxyacetone (DHA). DHA interacts with the dead surface cells in the epidermis to darken skin color and simulate a tan, and the result usually lasts for several days.

While the FDA allows DHA to be "externally applied" for skin coloring, there are restrictions on its use. DHA should not be inhaled, ingested, or exposed to areas covered by mucous membranes including the lips, nose, and areas in and around the eye (from the top of the cheek to above the eyebrow) because the risks, if any, are unknown.

Most sunless tanning sprays and lotions do not contain a skin protecting sunscreen. Make sure you apply an even coat of sunscreen to all exposed skin at least 30 minutes before going outdoors.

You should also take precautions if you're applying a self-tanner at home. Most self tanners contain the same DHA used in sunless tanning salons.

Self-tanners are available in many forms, including lotions, creams, and sprays that you apply and let soak into your skin. Follow the directions on the self-tanner label carefully and take care not to get the self-tanner in your eyes, nose, or mouth.

Tanning Pills

You may have seen ads that promise to give you a too-good-to-be-true golden glow just by swallowing a pill. These so-called tanning pills are unsafe and *none are approved by the FDA.*

Some tanning pills contain the color additive canthaxanthin. When large amounts of canthaxanthin are ingested, it can turn the skin a range of colors from orange to brown. It can also cause serious health problems including liver damage; hives; and an eye disorder called canthaxanthin retinopathy, in which yellow deposits form in the retinas.

Chapter 26

What Is Skin Cancer?

Cancer develops when DNA, the molecule found in cells that encodes genetic information, becomes damaged and the body cannot repair the damage. These damaged cells begin to grow and divide uncontrollably. When this occurs in the skin, skin cancer develops. As the damaged cells multiply, they form a tumor. Since skin cancer generally develops in the epidermis, the outermost layers of skin, a tumor is usually clearly visible. This makes most skin cancers detectable in the early stages.

Types Of Skin Cancer

Three types of skin cancer account for nearly 100 percent of all diagnosed cases. Each of these three cancers begins in a different type of cell within the skin, and each cancer is named for the type of cell in which it begins. Skin cancers are divided into one of two classes—nonmelanoma skin cancers and melanoma. Melanoma is the deadliest form of skin cancer.

The Different Types Of Skin Cancer

Basal Cell Carcinoma (BCC): The most common cancer in humans, BCC develops in more than one million people every year in the United States alone. About 80 percent of all skin cancers are BCC, a cancer that develops in the basal cells—skin cells located in the lowest layer of the epidermis. BCC can take several forms. It can appear as a shiny translucent or pearly nodule, a sore that continuously heals and then re-opens, a pink slightly elevated growth, reddish irritated patches of skin, or a waxy scar. Most BCCs appear on skin with a history of exposure to the sun, such as the face, ears, scalp, and upper trunk. These tumors tend to grow slowly and can take years to reach ½ inch in size. While these tumors very rarely metastasize (cancer spreads to other parts of the body), dermatologists encourage early diagnosis and treatment to prevent extensive damage to surrounding tissue.

Squamous Cell Carcinoma (SCC): About 16 percent of diagnosed skin cancers are SCC. This cancer begins in the squamous cells, which are found in the upper layer of the epidermis. About 200,000 cases are diagnosed every year. SCC tends to develop in fair-skinned, middle-aged and elderly people who have had long-term sun exposure. It most often appears as a crusted or scaly area of skin with a red inflamed base that resembles a growing tumor, non-healing ulcer, or crusted-over patch of skin. While most commonly found on sun-exposed areas of the body, it can develop anywhere, including the inside of the mouth and the genitalia. SCC may arise from actinic keratoses, which are dry, scaly lesions that may be skin-colored, reddish-brown or yellowish-black. SCC requires early treatment to prevent metastasis (spreading).

Melanoma: Accounting for about four percent of all diagnosed skin cancers, melanoma begins in the melanocytes, cells within the epidermis that give skin its color. Melanoma has been coined "the most lethal form of skin cancer" because it can rapidly spread to the lymph system and internal organs. In the United States alone, approximately one person dies from melanoma every hour. Older Caucasian men have the highest mortality rate. Dermatologists believe this is due to the fact that they are less likely to heed the early warning signs. With early detection and proper treatment, the cure rate for melanoma is about 95 percent. Once its spreads, the prognosis is poor. Melanoma most often develops in a pre-existing mole or looks like a new mole, which is why it is important for people to know what their moles look like and be able to detect changes to existing moles and spot new moles.

Other Nonmelanoma Skin Cancers: All other skin cancers combined account for less than one percent of diagnosed cases. These are classified as nonmelanoma skin cancers and include Merkel cell carcinoma, dermatofibrosarcoma protuberans, Paget's disease and cutaneous T-cell lymphoma.

Causes

Sun exposure is the leading cause of skin cancer. According to the American Cancer Society, "Many of the more than one million skin cancers diagnosed each year could be prevented with protection from the sun's rays." Scientists now know that exposure to the sun's ultraviolet (UV) rays damages DNA in the skin. The body can usually repair this damage before gene mutations occur and cancer develops. When a person's body cannot repair the damaged DNA, which can occur with cumulative sun exposure, cancer develops.

In some cases, skin cancer is an inherited condition. Between five and 10 percent of melanomas develop in people with a family history of melanoma.

Who Gets Skin Cancer?

Skin cancer develops in people of all colors, from the palest to the darkest. However, skin cancer is most likely to occur in those who have fair skin, light-colored eyes, blonde or red hair, a tendency to burn or freckle when exposed to the sun, and a history of sun exposure. Anyone with a family history of skin cancer also has an increased risk of developing skin cancer. In dark-skinned individuals, melanoma most often develops on non-sun-exposed areas, such as the foot, underneath nails, and on the mucous membranes of the mouth, nasal passages, or genitals. Those with fair skin also can have melanoma develop in these areas.

Skin Cancer Rates Rising

While Americans now recognize that overexposure to the sun is unhealthy, the fact remains that most do not protect their skin from the sun's harmful rays. As a result, skin cancer is common in the United States. More than one million nonmelanoma skin cancers are diagnosed each year, and approximately one person dies from melanoma every hour.

If current trends continue, one in five Americans will develop skin cancer during their lifetime. Melanoma continues to rise at an alarming rate. In 1930, one in 5,000 Americans was likely to develop melanoma during their lifetime. By 2004, this ratio jumped to one in 65. Today, melanoma is the second most common cancer in women aged 20 to 29.

Prevention And Early Detection Key

Sun protection can significantly decrease a person's risk of developing skin cancer. Sun protection

> ✎ **What's It Mean?**
>
> Basal Cells: Skin cells located in the lowest layer of the epidermis.
>
> Epidermis: The outermost layer of skin.
>
> Keratoses: Dry, scaly lesions that may be skin-colored, reddish-brown or yellowish-black.
>
> Melanocytes: Cells within the epidermis that give skin its color.
>
> Squamous Cells: Skin cells found in the upper layer of the epidermis.

practices include staying out of the sun between 10 a.m. and 4 p.m. when the rays are strongest, applying a broad-spectrum (offers UVA and UVB protection) sunscreen with a Sun Protection Factor (SPF) of 15 or higher year-round to all exposed skin, and wearing protective clothing, such as a wide-brimmed hat and sunglasses when outdoors.

Since skin cancer is so prevalent today, dermatologists also recommend that everyone learn how to recognize the signs of skin cancer, use this knowledge to perform regular examinations of their skin, and see a dermatologist annually (more frequently if at high risk) for an exam. Skin cancer is highly curable with early detection and proper treatment.

Chapter 27

Melanoma

Melanoma occurs when melanocytes (pigment cells) become malignant. Most pigment cells are in the skin; when melanoma starts in the skin, the disease is called *cutaneous* melanoma. Melanoma may also occur in the eye (ocular melanoma or intraocular melanoma). Rarely, melanoma may arise in the meninges, the digestive tract, lymph nodes, or other areas where melanocytes are found. Melanomas that begin in areas other than the skin are not discussed in this chapter.

Melanoma is one of the most common cancers. The chance of developing it increases with age, but this disease affects people of all ages. It can occur on any skin surface. In men, melanoma is often found on the trunk (the area between the shoulders and the hips) or the head and neck. In women, it often develops on the lower legs. Melanoma is rare in black people and others with dark skin. When it does develop in dark-skinned people, it tends to occur under the fingernails or toenails, or on the palms or soles.

When melanoma spreads, cancer cells may show up in nearby lymph nodes. Groups of lymph nodes are found throughout the body. Lymph nodes trap bacteria, cancer cells, or other harmful substances that may be in the lymphatic system. If the cancer has reached the lymph nodes, it may mean

About This Chapter: Information in this chapter is from "What You Need to Know about Melanoma," National Cancer Institute, March 2003.

that cancer cells have spread to other parts of the body such as the liver, lungs, or brain. In such cases, the cancer cells in the new tumor are still melanoma cells, and the disease is called *metastatic melanoma*, not liver, lung, or brain cancer.

Melanoma: Who's At Risk?

No one knows the exact causes of melanoma. Doctors can seldom explain why one person gets melanoma and another does not.

☞ Remember!!

Doctors recommend that people take steps to help prevent and reduce the risk of melanoma caused by UV radiation:

- Avoid exposure to the midday sun (from 10 a.m. to 4 p.m.) whenever possible. When your shadow is shorter than you are, remember to protect yourself from the sun.

- If you must be outside, wear long sleeves, long pants, and a hat with a wide brim.

- Protect yourself from UV radiation that can penetrate light clothing, windshields, and windows.

- Protect yourself from UV radiation reflected by sand, water, snow, and ice.

- Help protect your skin by using a lotion, cream, or gel that contains sunscreen. Many doctors believe sunscreens may help prevent melanoma, especially sunscreens that reflect, absorb, and/or scatter both types of ultraviolet radiation. These sunscreen products will be labeled with "broad-spectrum coverage." Sunscreens are rated in strength according to a sun protection factor (SPF). The higher the SPF, the more sunburn protection is provided. Sunscreens with an SPF value of two to 11 provide minimal protection against sunburns. Sunscreens with an SPF of 12 to 29 provide moderate protection. Those with an SPF of 30 or higher provide the most protection against sunburn.

- Wear sunglasses that have UV-absorbing lenses. The label should specify that the lenses block at least 99 percent of UVA and UVB radiation. Sunglasses can protect both the eyes and the skin around the eyes.

However, research has shown that people with certain risk factors are more likely than others to develop melanoma. A risk factor is anything that increases a person's chance of developing a disease. Still, many who do get this disease have no known risk factors.

Studies have found the following risk factors for melanoma:

- **Dysplastic Nevi:** Dysplastic nevi are more likely than ordinary moles to become cancerous. Dysplastic nevi are common, and many people have a few of these abnormal moles. The risk of melanoma is greatest for people who have a large number of dysplastic nevi. The risk is especially high for people with a family history of both dysplastic nevi and melanoma.

- **Many (More Than 50) Ordinary Moles:** Having many moles increases the risk of developing melanoma.

- **Fair Skin:** Melanoma occurs more frequently in people who have fair skin that burns or freckles easily (these people also usually have red or blond hair and blue eyes) than in people with dark skin. White people get melanoma far more often than do black people, probably because light skin is more easily damaged by the sun.

- **Personal History Of Melanoma Or Skin Cancer:** People who have been treated for melanoma have a high risk of a second melanoma. Some people develop more than two melanomas. People who had one or more of the common skin cancers (basal cell carcinoma or squamous cell carcinoma) are at increased risk of melanoma.

- **Family History Of Melanoma:** Melanoma sometimes runs in families. Having two or more close relatives who have had this disease is a risk factor. About 10 percent of all patients with melanoma have a family member with this disease. When melanoma runs in a family, all family members should be checked regularly by a doctor.

- **Weakened Immune System:** People whose immune system is weakened by certain cancers, by drugs given following organ transplantation, or by HIV are at increased risk of developing melanoma.

- **Severe, Blistering Sunburns:** People who have had at least one severe, blistering sunburn as a child or teenager are at increased risk of melanoma. Because of this, doctors advise that parents protect children's skin from the sun. Such protection may reduce the risk of melanoma later in life. Sunburns in adulthood are also a risk factor for melanoma.

- **Ultraviolet (UV) Radiation:** Experts believe that much of the worldwide increase in melanoma is related to an increase in the amount of time people spend in the sun. This disease is also more common in people who live in areas that get large amounts of UV radiation from the sun. In the United States, for example, melanoma is more common in Texas than in Minnesota, where the sun is not as strong. UV radiation from the sun causes premature aging of the skin and skin damage that can lead to melanoma. Artificial sources of UV radiation, such as sunlamps and tanning booths, also can cause skin damage and increase the risk of melanoma. Doctors encourage people to limit their exposure to natural UV radiation and to avoid artificial sources.

People who are concerned about developing melanoma should talk with their doctor about the disease, the symptoms to watch for, and an appropriate schedule for checkups. The doctor's advice will be based on the person's personal and family history, medical history, and other risk factors.

Signs and Symptoms

Often, the first sign of melanoma is a change in the size, shape, color, or feel of an existing mole. Most melanomas have a black or blue-black area. Melanoma also may appear as a new mole. It may be black, abnormal, or "ugly looking."

If you have a question or concern about something on your skin, see your doctor.

Melanomas can vary greatly in how they look. Many show all of the ABCD features. However, some may show changes or abnormalities in only one or two of the ABCD features.

Melanomas in an early stage may be found when an existing mole changes slightly, for example, when a new black area forms. Newly formed fine scales and itching in a mole also are common symptoms of early melanoma. In more advanced melanoma, the texture of the mole may change. For example, it may become hard or lumpy. Melanomas may feel different from regular moles. More advanced tumors may itch, ooze, or bleed. But melanomas usually do not cause pain.

✔ **Quick Tip**

Thinking of "ABCD" can help you remember what to watch for:

- **Asymmetry:** The shape of one half does not match the other.

- **Border:** The edges are often ragged, notched, blurred, or irregular in outline; the pigment may spread into the surrounding skin.

- **Color:** The color is uneven. Shades of black, brown, and tan may be present. Areas of white, grey, red, pink, or blue also may be seen.

- **Diameter:** There is a change in size, usually an increase. Melanomas are usually larger than the eraser of a pencil (1/4 inch or 5 millimeters).

A skin examination is often part of a routine checkup by a health care provider. People also can check their own skin for new growths or other changes. Changes in the skin, such as a change in a mole, should be reported to the health care provider right away. The person may be referred to a dermatologist, a doctor who specializes in diseases of the skin.

Melanoma can be cured if it is diagnosed and treated when the tumor is thin and has not deeply invaded the skin. However, if a melanoma is not removed at its early stages, cancer cells may grow downward from the skin surface and invade healthy tissue. When a melanoma becomes thick and deep, the disease often spreads to other parts of the body and is difficult to control.

People who have had melanoma have a high risk of developing a new melanoma. People at risk for any reason should check their skin regularly and have regular skin exams by a health care provider.

Dysplastic Nevi

Some people have certain abnormal-looking moles (called dysplastic nevi or atypical moles) that are more likely than normal moles to develop into melanoma. Most people with dysplastic nevi have just a few of these abnormal moles; some people have many. People with dysplastic nevi and their health care provider should examine these moles regularly to watch for changes.

Dysplastic nevi often look very much like melanoma. Doctors with special training in skin diseases are in the best position to decide whether an abnormal-looking mole should be closely watched or removed and checked for cancer.

In some families, many members have a large number of dysplastic nevi, and some have had melanoma. Members of these families have a very high risk of melanoma. Doctors often recommend that they have frequent checkups (every three to six months) so that any problems can be detected early. The doctor may take pictures of a person's skin to help show when changes occur.

Diagnosis

If the doctor suspects that a spot on the skin is melanoma, the patient will need to have a biopsy. A biopsy is the only way to make a definite diagnosis. In this procedure, the doctor tries to remove all of the suspicious-looking growth. This is an excisional biopsy. If the growth is too large to be removed entirely, the doctor removes a sample of the tissue. The doctor will never "shave off" or cauterize a growth that might be melanoma.

A biopsy can usually be done in the doctor's office using local anesthesia. A pathologist then examines the tissue under a microscope to check for cancer cells. Sometimes it is helpful for more than one pathologist to check the tissue for cancer cells.

Staging

If the diagnosis is melanoma, the doctor needs to learn the extent, or stage, of the disease before planning treatment. Staging is a careful attempt to learn how thick the tumor is, how deeply the melanoma has invaded the skin, and whether melanoma cells have spread to nearby lymph nodes or other parts of the body. The doctor may remove nearby lymph nodes to check for cancer cells. (Such surgery may be considered part of the treatment because removing cancerous lymph nodes may help control the disease.) The doctor also does a careful physical exam and, if the tumor is thick, may order chest x-rays, blood tests, and scans of the liver, bones, and brain.

Stages Of Melanoma

The following stages are used for melanoma:

Stage 0: In stage 0, the melanoma cells are found only in the outer layer of skin cells and have not invaded deeper tissues.

Stage I: Melanoma in stage I is thin:

- The tumor is no more than 1 millimeter (1/25 inch) thick. The outer layer (epidermis) of skin may appear scraped. (This is called an ulceration).

- Or, the tumor is between 1 and 2 millimeters (1/12 inch) thick. There is no ulceration.

- The melanoma cells have not spread to nearby lymph nodes.

✔ Quick Tip

A person who needs a biopsy may want to ask the doctor the following questions:

- Why do I need a biopsy?

- How long will it take? Will it hurt?

- Will the entire tumor be removed?

- What side effects can I expect?

- How soon will I know the results?

- If I do have cancer, who will talk to me about treatment? When?

Stage II: The tumor is at least 1 millimeter thick:

- The tumor is between 1 and 2 millimeters thick. There is ulceration.

- Or, the thickness of the tumor is more than 2 millimeters. There may be ulceration.

- The melanoma cells have not spread to nearby lymph nodes.

Stage III: The melanoma cells have spread to nearby tissues:

- The melanoma cells have spread to one or more nearby lymph nodes.

- Or, the melanoma cells have spread to tissues just outside the original tumor but not to any lymph nodes.

Stage IV: The melanoma cells have spread to other organs, to lymph nodes, or to skin areas far away from the original tumor.

Recurrent: Recurrent disease means that the cancer has come back (recurred) after it has been treated. It may have come back in the original site or in another part of the body.

Treatment

People with melanoma are often treated by a team of specialists. The team may include a dermatologist, surgeon, medical oncologist, radiation oncologist, and plastic surgeon.

Methods Of Treatment

People with melanoma may have surgery, chemotherapy, biological therapy, or radiation therapy. Patients may have a combination of treatments.

At any stage of disease, people with melanoma may have treatment to control pain and other symptoms of the cancer, to relieve the side effects of therapy, and to ease emotional and practical problems. This kind of treatment is called symptom management, supportive care, or palliative care.

The doctor is the best person to describe the treatment choices and discuss the expected results.

A patient may want to talk to the doctor about taking part in a clinical trial, a research study of new treatment methods. More information about clinical trials is included in the section called "The Promise Of Cancer Research" later in this chapter.

Surgery

Surgery is the usual treatment for melanoma. The surgeon removes the tumor and some normal tissue around it. This procedure reduces the chance that cancer cells will be left in the area. The width and depth of surrounding skin that needs to be removed depends on the thickness of the melanoma and how deeply it has invaded the skin:

- The doctor may be able to completely remove a very thin melanoma during the biopsy. Further surgery may not be necessary.

- If the melanoma was not completely removed during the biopsy, the doctor takes out the remaining tumor. In most cases, additional surgery is performed to remove normal-looking tissue around the tumor (called the margin) to make sure all melanoma cells are removed. This is often necessary, even for thin melanomas. If the melanoma is thick, the doctor may need to remove a larger margin of tissue.

If a large area of tissue is removed, the surgeon may do a skin graft. For this procedure, the doctor uses skin from another part of the body to replace the skin that was removed.

Lymph nodes near the tumor may be removed because cancer can spread through the lymphatic system. If the pathologist finds cancer cells in the lymph nodes, it may mean that the disease has also spread to other parts of the body. Two procedures are used to remove the lymph nodes:

- **Sentinel Lymph Node Biopsy:** The sentinel lymph node biopsy is done after the biopsy of the melanoma but before the wider excision of the tumor. A radioactive substance is injected near the melanoma. The surgeon follows the movement of the substance on a computer screen. The first lymph node(s) to take up the substance is called the sentinel lymph node(s). (The imaging study is called lymphoscintigraphy. The procedure to identify the sentinel node(s) is called sentinel lymph node mapping.) The surgeon removes the sentinel node(s) to check for cancer cells. If a sentinel node contains cancer cells, the surgeon removes the rest of the lymph nodes in the area. However, if a sentinel node does not contain cancer cells, no additional lymph nodes are removed.

- **Lymph Node Dissection:** The surgeon removes all the lymph nodes in the area of the melanoma.

Therapy may be given after surgery to kill cancer cells that remain in the body. This treatment is called adjuvant therapy. The patient may receive biological therapy.

Surgery is generally not effective in controlling melanoma that has spread to other parts of the body. In such cases, doctors may use other methods of treatment, such as chemotherapy, biological therapy, radiation therapy, or a combination of these methods.

Chemotherapy

Chemotherapy, the use of drugs to kill cancer cells, is sometimes used to treat melanoma. The drugs are usually given in cycles: a treatment period followed by a recovery period, then another treatment period, and so on. Usually a patient has chemotherapy as an outpatient (at the hospital, at the doctor's office, or at home). However, depending on which drugs are given and the patient's general health, a short hospital stay may be needed.

People with melanoma may receive chemotherapy in one of the following ways:

- **By Mouth Or Injection:** Either way, the drugs enter the bloodstream and travel throughout the body.

- **Isolated Limb Perfusion (Also Called Isolated Arterial Perfusion):** For melanoma on an arm or leg, chemotherapy drugs are put directly into the bloodstream of that limb. The flow of blood to and from the limb is stopped for a while. This allows most of the drug to reach the tumor directly. Most of the chemotherapy remains in that limb.

The drugs may be heated before injection. This type of chemotherapy is called hyperthermic perfusion.

Biological Therapy

Biological therapy (also called immunotherapy) is a form of treatment that uses the body's immune system, either directly or indirectly, to fight cancer or to reduce side effects caused by some cancer treatments. Biological therapy for melanoma uses substances called cytokines. The body normally produces cytokines in small amounts in response to infections and other diseases. Using modern laboratory techniques, scientists can produce cytokines in large amounts. In some cases, biological therapy given after surgery can help prevent melanoma from recurring. For patients with metastatic melanoma or a high risk of recurrence, interferon alpha and interleukin-2 (also called IL-2 or aldesleukin) may be recommended after surgery.

Radiation Therapy

Radiation therapy (also called radiotherapy) uses high-energy rays to kill cancer cells. A large machine directs radiation at the body. The patient usually has treatment at a hospital or clinic, five days a week for several weeks. Radiation therapy may be used to help control melanoma that has spread to the brain, bones, and other parts of the body. It may shrink the tumor and relieve symptoms.

Treatment Choices By Stage

The following are brief descriptions of the treatments most often used for each stage. (Other treatments may sometimes be appropriate.)

Stage 0: People with Stage 0 melanoma may have minor surgery to remove the tumor and some of the surrounding tissue.

Stage I: People with Stage I melanoma may have surgery to remove the tumor. The surgeon may also remove as much as 2 centimeters (3/4 inch) of tissue around the tumor. To cover the wound, the patient may have skin grafting.

Stage II Or Stage III: People with Stage II or Stage III melanoma may have surgery to remove the tumor. The surgeon may also remove as much as 3 centimeters (1 1/4 inches) of nearby tissue. Skin grafting may be done to cover the wound. Sometimes the surgeon removes nearby lymph nodes.

Stage IV: People with Stage IV melanoma often receive palliative care. The goal of palliative care is to help the patient feel better—physically and emotionally. This type of treatment is intended to control pain and other symptoms and to relieve the side effects of therapy (such as nausea), rather than to extend life.

The patient may have one of the following treatments:

- Surgery to remove lymph nodes that contain cancer cells or to remove tumors that have spread to other areas of the body

- Radiation therapy, biological therapy, or chemotherapy to relieve symptoms

Recurrent Melanoma

Treatment for recurrent melanoma depends on where the cancer came back, which treatments the patient has already received, and other factors. As with Stage IV melanoma, treatment usually cannot cure melanoma that recurs. Palliative care is often an important part of the treatment plan. Many patients have palliative care to ease their symptoms while they are getting anticancer treatments to slow the progress of the disease. Some receive only palliative care to improve their quality of life by easing pain, nausea, and other symptoms.

The patient may have one of the following treatments:

- Surgery to remove the tumor

- Radiation therapy, biological therapy, or chemotherapy to relieve symptoms

- Heated chemotherapy drugs injected directly into the tumor

Side Effects Of Treatment

Because treatment may damage healthy cells and tissues, unwanted side effects sometimes occur. These side effects depend on many factors, including the location of the tumor and the type and extent of the treatment. Side effects may not be the same for each person, and they may even change from one treatment session to the next. Before treatment starts, the health care team will explain possible side effects and suggest ways to help the patient manage them.

Surgery

The side effects of surgery depend mainly on the size and location of the tumor and the extent of the operation. Although patients may have some pain during the first few days after surgery, this pain can be controlled with medicine. People should feel free to discuss pain relief with the doctor or nurse. It is also common for patients to feel tired or weak for a while. The length of time it takes to recover from an operation varies for each patient.

Scarring may also be a concern for some patients. To avoid causing large scars, doctors remove as little tissue as they can (while still protecting against recurrence). In general, the scar from surgery to remove an early stage melanoma is a small line (often 1 to 2 inches long), and it fades with time. How noticeable the scar is depends on where the melanoma was, how well the person heals, and whether the person develops raised scars called keloids. When a tumor is large and thick, the doctor must remove more surrounding skin and other tissue (including muscle). Although skin grafts reduce scarring caused by the removal of large growths, these scars will still be quite noticeable.

Surgery to remove the lymph nodes from the underarm or groin may damage the lymphatic system and slow the flow of lymphatic fluid in the arm or leg. Lymphatic fluid may build up in a limb and cause swelling (lymphedema). The doctor or nurse can suggest exercises or other ways to reduce swelling if it becomes a problem. Also, it is harder for the body to fight infection in a limb after nearby lymph nodes have been removed, so the patient will need to protect the arm or leg from cuts, scratches, bruises, insect bites, or burns that may lead to infection. If an infection does develop, the patient should see the doctor right away.

Chemotherapy

The side effects of chemotherapy depend mainly on the specific drugs and the dose. In general, anticancer drugs affect cells that divide rapidly, especially:

- **Blood Cells:** These cells fight infection, help the blood to clot, and carry oxygen to all parts of the body. When drugs affect blood cells, patients are more likely to get infections, may bruise or bleed easily, and may feel very weak and tired.

- **Cells In Hair Roots:** Chemotherapy can lead to hair loss. The hair grows back, but the new hair may be somewhat different in color and texture.

- **Cells That Line The Digestive Tract:** Chemotherapy can cause poor appetite, nausea and vomiting, diarrhea, or mouth and lip sores. Many of these side effects can be controlled with drugs.

Biological Therapy

The side effects of biological therapy vary with the type of treatment. These treatments may cause flu-like symptoms, such as chills, fever, muscle aches, weakness, loss of appetite, nausea, vomiting, and diarrhea. Patients may also get a skin rash. These problems can be severe, but they go away after treatment stops.

Radiation Therapy

The side effects of radiation therapy depend on the amount of radiation given and the area being treated. Side effects that may occur in the treated area include red or dry skin and hair loss. Radiation therapy also may cause fatigue. Although the side effects of radiation therapy can be unpleasant, the doctor can usually treat or control them. It also helps to know that, in most cases, side effects are not permanent.

Nutrition

People with melanoma may not feel like eating, especially if they are uncomfortable or tired. Also, the side effects of treatment, such as poor appetite, nausea, or vomiting, can be a problem. Foods may taste different. Nevertheless, patients should try to eat well during cancer therapy. They need enough calories to maintain a good weight and protein to keep up strength. Good nutrition often helps people with cancer feel better and have more energy.

The doctor, dietitian, or other health care provider can suggest ways to maintain a healthy diet.

Follow-Up Care

Melanoma patients have a high risk of developing new melanomas. Some also are at risk of a recurrence of the original melanoma in nearby skin or in other parts of the body.

To increase the chance of detecting a new or recurrent melanoma as early as possible, patients should follow their doctor's schedule for regular check-ups. It is especially important for patients who have dysplastic nevi and a family history of melanoma to have frequent checkups. Patients also should examine their skin monthly (keeping in mind the "ABCD" guidelines in the "Signs and Symptoms" section). They should follow their doctor's advice about how to reduce their chance of developing another melanoma. General information about reducing the risk of melanoma is described in the "Melanoma: Who's at Risk?" section.

The chance of recurrence is greater for patients whose melanoma was thick or had spread to nearby tissue than for patients with very thin melanomas. Follow-up care for those who have a high risk of recurrence may include x-rays, blood tests, and scans of the chest, liver, bones, and brain.

A person who has been treated for melanoma may want to ask the doctor the following questions:

- How often should I have checkups?

- What special precautions should I take to avoid sun exposure?

- Are my family members at risk of melanoma? Should they schedule an appointment with their doctor for an examination?

Support For People With Melanoma

Living with a serious disease such as melanoma is not easy. Some people find they need help coping with the emotional and practical aspects of their disease. Support groups can help. In these groups, patients or their family members get together to share what they have learned about coping with the disease and the effects of treatment. Patients may want to talk with a member of their health care team about finding a support group. Groups may offer support in person, over the telephone, or on the internet.

People living with melanoma may worry about caring for their families, keeping their jobs, or continuing daily activities. Concerns about treatments and managing side effects, hospital stays, and medical bills also are common. Doctors, nurses, and other members of the health care team can answer questions about treatment, working, or other activities. Meeting with a social worker, counselor, or member of the clergy can be helpful to those who want to talk about their feelings or discuss their concerns. Often, a social worker can suggest resources for financial aid, transportation, home care, or emotional support.

The Cancer Information Service at 800-4-CANCER can send publications and provide information to help patients and their families locate programs and services.

The Promise Of Cancer Research

Doctors all over the country are conducting many types of clinical trials. These are research studies in which people take part voluntarily. Studies include new ways to treat melanomas. Research already has led to advances, and researchers continue to search for more effective approaches.

Patients who join these studies have the first chance to benefit from treatments that have shown promise in earlier research. They also make an important contribution to medical science by helping doctors learn more about the disease. Although clinical trials may pose some risks, researchers take very careful steps to protect their patients.

Researchers are testing new anticancer drugs. They are looking at combining chemotherapy with radiation therapy. Other studies are combining chemotherapy with biological therapy. Scientists also are studying several cancer vaccines and a type of gene therapy designed to help the immune system kill cancer cells.

Patients who are interested in being part of a clinical trial should talk with their doctor.

Chapter 28

Merkel Cell Carcinoma

What is Merkel cell carcinoma?

Merkel cell carcinoma (MCC) is a rare, aggressive type of skin cancer that forms on or just under the skin. It is also called primary small cell carcinoma of the skin, trabecular carcinoma, APUDoma, neuroendocrine carcinoma, endocrine carcinoma, or primary undifferentiated tumor of the skin. MCC is believed to start in neuroendocrine cells called Merkel cells. These cells release hormones into the blood when stimulated by the nervous system. They migrate from part of the nervous system called the neural crest to the skin. Merkel cells are believed to play a role in making the skin sensitive to touch.

How often does Merkel cell carcinoma occur?

Approximately 1,200 new cases of MCC are diagnosed in the United States each year, compared with almost 60,000 new cases of melanoma and more than one million new cases of nonmelanoma skin cancer. The incidence of MCC has been rising, with a threefold increase between 1986 and 2001. Most patients diagnosed with MCC are over age 50 at diagnosis (the average age is 69), with only five percent of cases diagnosed in those under age 50. MCC is

About This Chapter: Information in this chapter is from "Merkel Cell Carcinoma: Questions and Answers," National Cancer Institute, U.S. National Institutes of Health, January 2007.

more common in white people than in other racial and ethnic groups. Some cases have been reported in Japanese people, but very few have been seen in black people.

What are the possible causes of Merkel cell carcinoma?

The exact cause of MCC is unknown, but it appears to be linked to sun exposure and immunosuppression (suppression of the body's immune system and its ability to fight infections or disease). Sun exposure as a risk factor for MCC is supported by data that show a rise in incidence corresponding with the solar UVB index (scale indicating the intensity of solar ultraviolet-B (UVB) radiation at noon for a particular location). MCC has been linked to conditions such as HIV infection, chronic lymphocytic leukemia, Hodgkin lymphoma (cancer of the lymph system), ectodermal dysplasia (a disease involving abnormal tissue development), and

> ## ♣ It's A Fact!!
> - Merkel cell carcinoma (MCC) is a rare, aggressive type of skin cancer that forms on or just under the skin.
>
> - MCC has been linked to sun exposure, with most cases occurring on sun-exposed areas of the body. MCC has also been linked to immunosuppression, exposure to other sources of ultraviolet light, and certain diseases.
>
> - MCC differs from most other skin cancers in that it grows rapidly over a few weeks or months.
>
> - Surgery and radiation are the usual treatments for MCC.
>
> - People with cancer are encouraged to enroll in clinical trials (research studies with people) that explore new treatments.

Cowden disease (a disease in which masses of abnormal but benign tissues grow in multiple sites in the body). Other possible causes include exposure to arsenic and treatment for psoriasis that uses psoralens (a medication that causes the skin to become sensitive to light) and ultraviolet-A light (PUVA).

What are the symptoms of Merkel cell carcinoma?

The most common symptom of any skin cancer, including MCC, is a change in the skin, especially a change in an existing mole or a new growth. MCC appears as a firm, painless lump within the skin that may resemble a cyst but is fixed; i.e., cannot be moved. The lump is usually less than 2 cm (about ¾ inch) in size and can be red, pink, or blue-violet. MCC is different from other skin cancers in that it grows rapidly over a few weeks or months.

Where does Merkel cell carcinoma develop?

MCC is usually found on sun-exposed areas of the body. Fifty percent of cases occur on the head and neck, especially around the eye and on the eyelid. Forty percent of cases occur on the arms and legs. MCC has also been found on the trunk and other areas of the skin that are not usually exposed to the sun.

How is Merkel cell carcinoma diagnosed and staged?

The doctor may use the following procedures and tests to diagnose MCC. Some of these tests are also used to help determine the stage of the disease. Stage is a description of the extent of cancer.

Biopsy: A biopsy is the removal of cells or tissue from a tumor for examination by a pathologist. The pathologist may study tissue samples under a microscope or perform other tests on the cells or tissue. Biopsies are used for both diagnosis and staging. The surgeon may also remove lymph nodes (small, round organs that trap cancer cells, bacteria, or other harmful substances) to help determine the stage of the disease.

Sentinel Lymph Node Biopsy: Sentinel lymph node (SLN) biopsy is a procedure in which the sentinel lymph node is removed and examined under a microscope to determine whether cancer cells are present. The sentinel lymph node is the first lymph node to which cancer is likely to spread from the primary tumor. SLN biopsy is used to help determine the stage of the disease. SLN biopsy may cause fewer side effects than standard lymph node removal because fewer lymph nodes are taken out.

Immunohistochemistry: Immunohistochemistry (staining of cells with agents that react with antibodies on the surface of cancer cells) is a laboratory technique used to differentiate between MCC and other types of cancer.

Computed Tomography: Computed Tomography (CT), a procedure that uses special x-ray equipment to obtain cross-sectional pictures of the body, can distinguish MCC from small cell lung cancer and show whether the disease has metastasized (spread) to other parts of the body.

Octreotide Scan: In an octreotide scan (sometimes called somatostatin receptor scintigraphy or SRS), the doctor injects a small amount of a radioactive drug into a vein. The drug travels through the bloodstream and attaches to tumor cells. A machine called a scanner detects the radioactive material and creates scans (pictures) showing where the tumor cells are located in the body. For MCC, this test can be used for both diagnosis and staging.

PET Scan: A PET scan uses radioactive sugar, which is absorbed by cancer cells and appears as dark areas on the scan. It can be used for both diagnosis and staging of MCC.

How is Merkel cell carcinoma treated?

Surgery is the most common treatment for MCC. Surgery with wide margins (a large border of healthy tissue removed with the tumor) is the recommended treatment for MCC. Mohs micrographic surgery, a technique in which individual layers of tissue are removed and examined under a microscope until all cancerous tissue has been removed, may be used instead of traditional surgery with wide margins. Mohs micrographic surgery may be a good alternative for MCC tumors on highly visible areas such as the face, and in areas where the surgeon would not be able to obtain wide margins.

The surgeon may remove lymph nodes to help stage the disease or to prevent recurrence (cancer coming back). The patient may also receive adjuvant radiation therapy (treatment given after the primary therapy) to decrease the chance of recurrence. Chemotherapy is the usual treatment if the disease has spread beyond the lymph nodes to areas that are not treatable by radiation therapy.

Supportive care is treatment given to improve the quality of life of patients who have a serious or life-threatening disease, such as cancer. It prevents or treats as early as possible the symptoms of the disease, side effects caused by treatment of the disease, and psychological, social, and spiritual problems related to the disease or its treatment. For example, anticancer drugs such as carboplatin and etoposide may be given to relieve symptoms in some patients with MCC. Radiation may be used to relieve pain from MCC that has metastasized to the brain or bones, and to reduce discomfort from skin problems associated with MCC. Additionally, meeting with a social worker, counselor, or member of the clergy can be helpful to those who want to talk about their feelings or discuss their concerns. A social worker can often suggest resources for help with recovery, emotional support, financial aid, transportation, or home care.

Are clinical trials available?

Yes. The National Cancer Institute (NCI), a component of the National Institutes of Health, is sponsoring clinical trials that are designed to find new treatments and better ways to use current treatments. Before any new treatment can be recommended for general use, doctors conduct clinical trials to find out whether the treatment is safe for patients and effective against the disease. Participation in clinical trials may be a treatment option for patients with MCC.

People interested in taking part in a clinical trial should talk with their doctor. Information about clinical trials is available from the NCI's Cancer Information Service (CIS) at 1-800-4-CANCER.

What is the prognosis for patients with Merkel cell carcinoma?

Prognosis describes the likely course and outcome of a disease—that is, the chance that a patient will recover or have a recurrence. The prognosis for MCC patients depends greatly on the stage of the disease at the time of diagnosis. If the tumor is small (less than 2 cm or about ¾ inch) and cancer cells have not spread to the lymph nodes, the five-year survival rate is more than 90 percent. Patients with MCC that has spread to the lymph nodes have a five-year survival rate of about 50 percent. Overall five-year survival for patients diagnosed with MCC is 64 percent, but half of patients with advanced MCC will live only nine months. The disease recurs in about 50 percent of patients. It is important to keep in mind, however, that these statistics are averages based on large numbers of patients. Statistics cannot be used to predict what will happen to a particular patient because each person's situation is unique.

Chapter 29

Basal Cell And Squamous Cell Skin Cancer

Understanding Skin Cancer

Skin cancer begins in cells, the building blocks that make up the skin. Normally, skin cells grow and divide to form new cells. Every day skin cells grow old and die, and new cells take their place.

Sometimes, this orderly process goes wrong. New cells form when the skin does not need them, and old cells do not die when they should. These extra cells can form a mass of tissue called a *growth* or *tumor*.

Types Of Skin Cancer

Skin cancers are named for the type of cells that become cancerous. The two most common types of skin cancer are basal cell cancer and squamous cell cancer. These cancers usually form on the head, face, neck, hands, and arms. These areas are exposed to the sun. But skin cancer can occur anywhere.

• Basal cell skin cancer grows slowly. It usually occurs on areas of the skin that have been in the sun. It is most common on the face. Basal cell cancer rarely spreads to other parts of the body.

About This Chapter: Information in this chapter is from "What You Need To Know About Skin Cancer," National Cancer Institute, August 2005.

- Squamous cell skin cancer also occurs on parts of the skin that have been in the sun. But it also may be in places that are not in the sun. Squamous cell cancer sometimes spreads to lymph nodes and organs inside the body.

If skin cancer spreads from its original place to another part of the body, the new growth has the same kind of abnormal cells and the same name as the primary growth. It is still called skin cancer.

Symptoms

Most basal cell and squamous cell skin cancers can be cured if found and treated early.

A change on the skin is the most common sign of skin cancer. This may be a new growth, a sore that doesn't heal, or a change in an old growth. Not all skin cancers look the same. The following are some skin changes to watch for:

- Small, smooth, shiny, pale, or waxy lump

- Firm, red lump

- Sore or lump that bleeds or develops a crust or a scab

- Flat red spot that is rough, dry, or scaly and may become itchy or tender

---

♣ It's A Fact!!
Growths Or Tumors Can Be *Benign* Or *Malignant*

Benign growths are not cancer.

- Benign growths are rarely life-threatening.

- Generally, benign growths can be removed. They usually do not grow back.

- Cells from benign growths do not invade the tissues around them.

- Cells from benign growths do not spread to other parts of the body.

Malignant growths are cancer.

- Malignant growths are generally more serious than benign growths. They may be life-threatening. However, the two most common types of skin cancer cause only about one out of every thousand deaths from cancer.

- Malignant growths often can be removed. But sometimes they grow back.

- Cells from malignant growths can invade and damage nearby tissues and organs.

- Cells from some malignant growths can spread to other parts of the body. The spread of cancer is called metastasis.

- Red or brown patch that is rough and scaly

Sometimes skin cancer is painful, but usually it is not.

Checking your skin for new growths or other changes is a good idea. A guide for checking your skin is included in this chapter. Keep in mind that changes are not a sure sign of skin cancer. Still, you should report any changes to your health care provider right away. You may need to see a dermatologist, a doctor who has special training in the diagnosis and treatment of skin problems.

How To Do A Skin Self-Exam

Your doctor or nurse may suggest that you do a regular skin self-exam to check for skin cancer, including melanoma.

The best time to do this exam is after a shower or bath. You should check your skin in a room with plenty of light. You should use a full-length mirror and a hand-held mirror. It's best to begin by learning where your birthmarks, moles, and other marks are and their usual look and feel.

When you examine yourself, check for anything new, and look for the following types of changes:

- New mole (that looks different from your other moles)
- New red or darker color flaky patch that may be a little raised
- New flesh-colored firm bump
- Change in the size, shape, color, or feel of a mole
- Sore that does not heal

Check yourself from head to toe. Don't forget to check your back, scalp, genital area, and between your buttocks.

- Look at your face, neck, ears, and scalp. You may want to use a comb or a blow dryer to move your hair so that you can see better. You also may want to have a relative or friend check through your hair. It may be hard to check your scalp by yourself.
- Look at the front and back of your body in the mirror. Then, raise your arms and look at your left and right sides.

- Bend your elbows. Look carefully at your fingernails, palms, forearms (including the undersides), and upper arms.

- Examine the back, front, and sides of your legs. Also look around your genital area and between your buttocks.

- Sit and closely examine your feet, including your toenails, your soles, and the spaces between your toes.

By checking your skin regularly, you will learn what is normal for you. It may be helpful to record the dates of your skin exams and to write notes about the way your skin looks. If your doctor has taken photos of your skin, you can compare your skin to the photos to help check for changes. If you find anything unusual, see your doctor.

Diagnosis

If you have a change on the skin, the doctor must find out whether it is due to cancer or to some other cause. Your doctor removes all or part of the area that does not look normal. The sample goes to a lab. A pathologist checks the sample under a microscope. This is a biopsy. A biopsy is the only sure way to diagnose skin cancer.

You may have the biopsy in a doctor's office or as an outpatient in a clinic or hospital. Where it is done depends on the size and place of the abnormal area on your skin. You probably will have local anesthesia.

There are four common types of skin biopsies:

Punch Biopsy: The doctor uses a sharp, hollow tool to remove a circle of tissue from the abnormal area.

Incisional Biopsy: The doctor uses a scalpel to remove part of the growth.

Excisional Biopsy: The doctor uses a scalpel to remove the entire growth and some tissue around it.

Shave Biopsy: The doctor uses a thin, sharp blade to shave off the abnormal growth.

Chapter 30

How Is Nonmelanoma Skin Cancer Treated?

Treatment Option Overview

Different types of treatment are available for patients with nonmelanoma skin cancer and actinic keratosis. Some treatments are standard (the currently used treatment), and some are being tested in clinical trials. A treatment clinical trial is a research study meant to help improve current treatments or obtain information on new treatments for patients with cancer. When clinical trials show that a new treatment is better than the standard treatment, the new treatment may become the standard treatment. Patients may want to think about taking part in a clinical trial. Some clinical trials are open only to patients who have not started treatment. The four types of standard treatment are discussed next.

Surgery

One or more of the following surgical procedures may be used to treat nonmelanoma skin cancer or actinic keratosis:

- **Mohs Micrographic Surgery:** The tumor is cut from the skin in thin layers. During surgery, the edges of the tumor and each layer of tumor

About This Chapter: Information in this chapter is from "Skin Cancer Treatment (PDQ®): Patient Version." PDQ® Cancer Information Summary. National Cancer Institute; Bethesda, MD. Updated 10/17/2008. Available at: http://www.cancer.gov. Accessed February 2009.

removed are viewed through a microscope to check for cancer cells. Layers continue to be removed until no more cancer cells are seen. This type of surgery removes as little normal tissue as possible and is often used to remove skin cancer on the face.

- **Simple Excision:** The tumor is cut from the skin along with some of the normal skin around it.

- **Shave Excision:** The abnormal area is shaved off the surface of the skin with a small blade.

- **Electrodesiccation And Curettage:** The tumor is cut from the skin with a curette (a sharp, spoon-shaped tool). A needle-shaped electrode is then used to treat the area with an electric current that stops the bleeding and destroys cancer cells that remain around the edge of the wound. The process may be repeated one to three times during the surgery to remove all of the cancer.

- **Cryosurgery:** A treatment that uses an instrument to freeze and destroy abnormal tissue, such as carcinoma in situ. This type of treatment is also called cryotherapy.

- **Cryosurgery:** An instrument with a nozzle is used to spray liquid nitrogen or liquid carbon dioxide to freeze and destroy abnormal tissue.

- **Laser Surgery:** A surgical procedure that uses a laser beam (a narrow beam of intense light) as a knife to make bloodless cuts in tissue or to remove a surface lesion such as a tumor.

- **Dermabrasion:** Removal of the top layer of skin using a rotating wheel or small particles to rub away skin cells.

Radiation Therapy

Radiation therapy is a cancer treatment that uses high-energy x-rays or other types of radiation to kill cancer cells or keep them from growing. There are two types of radiation therapy. External radiation therapy uses a machine outside the body to send radiation toward the cancer. Internal radiation therapy uses a radioactive substance sealed in needles, seeds, wires, or catheters that are placed directly into or near the cancer. The way the radiation therapy is given depends on the type and stage of the cancer being treated.

Chemotherapy

Chemotherapy is a cancer treatment that uses drugs to stop the growth of cancer cells, either by killing the cells or by stopping them from dividing. When chemotherapy is taken by mouth or injected into a vein or muscle, the drugs enter the bloodstream and can reach cancer cells throughout the body (systemic chemotherapy). When chemotherapy is placed directly into the spinal column, an organ, or a body cavity such as the abdomen, the drugs mainly affect cancer cells in those areas (regional chemotherapy). Chemotherapy for nonmelanoma skin cancer and actinic keratosis is usually topical (applied to the skin in a cream or lotion). The way the chemotherapy is given depends on the condition being treated.

Retinoids (drugs related to vitamin A) are sometimes used to treat or prevent nonmelanoma skin cancer. The retinoids may be taken by mouth or applied to the skin. The use of retinoids is being studied in clinical trials for treatment of squamous cell carcinoma.

Photodynamic Therapy

Photodynamic therapy (PDT) is a cancer treatment that uses a drug and a certain type of laser light to kill cancer cells. A drug that is not active until it is exposed to light is injected into a vein. The drug collects more in cancer cells than in normal cells. For skin cancer, laser light is shined onto the skin and the drug becomes active and kills the cancer cells. Photodynamic therapy causes little damage to healthy tissue.

New Types Of Treatment Are Being Tested In Clinical Trials

This summary section describes treatments that are being studied in clinical trials. It may not mention every new treatment being studied. Information about clinical trials is available from the NCI web site.

Biologic Therapy: Biologic therapy is a treatment that uses the patient's immune system to fight cancer. Substances made by the body or made in a laboratory are used to boost, direct, or restore the body's natural defenses against cancer. This type of cancer treatment is also called biotherapy or immunotherapy.

Clinical Trials: For some patients, taking part in a clinical trial may be the best treatment choice. Clinical trials are part of the cancer research process. Clinical trials are done to find out if new cancer treatments are safe and effective or better than the standard treatment.

Many of today's standard treatments for cancer are based on earlier clinical trials. Patients who take part in a clinical trial may receive the standard treatment or be among the first to receive a new treatment.

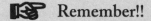 **Remember!!**

There are different types of treatment for patients with nonmelanoma skin cancer and actinic keratosis. Four types of standard treatment are used:

- Surgery
- Radiation therapy
- Chemotherapy
- Photodynamic therapy

Patients who take part in clinical trials also help improve the way cancer will be treated in the future. Even when clinical trials do not lead to effective new treatments, they often answer important questions and help move research forward.

Patients Can Enter Clinical Trials Before, During, Or After Starting Their Cancer Treatment: Some clinical trials only include patients who have not yet received treatment. Other trials test treatments for patients whose cancer has not gotten better. There are also clinical trials that test new ways to stop cancer from recurring (coming back) or reduce the side effects of cancer treatment. Clinical trials are taking place in many parts of the country.

Follow-Up Tests: Some of the tests that were done to diagnose the cancer or to find out the stage of the cancer may be repeated. Some tests will be repeated in order to see how well the treatment is working. Decisions about whether to continue, change, or stop treatment may be based on the results of these tests. This is sometimes called re-staging.

Some of the tests will continue to be done from time to time after treatment has ended. The results of these tests can show if your condition has changed or if the cancer has recurred (come back). These tests are sometimes called follow-up tests or check-ups.

Part Five

Other Diseases And Conditions That Affect The Skin And Scalp

Chapter 31

Cellulitis

Cellulitis is a spreading bacterial infection of the skin and the tissues immediately beneath the skin.

- Redness, pain, and tenderness are felt over an area of skin, and some people have a fever, chills, and other more serious symptoms.

- Antibiotics are needed to treat the infection.

Cellulitis may be caused by many different bacteria. The most common are those of the *Streptococcus* species. Streptococci spread rapidly in the skin because they produce enzymes that hinder the ability of the tissue to confine the infection. Staphylococcus bacteria can also cause cellulitis, as can many other bacteria, especially after bites by humans or animals or after injuries in water or dirt.

Bacteria usually enter through small breaks in the epidermis that result from scrapes, punctures, burns, and skin disorders. Areas of the skin that become swollen with fluid (edema) are especially vulnerable. Cellulitis is more common in people with poor blood circulation (chronic venous insufficiency). However, cellulitis can also occur in skin that is not obviously injured.

About This Chapter: Text in this chapter is from *The Merck Manual of Medical Information, Second Home Edition*, edited by Robert S. Porter. Copyright © 2007 by Merck & Co., Inc., Whitehouse Station, NJ. Available at: http://www.merck.com/mmhe. Accessed November 23, 2008.

Symptoms

Cellulitis most commonly develops on the legs but may occur anywhere. The first symptoms are redness, pain, and tenderness over an area of skin. These symptoms are caused both by the bacteria themselves and by the body's attempts to fight the infection. The infected skin becomes hot and swollen and may look slightly pitted, like an orange peel. Fluid-filled blisters, which may be small (vesicles) or large (bullae), sometimes appear on the infected skin. The borders of the affected area are not distinct, except in a form of cellulitis called *erysipelas*.

Most people with cellulitis feel only mildly ill, but some may have a fever, chills, rapid heart rate, headache, low blood pressure, and confusion.

As the infection spreads, nearby lymph nodes may become enlarged and tender (lymphadenitis), and the lymphatic vessels may become inflamed (lymphangitis). Sometimes, bacteria spread through the blood (bacteremia), which can cause more serious illness.

When cellulitis affects the same site repeatedly, especially the leg, lymphatic vessels may be damaged, causing permanent swelling of the affected tissue.

Diagnosis And Treatment

A doctor usually diagnoses cellulitis based on its appearance and symptoms. Laboratory identification of the bacteria from blood, pus, or tissue specimens usually is not necessary unless a person is seriously ill or the infection is not responding to drug therapy. Sometimes, doctors need to perform tests to differentiate cellulitis from a blood clot in the deep veins of the leg (deep vein thrombosis), because the symptoms of these disorders are similar.

Prompt treatment with antibiotics can prevent the infection from spreading rapidly and reaching the blood and internal organs. Antibiotics that are effective against both *streptococci* and *staphylococci* (such as dicloxacillin or cephalexin) are used. People with mild cellulitis may take antibiotics by mouth. Those with rapidly spreading cellulitis, high fever, or other evidence of serious infection often receive intravenous antibiotics (such as oxacillin or nafcillin). Also, the affected part of the body, when possible, is kept immobile and elevated to help reduce swelling. Cool, wet dressings applied to the infected area may relieve discomfort.

Symptoms of cellulitis usually disappear after a few days of antibiotic therapy. However, symptoms often get worse before they get better probably because, with the death of the bacteria, substances that cause tissue damage are released. When this occurs, the body continues to react even though the bacteria are dead. Antibiotics are continued for 10 days or longer even though the symptoms may disappear earlier.

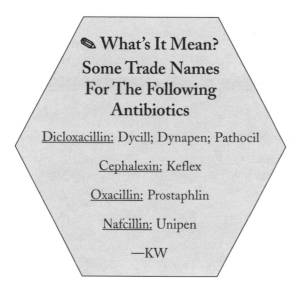

✎ What's It Mean?
Some Trade Names
For The Following
Antibiotics

Dicloxacillin: Dycill; Dynapen; Pathocil

Cephalexin: Keflex

Oxacillin: Prostaphlin

Nafcillin: Unipen

—KW

Chapter 32

Eczema

What's the difference between eczema and atopic dermatitis?

Eczema is a general term encompassing various inflamed skin conditions. One of the most common forms of eczema is atopic dermatitis (or "atopic eczema"). Approximately 10 to 20 percent of the world population is affected by this chronic, relapsing, and very itchy rash at some point during childhood. Fortunately, many children with eczema find that the disease clears and often disappears with age.

In general, atopic dermatitis will come and go, often based on external factors. Although its cause is unknown, the condition appears to be an abnormal response of the body's immune system. In people with eczema, the inflammatory response to irritating substances overacts, causing itching and scratching. Eczema is not contagious and, like many diseases, currently cannot be cured. However, for most patients the condition may be managed well with treatment and avoidance of triggers.

What does eczema look and feel like?

Although eczema may look different from person to person, it is most often characterized by dry, red, extremely itchy patches on the skin. Eczema is sometimes referred to as "the itch that rashes," since the itch, when scratched, results in the appearance of the rash.

About This Chapter: Text in this chapter is from "What Is Eczema?" reprinted with permission from the American Academy of Dermatology, © 2008. All rights reserved.

What makes patients with eczema itch?

Many substances have been identified as itch "triggers" in patients with eczema, and triggers are not the same for every person. Many times it is difficult to identify the exact trigger that causes a flare-up. For some, it seems that rough or coarse materials coming into contact with the skin causes itchiness. For others, feeling too hot and/or sweating will cause an outbreak. Other people find that certain soaps, detergents, disinfectants, contact with juices from fresh fruits and meats, dust mites, and animal saliva and dander may trigger itching. Upper respiratory infections (caused by viruses) may also be triggers. Stress can also sometimes aggravate an existing flare-up.

♣ It's A Fact!!

Eczema can occur on just about any part of the body; however, in infants, eczema typically occurs on the forehead, cheeks, forearms, legs, scalp, and neck. In children and adults, eczema typically occurs on the face, neck, and the insides of the elbows, knees, and ankles. In some people, eczema may "bubble up" and ooze. In others, the condition may appear more scaly, dry, and red. Chronic scratching causes the skin to take on a leathery texture because the skin thickens (lichenification).

Who gets eczema?

Eczema occurs in both children and adults, but usually appears during infancy. Although there is no known cause for the disease, it often affects people with a family history of allergies.

Those who are genetically predisposed and then exposed to environmental triggers may develop eczema. Many people who have eczema also suffer from allergic rhinitis and asthma, or have family members who do.

How common is eczema?

The National Institutes of Health estimates that 15 million people in the United States have some form of eczema. About 10 to 20 percent of all infants have eczema; however, in nearly half of these children, the disease will improve greatly by the time they are between five and 15 years of age. Others will have some form of the disease throughout their lives.

How can eczema be treated?

One of the most important components of an eczema treatment routine is to prevent scratching. Because eczema is usually dry and itchy, the most common treatment is the application of lotions or creams to keep the skin as moist as possible. These treatments are generally most effective when applied directly after bathing (within three minutes is a common recommendation) so that the moisture from the bath is "locked in." Cold compresses applied directly to itchy skin can also help relieve itching. If the condition persists, worsens, or does not improve satisfactorily, another effective treatment is the application of nonprescription corticosteroid creams and ointments to reduce inflammation.

Alternatives to nonprescription corticosteroids include more potent prescription corticosteroid creams and ointments, which are effective, but which may have some side effects. To prevent side effects such as skin thinning, your doctor may limit the length of treatment time and locations where you can apply treatment. For severe flare-ups, your doctor may prescribe oral corticosteroids, but be aware that side effects including new flare-ups can develop when treatment is discontinued (this treatment is not recommended for long-term use).

Skin affected by eczema may frequently become infected. If this happens to you, your doctor may prescribe topical or oral antibiotics to kill the bacteria causing the infection.

✔ **Quick Tip**

How can eczema be prevented?

Eczema outbreaks can usually be avoided with some simple precautions. The following suggestions may help to reduce the severity and frequency of flare-ups:

- Moisturize frequently
- Avoid sudden changes in temperature or humidity
- Avoid sweating or overheating
- Reduce stress
- Avoid scratchy materials (e.g., wool or other irritants)
- Avoid harsh soaps, detergents, and solvents
- Avoid environmental factors that trigger allergies (e.g., pollens, molds, mites, and animal dander)
- Be aware of any foods that may cause an outbreak and avoid those foods

For severe itching, sedative antihistamines are sometimes used to reduce the itch and are available in both prescription and over-the-counter varieties. Because drowsiness is a common side effect, antihistamines are often used in the evening to help a person restless from eczema get to sleep. Because of the same sedative effect, though, persons taking these agents should not drive. Tar treatments and phototherapy are also used and can have positive effects; however, tar can be messy. Phototherapy requires special equipment (lights). Finally, in cases where eczema is resistant to therapy, your physician may prescribe the drug cyclosporine A, which modifies immune response; however, this is used only in extreme cases because of its association with serious side effects.

Two topical medications, tacrolimus and pimecrolimus, have been approved by the U.S. Food and Drug Administration (FDA) to treat atopic dermatitis. These medications belong to a class of drugs called calcineurin inhibitors and work by modulating the immune response. Pimecrolimus and tacrolimus are a much-welcomed addition because they have not produced some of the side effects associated with long-term topical corticosteroid use, such as thinning skin and loss of effectiveness.

What can be done for children with eczema?

Children are unique patients because it may be difficult for them to resist scratching their eczema, thereby making the condition worse. Fortunately, for mild to moderate cases, the application of moisturizer on a regular basis can be very helpful. And, in most cases, the eczema will disappear as the child ages. In the meantime, avoid as many eczema triggers as possible. Keep the child's skin moist. After bathing, apply moisturizer within three minutes to retain the moisture in the skin. Avoid sudden temperature changes. Keep the child's bedroom and play areas free of dust mites (a common trigger). Use mild soaps—both on the child's skin and clothing. Dress the child in breathable, preferably cotton, clothing.

If these methods fail to help the child, you should seek further advice from a dermatologist. After consultation, an over-the-counter cream, a prescription cream, ointment, antihistamines, or antibiotics may be advised. Regardless, most children will see improvement as time goes by.

Chapter 33

Fever Blisters And Canker Sores

Fever blisters and canker sores are two of the most common disorders of the mouth, causing discomfort and annoyance to millions of Americans. Both cause small sores to develop in or around the mouth, and often are confused with each other. Canker sores, however, occur only inside the mouth—on the tongue and the inside linings of the cheeks, lips and throat. Fever blisters, also called cold sores, usually occur outside the mouth—on the lips, chin, cheeks or in the nostrils. When fever blisters do occur inside the mouth, it is usually on the gums or the roof of the mouth. Inside the mouth, fever blisters are smaller than canker sores, heal more quickly, and often begin as a blister.

Both canker sores and fever blisters have plagued mankind for thousands of years. Scientists at the National Institute of Dental and Craniofacial Research, one of the federal government's National Institutes of Health, are seeking ways to better control and ultimately prevent these and other oral disorders.

Fever Blisters

In ancient Rome, an epidemic of fever blisters prompted Emperor Tiberius to ban kissing in public ceremonies. Today fever blisters still occur in epidemic proportions. About 100 million episodes of recurrent fever blisters

About This Chapter: From "Fever Blisters and Canker Sores," © 1992 National Institute of Dental and Craniofacial Research. Updated by David A. Cooke, MD, FACP, February 2009.

occur yearly in the United States alone. An estimated 45 to 80 percent of adults and children in this country have had at least one bout with the blisters.

What causes fever blisters?

Fever blisters are caused by a contagious virus called herpes simplex. There are two types of herpes simplex virus. Type 1 usually causes oral herpes, or fever blisters. Type 2 usually causes genital herpes. Although both type 1 and type 2 viruses can infect oral tissues, more than 95 percent of recurrent fever blister outbreaks are caused by the type 1 virus.

♣ **It's A Fact!!**
Fever blisters and canker sores are often confused with each other. Fever blisters, also known as *cold sores*, usually occur outside the mouth—on the lips, chin, cheeks or in the nostrils. Canker sores occur *only* inside the mouth—on the tongue and the inside linings of the cheeks, lips, and throat. Fever blisters are highly contagious, canker sores are not.

Herpes simplex virus is highly contagious when fever blisters are present, and the virus frequently is spread by kissing. Children often become infected by contact with parents, siblings or other close relatives who have fever blisters.

A child can spread the virus by rubbing his or her cold sore and then touching other children. About 10 percent of oral herpes infections in adults result from oral-genital sex with a person who has active genital herpes (type 2). These infections, however, usually do not result in repeat bouts of fever blisters.

Most people infected with the type 1 herpes simplex virus became infected before they were 10 years old. The virus usually invades the moist membrane cells of the lips, throat or mouth. In most people, the initial infection causes no symptoms. About 15 percent of patients, however, develop many fluid-filled blisters inside and outside the mouth three to five days after they are infected with the virus. These may be accompanied by fever, swollen neck glands and general aches. The blisters tend to merge and then collapse. Often a yellowish crust forms over the sores, which usually heal without scarring within two weeks.

The herpes virus, however, stays in the body. Once a person is infected with oral herpes, the virus remains in a nerve located near the cheekbone. It may stay permanently inactive in this site, or it may occasionally travel down the nerve to the skin surface, causing a recurrence of fever blisters. Recurring blisters usually erupt at the outside edge of the lip or the edge of the nostril, but can also occur on the chin, cheeks, or inside the mouth.

The symptoms of recurrent fever blister attacks usually are less severe than those experienced by some people after an initial infection. Recurrences appear to be less frequent after age 35. Many people who have recurring fever blisters feel itching, tingling or burning in the lip one to three days before the blister appears.

What causes a recurrence of fever blisters?

Several factors weaken the body's defenses and trigger an outbreak of herpes. These include emotional stress, fever, illness, injury, and exposure to sunlight. Many women have recurrences only during menstruation. One study indicates that susceptibility to herpes recurrences is inherited. Research is under way to discover exactly how the triggering factors interact with the immune system and the virus to prompt a recurrence of fever blisters.

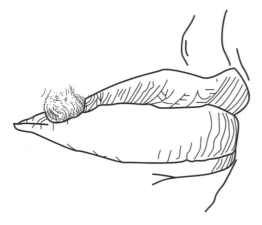

Figure 33.1. Fever blister.

What are the treatments for fever blisters?

Several antiviral medications are available for treatment of fever blisters. They include several oral drugs, such as acyclovir (Zovirax™), valacyclovir (Valtrex™), and famciclovir (Famvir™). There are also several antiviral drugs available in cream or ointment form, including penciclovir (Denavir™) and acyclovir (Zovirax™). Docosanol is sold as an over-the-counter medication called Abreva™. These drugs can shorten a herpes outbreak somewhat, but only if they are started soon after the symptoms develop. Additionally, there are a number of over-the-counter medications that can relieve some of the pain and discomfort associated with the sores. These include ointments that numb the blisters and ointments that soften the crusts of the sores.

Is there a vaccine for fever blisters?

Currently there is no vaccine for herpes simplex virus available to the public. Many research laboratories, however, are working on this approach to preventing fever blisters. For example, scientists at the National Institute of Dental and Craniofacial Research and the National Institute of Allergy and Infectious Diseases have developed a promising experimental herpes vaccine. In tests on laboratory mice, the vaccine has prevented the herpes simplex virus from infecting the animals and establishing itself in the nerves.

Although these findings are encouraging, the scientists must complete more animal studies on the safety and effectiveness of the vaccine before a decision can be made whether to test it in humans. The vaccine would be useful only for those not already infected with herpes simplex virus.

What can the patient do?

If fever blisters erupt, keep them clean and dry to prevent bacterial infections. Eat a soft, bland diet to avoid irritating the sores and surrounding sensitive areas. Be careful not to touch the sores and spread the virus to new sites, such as the eyes or genitals. To make sure you do not infect others, avoid kissing them or touching the sores and then touching another person.

Little is known about how to prevent recurrences of fever blisters triggered by factors other than sunlight. People whose cold sores appear in response to stress should try to avoid stressful situations. Some investigators have suggested adding lysine to the diet or eliminating foods such as nuts, chocolate, seeds or gelatin. These measures have not, however, been proven effective in controlled studies.

The oral drugs acyclovir (Zovirax™), valacyclovir (Valtrex™), and famciclovir (Famvir™) are approved by the Food and Drug Administration for prevention of recurrent genital herpes infections. While they are not approved for prevention of oral herpes recurrences, there is data that suggests that they are also effective for this purpose.

✔ Quick Tip

There is good news for people whose fever blister outbreaks are triggered by sunlight. Scientists at the National Institute of Dental and Craniofacial Research have confirmed that sunscreen on the lips can prevent sun-induced recurrences of herpes. They recommend applying the sunscreen before going outside and reapplying it frequently during sun exposure. The researchers used a sunblock with a protection factor of 15 in their studies.

What research is being done?

Researchers are working on several approaches to preventing or treating fever blisters. As mentioned earlier, they are trying to develop a vaccine against herpes simplex virus. Researchers are also trying to develop ointments that make it easier for antiviral drugs to penetrate the skin.

Basic research on how the immune system interacts with herpes simplex viruses may lead to new therapies for fever blisters. The immune system uses a wide array of cells and chemicals to defend the body against infections. Scientists are trying to identify the immune components that prevent recurrent attacks of oral herpes.

Scientists are also trying to determine the precise form and location of the inactive herpes virus in nerve cells. This information might allow them to design antiviral drugs that can attack the herpes virus while it lies dormant in nerves.

In addition, researchers are trying to understand how sunlight, skin injury and stress can trigger recurrences of fever blisters. They hope to develop methods for blocking reactivation of the virus.

Canker Sores

Recurrent canker sores afflict about 20 percent of the general population. The medical term for the sores is aphthous stomatitis.

Canker sores are usually found on the movable parts of the mouth such as the tongue or the inside linings of the lips and cheeks. They begin as small oval or round reddish swellings, which usually burst within a day. The ruptured sores are covered by a thin white or yellow membrane and edged by a red halo. Generally, they heal within two weeks. Canker sores range in size from an eighth of an inch wide in mild cases to more than an inch wide in severe cases. Severe canker sores may leave scars. Fever is rare, and the sores are rarely associated with other diseases. Usually a person will have only one or a few canker sores at a time.

Most people have their first bout with canker sores between the ages of 10 and 20. Children as young as two, however, may develop the condition. The frequency of canker sore recurrences varies

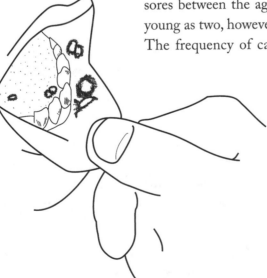

Figure 33.2. Canker sores.

considerably. Some people have only one or two episodes a year, while others may have a continuous series of canker sores.

What causes canker sores?

The cause of canker sores is not well understood. More than one cause is likely, even for individual patients. Canker sores do not appear to be caused by viruses or bacteria, although an allergy to a type of bacterium commonly found in the mouth may trigger them in some people. The sores may be an allergic reaction to certain foods. In addition, there is research suggesting that canker sores may be caused by a faulty immune system that uses the body's defenses against disease to attack and destroy the normal cells of the mouth or tongue.

It has been reported in some British studies that, in about 20 percent of patients, canker sores are due partly to nutritional deficiencies, especially lack of vitamin B12, folic acid, and iron. Similar studies performed in the United States, however, have not confirmed this finding. Currently, most experts do not believe nutritional deficiencies to be a cause of canker sores.

In a small percentage of patients, canker sores occur with gastrointestinal problems, such as an inability to digest certain cereals. In these patients, canker sores appear to be part of a generalized disorder of the digestive tract.

Female sex hormones apparently play a role in causing canker sores. Many women have bouts of the sores only during certain phases of their menstrual cycles. Most women experience improvement or remission of their canker sores during pregnancy. Researchers have used hormone therapy successfully in clinical studies to treat some women.

Both emotional stress and injury to the mouth can trigger outbreaks of canker sores, but these factors probably do not cause the disorder.

Who is susceptible?

Women are more likely than men to have recurrent canker sores. Genetic studies show that susceptibility to recurrent outbreaks of the sores is inherited in some patients. This partially explains why the disorder is often shared by family members.

What are the treatments for canker sores?

Most doctors recommend that patients who have frequent bouts of canker sores undergo blood and allergy tests to determine if their sores are caused by a nutritional deficiency, an allergy, or some other preventable cause. Vitamins and other nutritional supplements often prevent recurrences or reduce the severity of canker sores in patients with a nutritional deficiency. Patients with food allergies can reduce the frequency of canker sores by avoiding those foods.

✔ Quick Tip
What can the canker sore patient do?

If you have canker sores, avoid abrasive foods such as potato chips that can stick in the cheek or gum and aggravate the sores. Take care when brushing your teeth not to stab the gums or cheek with a toothbrush bristle. Avoid acidic and spicy foods. Canker sores are not contagious, so patients do not have a worry about spreading them to other people.

There are several treatments for reducing the pain and duration of canker sores for patients whose outbreaks cannot be prevented. These include numbing ointments such as benzocaine, which are available in drug stores without a prescription. Anti-inflammatory steroid mouth rinses or gels can be prescribed for patients with severe sores.

A topical prescription medication called Amlexanox (Aphthasol™) is approved for the treatment of cold sores. It has antiallergy properties, which are thought to aid in healing. It does appear to reduce pain and healing time, but it is unclear how it compares to other therapies for canker sores.

Mouth rinses containing the antibiotic tetracycline may reduce the unpleasant symptoms of canker sores and speed healing by preventing bacterial infections in the sores. Clinical studies at the National Institute of Dental and Craniofacial Research have shown that rinsing the mouth with tetracycline several times a day usually relieves pain in 24 hours and allows complete healing in five to seven days. The U.S. Food and Drug Administration warns, however, that tetracycline given to pregnant women and young children can permanently stain youngsters' teeth. Both steroid and tetracycline treatments require a prescription and care of a dentist or physician.

Patients with severe recurrent canker sores may need to take steroid or other immunosuppressant drugs orally. These potent drugs can cause many undesirable side effects, and should be used only under the close supervision of a dentist or physician.

What research is being done?

Researchers are trying to identify the malfunctions in patients' immune systems that make them susceptible to recurrent bouts of canker sores. By analyzing the blood of people with and without canker sores, scientists have found several differences in immune function between the two groups. Whether these differences cause canker sores is not yet known.

Researchers also are developing and testing new drugs designed to treat canker sores. Most of these drugs alter the patients' immune function. Although some of the drugs appear to be effective in treating canker sores in some patients, the data are still inconclusive. Until these drugs are proven to be absolutely safe and effective, they will not be available for general use.

Chapter 34

Genetic Conditions That Affect The Skin

Androgenetic Alopecia

Androgenetic alopecia is a common form of hair loss in both men and women. In men, this condition is also known as male pattern baldness. Hair is lost in a well-defined pattern, beginning above both temples. Over time, the hairline recedes to form a characteristic "M" shape. Hair also thins at the crown (near the top of the head), often progressing to partial or complete baldness.

Androgenetic alopecia in men has been associated with several other medical conditions including coronary heart disease and enlargement of the prostate, a walnut-sized gland in males that is located below the bladder. Additionally, prostate cancer, disorders of insulin resistance (such as diabetes and obesity), and high blood pressure (hypertension) have been related to androgenetic alopecia. In women, androgenetic alopecia is associated with an increased risk of polycystic ovary syndrome (PCOS). PCOS is characterized by a hormonal imbalance that can lead to irregular menstruation, acne, excess body hair (hirsutism), and weight gain.

About This Chapter: This chapter includes excerpts from "Androgenetic Alopecia," May 2006; "Harlequin Ichthyosis," November 2008; "Oculocutaneous Albinism," March 2007; and "Tuberous Sclerosis," November 2005; from *Genetics Home Reference*, a service of the U.S. National Library of Medicine.

How common is androgenetic alopecia?

Although androgenetic alopecia is a frequent cause of hair loss in both men and women, it is more common in men. This form of hair loss affects an estimated 35 million men in the United States. Androgenetic alopecia can start as early as a person's teens and risk increases with age; more than 50 percent of men over age 50 have some degree of hair loss. In women, hair loss is most likely after menopause.

❧ It's A Fact!!

The pattern of hair loss in women differs from male pattern baldness. In women, the hair becomes thinner all over the head, and the hairline does not recede. Androgenetic alopecia in women rarely leads to total baldness.

Source: *Genetics Home Reference*, a service of the U.S. National Library of Medicine, May 2006.

What genes are related to androgenetic alopecia?

The AR gene is associated with androgenetic alopecia.

A variety of genetic and environmental factors likely play a role in causing androgenetic alopecia. Although researchers are studying risk factors that may contribute to this condition, most of these factors remain unknown. Researchers have determined that this form of hair loss is related to hormones called androgens, particularly an androgen called dihydrotestosterone. Androgens are important for normal male sexual development before birth and during puberty. Androgens also have other important functions in both males and females, such as regulating hair growth and sex drive.

Hair growth begins under the skin in structures called follicles. Each strand of hair normally grows for two to six years, goes into a resting phase for several months, and then falls out. The cycle starts over when the follicle begins growing a new hair. Increased levels of androgens in hair follicles can lead to a shorter cycle of hair growth and the growth of shorter and thinner strands of hair. Additionally, there is a delay in the growth of new hair to replace strands that are shed.

Although researchers suspect that several genes play a role in androgenetic alopecia, variations in only one gene, AR, have been identified in people with this condition. The AR gene provides instructions for making a protein called an androgen receptor. Androgen receptors allow the body to respond appropriately to dihydrotestosterone and other androgens. Studies suggest that variations in the AR gene lead to increased activity of androgen receptors in hair follicles. It remains unclear, however, how these genetic changes increase the risk of patterned hair loss in men and women with androgenetic alopecia.

Researchers continue to investigate the connection between androgenetic alopecia and other medical conditions, such as coronary heart disease and prostate cancer in men and polycystic ovary syndrome in women. They believe that some of these disorders may be associated with elevated androgen levels, which may help explain why they tend to occur with androgen-related hair loss. Other hormonal, environmental, and genetic factors that have not been identified also may be involved.

How do people inherit androgenetic alopecia?

The inheritance pattern of androgenetic alopecia is unclear because many genetic and environmental factors are likely to be involved. This condition tends to cluster in families, however, and having a close relative with patterned hair loss appears to be a risk factor for developing the condition.

Harlequin Ichthyosis

Harlequin ichthyosis is a severe genetic disorder that mainly affects the skin. Infants with this condition are born with very hard, thick skin covering most of their bodies. The skin forms large, diamond-shaped plates that are separated by deep cracks (fissures). These skin abnormalities affect the shape of the eyelids, nose, mouth, and ears, and limit movement of the arms and legs. Restricted movement of the chest can lead to breathing difficulties and respiratory failure.

The skin normally forms a protective barrier between the body and its surrounding environment. The skin abnormalities associated with harlequin ichthyosis disrupt this barrier, making it more difficult for affected infants to control water loss, regulate their body temperature, and fight infections. Infants with harlequin ichthyosis often experience an excessive loss of fluids (dehydration) and develop life-threatening infections in the first few weeks of life. It used to be very rare for affected infants to survive the newborn period. However, with intensive medical support and improved treatment, people with this disorder now have a better chance of living into childhood and adolescence.

How do people inherit harlequin ichthyosis?

This condition is inherited in an autosomal recessive pattern, which means both copies of the gene in each cell have mutations. The parents of an individual with an autosomal recessive condition each carry one copy of the mutated gene, but they typically do not show signs and symptoms of the condition.

❖ **It's A Fact!!**
How common is harlequin ichthyosis?

Harlequin ichthyosis is very rare; its exact incidence is unknown.

Source: *Genetics Home Reference*, a service of the U.S. National Library of Medicine, November 2008.

Oculocutaneous Albinism

Oculocutaneous albinism is a group of conditions that affect coloring (pigmentation) of the skin, hair, and eyes. Affected individuals typically have very fair skin and white or light-colored hair. Long-term sun exposure greatly increases the risk of skin damage and skin cancers, including an aggressive form of skin cancer called melanoma, in people with this condition. Oculocutaneous albinism also reduces pigmentation of the colored part of the eye (the iris) and the light-sensitive tissue at the back of the eye (the retina). People with this condition usually have vision problems such as reduced sharpness; rapid, involuntary eye movements (nystagmus); and increased sensitivity to light (photophobia).

The four types of oculocutaneous albinism are designated as type 1 (OCA1) through type 4 (OCA4):

- Oculocutaneous albinism type 1 is characterized by white hair, very pale skin, and light-colored irises.

- Type 2 is typically less severe than type 1—the skin is usually a creamy white color and hair may be light yellow, blond, or light brown.

- Type 3 includes a form of albinism called rufous oculocutaneous albinism, which usually affects dark-skinned people. Affected individuals have reddish-brown skin, ginger or red hair, and hazel or brown irises. Type 3 is often associated with milder vision abnormalities than the other forms of oculocutaneous albinism.

- Type 4 has signs and symptoms similar to those seen with type 2.

Because their features overlap, the four types of oculocutaneous albinism are most accurately distinguished by their genetic cause.

How common is oculocutaneous albinism?

Overall, an estimated one in 20,000 people worldwide are born with oculocutaneous albinism. The condition affects people in many ethnic groups and geographical regions. Types 1 and 2 are the most common forms of this condition; types 3 and 4 are less common. Type 2 occurs more frequently in African Americans, some Native American groups, and people from sub-Saharan Africa. Type 3, specifically rufous oculocutaneous albinism, has been described primarily in people from southern Africa. Studies suggest that type 4 occurs more frequently in the Japanese and Korean populations than in people from other parts of the world.

How do people inherit oculocutaneous albinism?

Each of the four types of oculocutaneous albinism is inherited in an autosomal recessive pattern, which means both copies of the gene in each cell have mutations. Most often, the parents of an individual with an autosomal recessive condition each carry one copy of the mutated gene, but do not show signs and symptoms of the condition.

Tuberous Sclerosis

Tuberous sclerosis is a genetic disorder characterized by the growth of numerous noncancerous tumors in many parts of the body. These tumors can occur in the skin, brain, kidneys, and other organs, in some cases leading to significant medical problems.

The signs and symptoms of tuberous sclerosis vary according to the location of tumor growth. Virtually all affected people have skin abnormalities, including patches of unusually light-colored skin, areas of raised and thick-

ened skin, and growths under the nails. Tumors on the face (facial angio-fibromas) are also common, beginning in childhood. Many people with tuberous sclerosis have noncancerous brain tumors. Neurologic symptoms can include seizures, behavioral problems such as hyperactivity and aggression, and intellectual disability or learning problems. Some affected children have the characteristic features of autism, a developmental disorder that affects communication and social interaction. Kidney tumors are also common in people with tuberous sclerosis; these growths can cause serious problems with kidney function and may be life-threatening in some cases. Additionally, tumors can develop in the heart, lungs, and the light-sensitive tissue at the back of the eye (the retina).

How do people inherit tuberous sclerosis?

Tuberous sclerosis is inherited in an autosomal dominant pattern, which means one copy of the altered gene in each cell is sufficient to cause the disorder. About two thirds of cases result from new mutations in the TSC1 or TSC2 gene. These cases occur in people with no history of tuberous sclerosis in their family. In the remaining cases, an affected person inherits an altered TSC1 or TSC2 gene from a parent who has the disorder. TSC1 mutations appear to be more common in familial cases of tuberous sclerosis, while mutations in the TSC2 gene tend to occur more frequently in affected individuals with no family history of the disorder.

♣ It's A Fact!!
How common is tuberous sclerosis?
Tuberous sclerosis affects about one in 6,000 people.

Source: *Genetics Home Reference*, a service of the U.S. National Library of Medicine, November 2005.

Chapter 35

Hives

After eating some big, red strawberries, you decide to walk to your friend's house. Just as you're turning the corner, you notice reddish bumps and patches on your arms and chest. What are these itchy welts or blotches on your skin? Should you turn around and head home?

What Are Hives?

Hives are pink or red bumps or slightly raised patches of skin. Sometimes, they have a pale center. Hives usually itch, but they also can burn or sting.

Hives can occur anywhere on the body and vary in size and shape. They can be small like a mosquito bite or big like a dinner plate. Hives also might look like rings or groups of rings joined together. Hives can appear in clusters and might change locations in a matter of hours. A bunch of hives might be on a person's face, then those might go away. Later some more may appear on a person's arms.

The medical term for hives is urticaria (say: ur-tuh-kar-ee-uh). When a person is exposed to something that can trigger hives, certain cells in the

About This Chapter: Text in this chapter is from "Help with Hives," October 2007, reprinted with permission from www.kidshealth.org. Copyright © 2007 The Nemours Foundation. This information was provided by KidsHealth, one of the largest resources online for medically reviewed health information written for parents, kids, and teens. For more articles like this one, visit www.KidsHealth.org, or www.TeensHealth.org.

body release histamine (say: his-tuh-meen) and other substances. This causes fluid to leak from the small blood vessels under the skin. When this fluid collects under the skin, it forms the blotches, which we call hives.

Why Do I Get Hives?

People can get hives for lots of different reasons. Often, the cause is not known. One common reason for getting hives is an allergic reaction. Some common allergic triggers are certain foods (like milk, shellfish, berries, and nuts), medications (such as antibiotics), and insect stings or bites. Other causes of hives are not related to allergies and these can include:

- exposure to the cold (like diving into a cold pool);

- exercise;

- sun exposure;

- nervousness or stress;

- infections caused by viruses.

No matter what the cause, a case of hives can last for a few minutes, a few hours, or even days.

What Will The Doctor Do?

Doctors usually can diagnose hives just by looking at you and hearing your story about what happened. The doctor can try to help figure out what might be causing your hives, although often the cause will remain a mystery. If you're getting hives a lot, or your reaction was serious, your doctor might send you to another doctor who specializes in allergies.

♣ **It's A Fact!!**
Hives are common—between 10 and 25 percent of people get them at least once in their lives. They are usually harmless, though they may occasionally be a sign of a serious allergic reaction. (So, yes, you should go home and tell your mom or dad.)

Sometimes, doctors will suggest you take a type of medication called an antihistamine to relieve the itchiness. In many cases, hives clear up on their own without any medication or doctor visits.

Less often, hives can be a sign of a more serious allergic reaction that can affect breathing and other body functions. In these cases, the person needs immediate medical care. Some people who know they have serious allergies carry a special medicine to use in an emergency. This medicine, called epinephrine, is given by a shot. Ordinarily, a nurse gives you a shot, but because some allergic reactions can happen really fast, many adults and kids carry this emergency shot with them and know how to use it, just in case they ever need it in a hurry.

Can I Prevent Hives?

Yes and no. The answer is "yes" if you know what causes your hives—the strawberries at the start of this chapter, for example. If you know they cause you trouble, you can just avoid them. If you get hives when you're nervous, relaxation breathing exercises may help. But if you don't know why you get hives, it's tough to prevent them.

Some kids get hives when they have a virus, such as a bad cold or a stomach flu. Other than washing your hands regularly, there's not much you can do to avoid getting sick occasionally. The good news is that hives usually aren't serious and you might even grow out of them. Who wouldn't want to give hives the heave-ho?

Chapter 36

Hyperhidrosis (Excessive Sweating)

Sweat Facts

Hy•per•hi•dro•sis: n. Extreme sweating.

- Four or five times the amount of sweat that's normal—or needed—to keep the body cool.

- Sweating that's so excessive that it's embarrassing, depressing, and prevents you from living life.

Messages from your brain tell your body "It's getting hot in here! Cool me off with sweat!" But if you have hyperhidrosis, you keep on sweating no matter what.

Think you're alone? You're not. At least 176 million people have hyperhidrosis. (that's a lot of sweat.)

♣ **It's A Fact!!**

Your body has four million sweat glands.

Most of your sweat glands are on your hands, feet, face, and (of course) in your armpits.

About This Chapter: Text in this chapter is from "Sweat Facts" and "Treatments," © 2008 International Hyperhidrosis Society (www.sweathelp.org). Reprinted with permission.

Treatments

Whether You Sweat A Little Or A Lot, There's Stuff You Can Do To Dry Up

Antiperspirants: These gems are for practically everybody. You can buy antiperspirants at the drug store or a dermatologist can give you a prescription for stronger ones. Antiperspirants work by plugging your sweat ducts so that the sweat doesn't reach the surface of your skin. The "plugging" is safe and too small to see. Most people use them for their armpits, but antiperspirants also work on hands, feet, other body parts, and even your face (talk to a doctor before you start spreading that stick on your head, though, because your face could get irritated and red). Antiperspirants work best if you apply them every day, both in the morning *and* in the evening before bed, and make sure your skin is dry first. When buying an antiperspirant, be sure to read the label so you know you're getting an antiperspirant and not just a deodorant. Deodorants cover body odor—they don't stop sweat.

Iontophoresis: Electricity turns on your lights but it can also turn off your sweat. Iontophoresis is for people who have extremely sweaty hands or feet (or both). A doctor can prescribe a special iontophoresis machine for you. During iontophoresis, you sit with hands or feet, or both, immersed in shallow trays filled with water for about a half-hour while the small machine

♣ **It's A Fact!!**

Scientists think hyperhidrosis can be passed on from parents to kids through genetics.

Hyperhidrosis often starts in junior high—as if junior high wasn't hard enough.

Oh, and by the way, body odor isn't really caused by sweat. It's caused by bacteria on your skin mixing with sweat.

sends a mild electrical current through the water. Don't worry, the electric current is safe. No one totally understands how or why iontophoresis works, but scientists believe the electric current and particles in the water work together to invisibly thicken the outer layer of the skin, which blocks the flow of sweat to the surface. The process is repeated every other day for five or ten days or until sweating is reduced to a comfortable level. Once dry, most people only have to continue doing iontophoresis once a week or even just once every four weeks.

Botox: Botox is the newest way to stop excessive sweating. You've heard of the rich-and-famous getting Botox injected into their wrinkles, right? Well Botox also has amazing medical uses. Neurologists use Botox to help people with disabling muscle problems, and dermatologists use Botox to stop hyperhidrosis. It can be injected into the armpits, hands, feet, and face to help stop uncomfortable, embarrassing, and dripping sweat. Botox is a natural, purified protein that can temporarily block the secretion of the chemical in your body that is responsible for "turning on" your sweat glands. By blocking this chemical messenger, Botox "turns off" sweating at the area where it has been injected. Follow-up injections are required every seven to sixteen months to maintain dryness. The injections can be a little uncomfortable but teens who've had it done say it's not that bad and totally worth it.

Here's The Skinny

Antiperspirants, iontophoresis, and Botox are the most useful and safe ways to treat hyperhidrosis (and of course, antiperspirants are great for "regular" sweating, too). You may hear some people talking about getting surgery to stop excessive sweating. We think that's pretty extreme and because the side effects can be awfully bad, most doctors don't recommend surgery, particularly for young people. Oral medications that a doctor can give you may work for a short time but they have side effects too, so they're not a good choice for long-term use.

Chapter 37

Impetigo

What is impetigo?

Impetigo is an infection of the skin caused primarily by the bacterium *Streptococcus pyogenes*, also known as group A beta-hemolytic streptococci (GABS). Sometimes another bacterium, *Staphylococcus aureus*, can also be isolated from impetigo lesions.

What are the symptoms of impetigo?

Impetigo begins as a cluster of small blisters that expand and rupture within the first 24 hours. The thin yellow fluid that drains from the ruptured blisters quickly dries, forming a honey-colored crust. Impetigo develops most frequently on the legs, but may also be found on the arms, face, and trunk. There is usually no fever.

> ♣ It's A Fact!!
> *How long does it take to develop impetigo following exposure?*
>
> Impetigo may develop up to 10 days after the skin becomes infected with group A beta-hemolytic streptococci (GABS).

How does a person get impetigo?

Impetigo may develop after the skin is infected with GABS. The bacterium is usually acquired from skin-to-skin contact with

About This Chapter: Text in this chapter is from "Impetigo," reprinted from Wisconsin Department of Health and Family Services, www.dhs.wisconsin.gov, © March 20, 2008.

another person with impetigo. Less commonly, impetigo may develop when open skin lesions (such as insect bites or burns) are infected following exposure to a person with *streptococcal pharyngitis* ("strep throat").

Who gets impetigo?

The infection is most common in settings where there is crowding or activities leading to close person-to-person contact such as in schools and military installations. Impetigo occurs more commonly during the summer and early fall.

How is impetigo treated?

Impetigo may be treated with an antibiotic taken by mouth or by application of an antibiotic ointment to the affected areas.

How long is a person considered infectious?

A person with impetigo is probably no longer infectious after 24 hours of adequate antibiotic treatment. Without treatment, a person may be infectious for several weeks.

> ✔ **Quick Tip**
> **What can be done to prevent impetigo?**
> Simple cleanliness and prompt attention to minor wounds will do much to prevent impetigo. Persons with impetigo or symptoms of group A beta-hemolytic streptococci (GABS) infections should seek medical care and if necessary begin antibiotic treatment as soon as possible to prevent spread to others. Individuals with impetigo should be excluded from school, day care, or other situations where close person-to-person contact is likely to occur until at least 24 hours after beginning appropriate antibiotic therapy. Sharing of towels, clothing, and other personal articles should be discouraged.

What are the complications of impetigo?

Rarely, GABS may invade beyond the skin of a person with impetigo and cause more serious illnesses. Persons with impetigo may also develop post-streptococcal scarlet fever, or glomerulonephritis, a condition that may result in temporary kidney failure. Post-streptococcal glomerulonephritis follows roughly 10 days after the onset of streptococcal infection. However, the long-term prognosis is excellent. Scarlet fever is caused by a toxin produced by certain strains of GABS and is characterized by high fever, chills, sore throat, headache, vomiting, and a fine red rash.

Chapter 38

Lichen Sclerosus

What is lichen sclerosus?

Lichen sclerosus (LIKE-in skler-O-sus) is a chronic inflammatory skin disorder that can affect men, women, or children, but is most common in women. It usually affects the vulva (the outer genitalia or sex organ) and the anal area. While lichen sclerosus appears predominantly in postmenopausal women, this skin condition is also known to develop on the head of the penis in men. Occasionally, lichen sclerosus is seen on other parts of the body, especially the upper body, breasts, and upper arms.

The symptoms are the same in children and adults. Early in the disease, small, subtle white spots appear. These areas are usually slightly shiny and smooth. As time goes on, the spots develop into bigger patches, and the skin surface becomes thinned and crinkled. As a result, the skin tears easily, and bright red or purple discoloration from bleeding inside the skin is common. More severe cases of lichen sclerosus produce scarring that may cause the inner lips of the vulva to shrink and disappear, the clitoris to become covered with scar tissue, and the opening of the vagina to narrow.

About This Chapter: Text in this chapter is from "Lichen Sclerosus," National Institute of Arthritis and Musculoskeletal and Skin Diseases, June 2004. Brand names included in this chapter are provided as examples only, and their inclusion does not mean that these products are endorsed by the National Institutes of Health or any other government agency. Also, if a particular brand name is not mentioned, this does not mean or imply that the product is unsatisfactory.

Lichen sclerosus of the penis occurs almost exclusively in uncircumcised men (those who have not had the foreskin removed). Affected foreskin can scar, tighten, and shrink over the head of the penis. Skin on other areas of the body affected by lichen sclerosus usually does not develop scarring.

How common is it?

Although definitive data are not available, lichen sclerosus is considered a rare disorder that can develop in people of all ages. It usually appears in postmenopausal women and primarily affects the vulva. It is uncommon for women who have vulvar lichen sclerosus to have the disease on other skin surfaces. The disease is much less common in childhood. In boys, it is a major cause of tightening of the foreskin, which requires circumcision. Otherwise, it is very uncommon in men.

What are the symptoms?

Symptoms vary depending on the area affected. Patients experience different degrees of discomfort. When lichen sclerosus occurs on parts of the body other than the genital area, most often there are no symptoms, other than itching. If the disease is severe, bleeding, tearing, and blistering caused by rubbing or bumping the skin can cause pain.

Very mild lichen sclerosus of the genital area often causes no symptoms at all. If the disease worsens, itching is the most common symptom. Rarely, lichen sclerosus of the vulva may cause extreme itching that interferes with sleep and daily activities. Rubbing or scratching to relieve the itching can create painful sores and bruising, so that many women must avoid sexual intercourse, tight clothing, tampons, riding bicycles, and other common activities that involve pressure or friction. Urination can be accompanied by burning or pain, and bleeding can occur, especially

♣ It's A Fact!!
Most men with genital lichen sclerosus have not been circumcised. They sometimes experience difficulty pulling back the foreskin and have decreased sensation at the tip of the penis. Occasionally, erections are painful, and the urethra (the tube through which urine flows) can become narrow or obstructed.

during intercourse. When lichen sclerosus develops around the anus, the discomfort can lead to constipation that is difficult to relieve. This is particularly common in children. It is important to note that the signs of lichen sclerosus in children may sometimes be confused with those of sexual abuse.

What causes lichen sclerosus?

The cause is unknown, although an overactive immune system may play a role. Some people may have a genetic tendency toward the disease, and studies suggest that abnormal hormone levels may also play a role. Lichen sclerosus has also been shown to appear at sites of previous injury or trauma where the skin has already experienced scarring or damage.

Is it contagious?

No, lichen sclerosus is not contagious.

How is it diagnosed?

Doctors can diagnose an advanced case by looking at the skin. However, early or mild disease often requires a biopsy (removal and examination of a small sample of affected skin). Because other diseases of the genitalia can look like lichen sclerosus, a biopsy is advised whenever the appearance of the skin is not typical of lichen sclerosus.

How is it treated?

Patients with lichen sclerosus of nongenital skin often do not need treatment because the symptoms are very mild and usually go away over time. The amount of time involved varies from patient to patient.

However, lichen sclerosus of the genital skin should be treated, even when it is not causing itching or pain, because it can lead to scarring that may narrow openings in the genital area and interfere with either urination or sexual intercourse or both. There is also a very small chance that skin cancer may develop within the affected areas.

In uncircumcised men, circumcision is the most widely used therapy for lichen sclerosus. This procedure removes the affected skin, and the disease usually does not recur.

Prescription medications are required to treat vulvar lichen sclerosus, nongenital lichen sclerosus that is causing symptoms, and lichen sclerosus of the penis that is not cured by circumcision. The treatment of choice is an ultrapotent topical corticosteroid (a very strong cortisone cream or ointment). These creams or ointments may be applied daily for several weeks, which will be sufficient to stop the itching. However, long-term but less frequent applications (sometimes as infrequently as twice a week) will be needed to keep the lesions from reactivating and to help restore the skin's normal texture and strength. Treatment does not reverse the scarring that may have already occurred.

Because prolonged use of ultrapotent corticosteroid creams and ointments can cause thinning and redness of the skin, give rise to "stretch marks" around the area of application, and predispose individuals to vulvar yeast infections, periodic follow-up by a doctor is necessary.

Young girls may not require lifelong treatment, since lichen sclerosus can sometimes, but not always, disappear permanently at puberty. Scarring and changes in skin color, however, may remain even after the symptoms have disappeared.

Ultrapotent topical corticosteroids are so effective that other therapies are rarely prescribed. The previous standard therapy was testosterone cream or ointment, but this has been proven to produce no more benefit than a placebo (inactive) cream. Prolonged use of the testosterone cream or ointment can cause masculinization (low-pitched voice, increased coarse facial hairs). Another hormone cream, progesterone, was previously used to treat the disease, but has also been shown to be ineffective. Retinoids, or vitamin A-like medications, may be helpful for patients who cannot tolerate or are not helped by ultrapotent topical corticosteroids.

Tacrolimus (Protopic) ointment has been reported to benefit some patients, but more research is needed to confirm this. Tacrolimus is a steroid-free ointment; it is not a corticosteroid. Tacrolimus has no apparent side effects other than local irritation in some patients.

There are some early indications that different forms of ultraviolet light treatments, with or without psoralens (pills that intensify the effect of ultraviolet A light), may be effective and well-tolerated treatments for some patients with lichen sclerosus on nongenital skin.

Patients who need medication should ask their doctor how the medication works, what its side effects might be, and why it is the best treatment for their lichen sclerosus.

For women and girls, surgery to remove the affected skin is not an acceptable option because lichen sclerosus comes back after removal. Surgery may be useful for scarring, but only after lichen sclerosus is controlled with medication.

Sometimes, people do not respond to the ultrapotent topical corticosteroid. Other factors, such as low estrogen levels, an infection, irritation, or allergy to the medication, can keep symptoms from clearing up. Your doctor may need to treat these as well. If you feel that you are not improving as you would expect, talk to your doctor.

Can people with lichen sclerosus have sexual intercourse?

Women with severe lichen sclerosus may not be able to have sexual intercourse because of pain or scarring that narrows the entrance to the vagina. However, proper treatment with an ultrapotent topical corticosteroid can help restore normal sexual functioning, unless severe scarring has already narrowed the vaginal opening. In this case, surgery may be needed to correct the problem, but only after the disease has been controlled.

Is lichen sclerosus related to cancer?

Lichen sclerosus does not cause skin cancer. However, skin that is scarred by lichen sclerosus is more likely to develop skin cancer. The frequency of skin cancer in men with lichen sclerosus is not known. It is important for people who have the disease to receive proper treatment and to see the doctor every six to 12 months, so that the doctor can monitor and treat any changes that might signal skin cancer.

What kind of doctor treats lichen sclerosus?

Lichen sclerosus is treated by dermatologists (doctors who treat the skin) and by gynecologists if the female genitalia are involved. Urologists (a specialist of the urinary or urogenital tract) and primary health care providers with a special interest in genital diseases also treat this disease. To find a doctor who treats lichen sclerosus, ask your family doctor for a referral, call a local or state department of health, look in the local telephone directory, or contact a local medical center. The American Academy of Dermatology also provides referrals to dermatologists in your area, and the American College of Obstetricians and Gynecologists can refer you to a gynecologist. The Directory of Medical Specialists, available at most public libraries, lists dermatologists, gynecologists, and urologists in your area.

Chapter 39

Lupus

Defining Lupus

Lupus is one of many disorders of the immune system known as *auto-immune diseases*. In autoimmune diseases, the immune system turns against parts of the body it is designed to protect. This leads to inflammation and damage to various body tissues. Lupus can affect many parts of the body, including the joints, skin, kidneys, heart, lungs, blood vessels, and brain. Although people with the disease may have many different symptoms, some of the most common ones include extreme fatigue, painful or swollen joints (arthritis), unexplained fever, skin rashes, and kidney problems.

At present, there is no cure for lupus. However, lupus can be effectively treated with drugs, and most people with the disease can lead active, healthy lives. Lupus is characterized by periods of illness, called flares, and periods of wellness, or remission. Understanding how to prevent flares and how to treat them when they do occur helps people with lupus maintain better health. Intense research is underway, and scientists funded by the National Institutes

About This Chapter: Text in this chapter is from "Lupus," National Institute of Arthritis and Musculoskeletal and Skin Diseases, August 2003. Brand names included in this chapter are provided as examples only, and their inclusion does not mean that these products are endorsed by the National Institutes of Health or any other government agency. Also, if a particular brand name is not mentioned, this does not mean or imply that the product is unsatisfactory.

of Health are continuing to make great strides in understanding the disease, which may ultimately lead to a cure.

Two of the major questions researchers are studying are who gets lupus and why. We know that many more women than men have lupus. Lupus is three times more common in African American women than in Caucasian women and is also more common in women of Hispanic, Asian, and Native American descent. In addition, lupus can run in families, but the risk that a child or a brother or sister of a patient will also have lupus is still quite low. It is difficult to estimate how many people in the United States have the disease because its symptoms vary widely and its onset is often hard to pinpoint.

There are several kinds of lupus:

Systemic Lupus Erythematosus: Systemic lupus erythematosus (SLE) is the form of the disease that most people are referring to when they say "lupus." The word *systemic* means the disease can affect many parts of the body. The symptoms of SLE may be mild or serious. Although SLE usually first affects people between the ages of 15 and 45, it can occur in childhood or later in life as well. This chapter focuses on SLE.

Discoid Lupus Erythematosus: This is a chronic skin disorder in which a red, raised rash appears on the face, scalp, or elsewhere. The raised areas may become thick and scaly and may cause scarring. The rash may last for

> ### ✎ What's It Mean?
>
> Anemia: A decrease in red blood cells.
>
> Arthritis: Painful or swollen joints.
>
> Autoantibodies: Blood proteins that act against the body's own parts.
>
> Leukopenia: A decreased number of white blood cells.
>
> Nephritis: Inflammation of the kidneys.
>
> Photosensitivity: Sensitivity to sunlight.
>
> Pleuritis: An inflammation of the lining of the chest cavity that causes chest pain, particularly with breathing.
>
> Rheumatologist: A doctor who specializes in rheumatic diseases (arthritis and other inflammatory disorders, often involving the immune system).

days or years and may recur. A small percentage of people with discoid lupus have or develop SLE later.

Subacute Cutaneous Lupus Erythematosus: This type of lupus refers to skin lesions that appear on parts of the body exposed to sun. The lesions do not cause scarring.

Drug-Induced Lupus: This form of lupus is caused by medications. Many different drugs can cause drug-induced lupus. Symptoms are similar to those of SLE (arthritis, rash, fever, and chest pain) and they typically go away completely when the drug is stopped. The kidneys and brain are rarely involved.

Neonatal Lupus: This type of lupus is a rare disease that can occur in newborn babies of women with SLE, Sjögren's syndrome, or no disease at all. Scientists suspect that neonatal lupus is caused by autoantibodies in the mother's blood called anti-Ro (SSA) and anti-La (SSB). Autoantibodies ("auto" means self) are blood proteins that act against the body's own parts. At birth, the babies have a skin rash, liver problems, and low blood counts. These symptoms gradually go away over several months. In rare instances, babies with neonatal lupus may have a serious heart problem that slows down the natural rhythm of the heart. Neonatal lupus is rare, and most infants of mothers with SLE are entirely healthy. All women who are pregnant and known to have anti-Ro (SSA) or anti-La (SSB) antibodies should be monitored by echocardiograms (a test that monitors the heart and surrounding blood vessels) during the 16th and 30th weeks of pregnancy.

It is important for women with SLE or other related autoimmune disorders to be under a doctor's care during pregnancy. Physicians can now identify mothers at highest risk for complications, allowing for prompt treatment of the infant at or before birth. SLE can also flare during pregnancy, and prompt treatment can keep the mother healthier longer.

Understanding What Causes Lupus

Lupus is a complex disease, and its cause is unknown. It is likely that a combination of genetic, environmental, and possibly hormonal factors work together to cause the disease. The fact that lupus can run in families indicates that its development has a genetic basis. Recent research suggests that genetics plays an important role; however, no specific "lupus gene" has been identified yet. Studies suggest that several different genes may be involved in determining a person's likelihood of developing the disease, which tissues and organs are affected, and the severity of disease. However, scientists believe that genes alone do not determine who gets lupus and that other factors also play a role. Some of the factors scientists are studying include sunlight, stress, certain drugs, and infectious agents such as viruses.

In lupus, the body's immune system does not work as it should. A healthy immune system produces proteins called antibodies and specific cells called lymphocytes that help fight and destroy viruses, bacteria, and other foreign substances that invade the body. In lupus, the immune system produces antibodies against the body's healthy cells and tissues. These antibodies, called autoantibodies, contribute to the inflammation of various parts of the body and can cause damage to organs and tissues. The most common type of autoantibody that develops in people with lupus is called an antinuclear antibody (ANA) because it reacts with parts of the cell's nucleus (command center). Doctors and scientists do not yet understand all of the factors that cause inflammation and tissue damage in lupus, and researchers are actively exploring them.

Symptoms Of Lupus

Each person with lupus has slightly different symptoms that can range from mild to severe and may come and go over time. However, some of the most common symptoms of lupus include painful or swollen joints (arthritis), unexplained fever, and extreme fatigue. A characteristic red skin rash—the so-called butterfly or malar rash—may appear across the nose and cheeks. Rashes may also occur on the face and ears, upper arms, shoulders, chest, and hands. Because many people with lupus are sensitive to sunlight, skin rashes often first develop or worsen after sun exposure.

Common Symptoms Of Lupus

The following are some common symptoms of lupus:

- Painful or swollen joints and muscle pain
- Unexplained fever

- Red rashes, most commonly on the face

- Chest pain upon deep breathing

- Unusual loss of hair

- Pale or purple fingers or toes from cold or stress (Raynaud's phenomenon)

- Sensitivity to the sun

- Swelling (edema) in legs or around eyes

- Mouth ulcers

- Swollen glands

- Extreme fatigue

Other symptoms of lupus include chest pain, hair loss, anemia (a decrease in red blood cells), mouth ulcers, and pale or purple fingers and toes from cold and stress. Some people also experience headaches, dizziness, depression, confusion, or seizures. New symptoms may continue to appear years after the initial diagnosis, and different symptoms can occur at different times. In some people with lupus, only one system of the body, such as the skin or joints, is affected. Other people experience symptoms in many parts of their body. Just how seriously a body system is affected varies from person to person. The following systems in the body also can be affected by lupus:

- **Kidneys:** Inflammation of the kidneys (nephritis) can impair their ability to get rid of waste products and other toxins from the body effectively. There is usually no pain associated with kidney involvement, although some patients may notice swelling in their ankles. Most often, the only indication of kidney disease is an abnormal urine or blood test. Because the kidneys are so important to overall health, lupus affecting the kidneys generally requires intensive drug treatment to prevent permanent damage.

- **Lungs:** Some people with lupus develop pleuritis, an inflammation of the lining of the chest cavity that causes chest pain, particularly with breathing. Patients with lupus also may get pneumonia.

- **Central Nervous System:** In some patients, lupus affects the brain or central nervous system. This can cause headaches, dizziness, memory disturbances, vision problems, seizures, stroke, or changes in behavior.

- **Blood Vessels:** Blood vessels may become inflamed (vasculitis), affecting the way blood circulates through the body. The inflammation may be mild and may not require treatment or may be severe and require immediate attention.

- **Blood:** People with lupus may develop anemia, leukopenia (a decreased number of white blood cells), or thrombocytopenia (a decrease in the number of platelets in the blood, which assist in clotting). Some people with lupus may have an increased risk for blood clots.

- **Heart:** In some people with lupus, inflammation can occur in the heart itself (myocarditis and endocarditis) or the membrane that surrounds it (pericarditis), causing chest pains or other symptoms. Lupus can also increase the risk of atherosclerosis (hardening of the arteries).

Diagnosing Lupus

Diagnosing lupus can be difficult. It may take months or even years for doctors to piece together the symptoms to diagnose this complex disease accurately. Making a correct diagnosis of lupus requires knowledge and awareness on the part of the doctor and good communication on the part of the patient. Giving the doctor a complete, accurate medical history (for example, what health problems you have had and for how long) is critical to the process of diagnosis. This information, along with a physical examination and the results of laboratory tests, helps the doctor consider other diseases that may mimic lupus, or determine if the patient truly has the disease. Reaching a diagnosis may take time as new symptoms appear.

No single test can determine whether a person has lupus, but several laboratory tests may help the doctor to make a diagnosis. The most useful tests identify certain autoantibodies often present in the blood of people with lupus. For example, the antinuclear antibody (ANA) test is commonly used to look for autoantibodies that react against components of the nucleus, or "command center," of the body's cells.

Other laboratory tests are used to monitor the progress of the disease once it has been diagnosed. A complete blood count, urinalysis, blood chemistries, and the erythrocyte sedimentation rate (ESR) test can provide valuable information. Another common test measures the blood level of a group of substances called *complement*. People with lupus often have increased ESRs and low complement levels, especially during flares of the disease. X-rays and other imaging tests can help doctors see the organs affected by SLE.

Diagnostic Tools For Lupus

- Medical history

- Complete physical examination

- Laboratory tests:

  1. Complete blood count

  2. Erythrocyte sedimentation rate

  3. Urinalysis

  4. Blood chemistries

  5. Complement levels

  6. Antinuclear antibody test

  7. Other autoantibody tests (anti-DNA, anti-Sm, anti-RNP, anti-Ro [SSA], anti-La [SSB])

  8. Anticardiolipin antibody test

- Skin biopsy

- Kidney biopsy

Treating Lupus

Diagnosing and treating lupus are often a team effort between the patient and several types of health care professionals. A person with lupus can go to his or her family doctor or internist, or can visit a rheumatologist. A rheumatologist is a doctor who specializes in rheumatic diseases (arthritis and other inflammatory disorders, often involving the immune system). Clinical immunologists (doctors specializing in immune system disorders) may also treat people with lupus. As treatment progresses,

☞ Remember!!

In developing a treatment plan, the doctor has several goals: to prevent flares, to treat them when they do occur, and to minimize organ damage and complications. The doctor and patient should reevaluate the plan regularly to ensure it is as effective as possible.

other professionals often help. These may include nurses, psychologists, social workers, nephrologists (doctors who treat kidney disease), hematologists (doctors specializing in blood disorders), dermatologists (doctors who treat skin disease), and neurologists (doctors specializing in disorders of the nervous system).

Once lupus has been diagnosed, the doctor will develop a treatment plan based on the patient's age, sex, health, symptoms, and lifestyle. Treatment plans are tailored to the individual's needs and may change over time.

NSAIDs: For people with joint or chest pain or fever, drugs that decrease inflammation, called nonsteroidal anti-inflammatory drugs (NSAIDs), are often used. While some NSAIDs, such as ibuprofen and naproxen, are available over the counter, a doctor's prescription is necessary for others. NSAIDs may be used alone or in combination with other types of drugs to control pain, swelling, and fever. Even though some NSAIDs may be purchased without a prescription, it is important that they be taken under a doctor's direction.

Antimalarials: Antimalarials are another type of drug commonly used to treat lupus. These drugs were originally used to treat malaria, but doctors have found that they also are useful for lupus. A common antimalarial used to treat lupus is hydroxychloroquine (Plaquenil). It may be used alone or in combination with other drugs and generally is used to treat fatigue, joint pain, skin rashes, and inflammation of the lungs.

Corticosteroids: The mainstay of lupus treatment involves the use of corticosteroid hormones, such as prednisone (Deltasone), hydrocortisone, methylprednisolone (Medrol), and dexamethasone (Decadron, Hexadrol). Corticosteroids are related to cortisol, which is a natural anti-inflammatory hormone. They work by rapidly suppressing inflammation. Corticosteroids can be given by mouth, in creams applied to the skin, or by injection. Because they are potent drugs, the doctor will seek the lowest dose with the greatest benefit. Short-term side effects of corticosteroids include swelling, increased appetite, and weight gain. These side effects generally stop when the drug is stopped. It is dangerous to stop taking corticosteroids suddenly, so it is very important that the doctor and patient work together in changing the corticosteroid dose. Sometimes doctors give very large amounts of corticosteroid by vein over a brief period of time (days) ("bolus" or "pulse" therapy). With this treatment, the typical side effects are less likely and slow with-drawal is unnecessary.

Immunosuppressives: For some patients whose kidneys or cen-tral nervous systems are affected by lupus, a type of drug called an immunosuppressive may be

> **☞ Remember!!**
>
> It is dangerous to stop taking corticosteroids suddenly, so it is very important that the doctor and patient work together in changing the dose.

used. Immunosuppressives, such as cyclophosphamide (Cytoxan) and mycophenolate mofetil (CellCept), restrain the overactive immune system by blocking the production of immune cells. These drugs may be given by mouth or by infusion (dripping the drug into the vein through a small tube). Side effects may include nausea, vomiting, hair loss, bladder problems, de-creased fertility, and increased risk of cancer and infection. The risk for side effects increases with the length of treatment. As with other treatments for lupus, there is a risk of relapse after the immunosuppressives have been stopped.

Alternative And Complementary Therapies: Because of the nature and cost of the medications used to treat lupus and the potential for serious side effects, many patients seek other ways of treating the disease. Some alterna-tive approaches people have tried include special diets, nutritional supple-ments, fish oils, ointments and creams, chiropractic treatment, and homeopathy. Although these methods may not be harmful in and of them-selves, and may be associated with symptomatic or psychosocial benefit, no research to date shows that they affect the disease process or prevent organ damage. Some alternative or complementary approaches may help the pa-tient cope or reduce some of the stress associated with living with a chronic illness. If the doctor feels the approach has value and will not be harmful, it can be incorporated into the patient's treatment plan. However, it is impor-tant not to neglect regular health care or treatment of serious symptoms. An open dialogue between the patient and physician about the relative values of complementary and alternative therapies allows the patient to make an in-formed choice about treatment options.

Lupus And Quality Of Life

Despite the symptoms of lupus and the potential side-effects of treatment, people with lupus can maintain a high quality of life overall. One key to managing lupus is to understand the disease and its impact. Learning to recognize the warning signs of a flare can help the patient take steps to ward it off or reduce its intensity. Many people with lupus experience increased fatigue, pain, a rash, fever, abdominal discomfort, headache, or dizziness just before a flare. Developing strategies to prevent flares can also be helpful, such as learning to recognize your warning signals and maintaining good communication with your doctor.

It is also important for people with lupus to receive regular health care, instead of seeking help only when symptoms worsen. Results from a medical exam and laboratory work on a regular basis allows the doctor to note any changes and to identify and treat flares early. The treatment plan, which is tailored to the individual's specific needs and circumstances, can be adjusted accordingly. If new symptoms are identified early, treatments may be more effective. Other concerns also can be addressed at regular checkups. The doctor can provide guidance about such issues as the use of sunscreens, stress reduction, and the importance of structured exercise and rest, as well as birth control and family planning. Because people with lupus can be more susceptible to infections, the doctor may recommend yearly influenza vaccinations or pneumococcal vaccinations for some patients.

Women with lupus should receive regular preventive health care, such as gynecological and breast examinations. Men with lupus should have the prostate-specific antigen (PSA) test. Both men and women need to have their blood pressure and cholesterol checked on a regular basis. If a person is taking corticosteroids or antimalarial medications, an eye exam should be done at least yearly to screen for and treat eye problems.

Staying healthy requires extra effort and care for people with lupus, so it becomes especially important to develop strategies for maintaining wellness. Wellness involves close attention to the body, mind, and spirit. One of the primary goals of wellness for people with lupus is coping with the stress of having a chronic disorder. Effective stress management varies from person to person. Some approaches that may help include exercise, relaxation techniques such as meditation, and setting priorities for spending time and energy.

Developing and maintaining a good support system is also important. A support system may include family, friends, medical professionals, community organizations, and support groups. Participating in a support group can provide emotional help, boost self-esteem and morale, and help develop or improve coping skills.

Warning Signs Of A Flare

The warning signs of a flare of lupus include the following:

- Increased fatigue
- Pain
- Rash
- Fever
- Abdominal discomfort
- Headache
- Dizziness

✔ **Quick Tip**
Learning to recognize the warning signs of a flare can help the patient take steps to ward it off or reduce its intensity.

Preventing A Flare

- Learn to recognize your warning signals
- Maintain good communication with your doctor

Learning more about lupus may also help. Studies have shown that patients who are well-informed and participate actively in their own care experience less pain, make fewer visits to the doctor, build self-confidence, and remain more active.

Pregnancy For Women With Lupus

Although a lupus pregnancy is considered high risk, most women with lupus carry their babies safely to the end of their pregnancy. Women with lupus have a higher rate of miscarriage and premature births compared with the general population. In addition, women who have antiphospholipid

Tips For Working With Your Doctor

- Seek a health care provider who is familiar with SLE and who will listen to and address your concerns.

- Provide complete, accurate medical information.

- Make a list of your questions and concerns in advance.

- Be honest and share your point of view with the health care provider.

- Ask for clarification or further explanation if you need it.

- Talk to other members of the health care team, such as nurses, therapists, or pharmacists.

- Do not hesitate to discuss sensitive subjects (for example, birth control, intimacy) with your doctor.

- Discuss any treatment changes with your doctor before making them.

antibodies are at a greater risk of miscarriage in the second trimester because of their increased risk of blood clotting in the placenta. Lupus patients with a history of kidney disease have a higher risk of preeclampsia (hypertension with a buildup of excess watery fluid in cells or tissues of the body). Pregnancy counseling and planning before pregnancy are important. Ideally, a woman should have no signs or symptoms of lupus and be taking no medications for at least six months before she becomes pregnant.

Some women may experience a mild to moderate flare during or after their pregnancy; others do not. Pregnant women with lupus, especially those taking corticosteroids, also are more likely to develop high blood pressure, diabetes, hyperglycemia (high blood sugar), and kidney complications, so regular care and good nutrition during pregnancy are essential. It is also advisable to have access to a neonatal (newborn) intensive care unit at the time of delivery in case the baby requires special medical attention.

Chapter 40

Poison Ivy, Poison Oak, And Poison Sumac

First comes the itching, then a red rash, and then blisters. These symptoms of poison ivy, poison oak, and poison sumac can start from a few hours to several days after exposure to the plant oil found in the sap of these poisonous plants.

Recognizing Poison Ivy, Poison Oak, And Poison Sumac

Poison Ivy: Poison ivy is found throughout the United States except Alaska, Hawaii, and parts of the West Coast. It can grow as a vine or shrub. Each leaf has three glossy leaflets, with smooth or toothed edges. Leaves are reddish in spring, green in summer, and yellow, orange, or red in fall. It may have white berries.

Poison Oak: Poison oak grows as a low shrub in the eastern United States, and in tall clumps or long vines on the Pacific Coast. Fuzzy green leaves in clusters of three are lobed or deeply toothed with rounded tips. It may have yellow-white berries.

Poison Sumac: Poison sumac grows as a tall shrub or small tree in bogs or swamps in the Northeast, Midwest, and parts of the Southeast. Each leaf

About This Chapter: Text in this chapter is from "Outsmarting Poison Ivy and Other Poisonous Plants," U.S. Food and Drug Administration, September 2008.

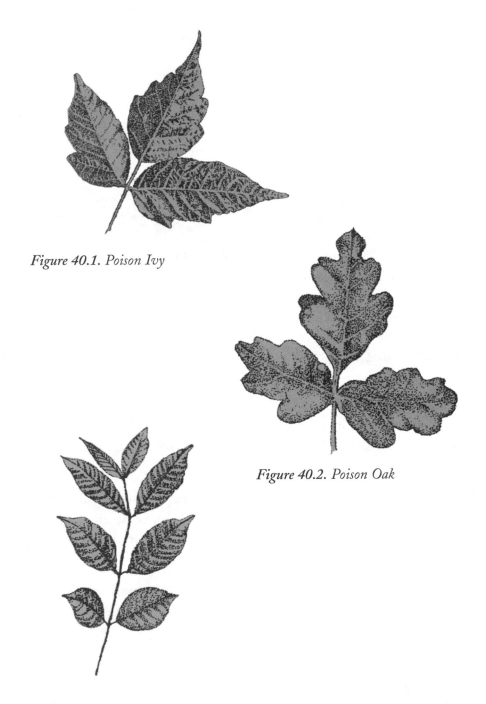

Figure 40.1. Poison Ivy

Figure 40.2. Poison Oak

Figure 40.3. Poison Sumac

has clusters of seven to 13 smooth-edged leaflets. Leaves are orange in spring, green in summer, and yellow, orange, or red in fall. It may have yellow–white berries.

Not Contagious

Poison ivy and other poison plant rashes can't be spread from person to person. But it is possible to pick up the rash from plant oil that may have stuck to clothing, pets, garden tools, and other items that have come in contact with these plants. The plant oil lingers (sometimes for years) on virtually any surface until it's washed off with water or rubbing alcohol.

> **♣ It's A Fact!!**
> The plant oil lingers (sometimes for years) on virtually any surface until it's washed off with water or rubbing alcohol.

The rash will only occur where the plant oil has touched the skin, so a person with poison ivy can't spread it on the body by scratching. It may seem like the rash is spreading if it appears over time instead of all at once. But this is either because the plant oil is absorbed at different rates in different parts of the body or because of repeated exposure to contaminated objects or plant oil trapped under the fingernails. Even if blisters break, the fluid in the blisters is not plant oil and cannot further spread the rash.

Tips For Prevention

- Learn what poison ivy, oak, and sumac plants look like so you can avoid them.

- Wash your garden tools and gloves regularly. If you think you may be working around poison ivy, wear long sleeves, long pants tucked into boots, and gloves.

- Wash your pet if it may have brushed up against poison ivy, oak, or sumac. Use pet shampoo and water while wearing rubber gloves, such as dishwashing gloves. Most pets are not sensitive to poison ivy, but the oil can stick to their fur and cause a reaction in someone who pets them.

- Wash your skin in cool water as soon as possible if you come in contact with a poisonous plant. The sooner you cleanse the skin, the greater

Remember!!

See A Doctor

- If you have a temperature over 100° F

- If there is pus, soft yellow scabs, or tenderness on the rash

- If the itching gets worse or keeps you awake at night

- If the rash spreads to your eyes, mouth, genital area, or covers more than one-fourth of your skin area

- If the rash is not improving within a few days

Source [cited in FDA document]: "Poison Ivy," Minnesota Poison Control System website, 2004.

the chance that you can remove the plant oil or help prevent further spread.

- Use the topical product "Ivy Block" if you know you will come into contact with the poisonous plants. This FDA-approved product is available over the counter.

Tips For Treatment

Don't scratch the blisters. Bacteria from under your fingernails can get into the blisters and cause an infection. The rash, blisters, and itch normally disappear in several weeks without any treatment. The following are some ways you can relieve the itch:

- Using wet compresses or soaking in cool water

- Applying over-the-counter topical corticosteroid preparations or taking prescription oral corticosteroids

- Applying topical over-the-counter skin protectants, such as calamine, labeled to dry oozing and weeping or to relieve itching and irritation caused by poison ivy, poison oak, and poison sumac

Chapter 41

Psoriasis

What Exactly Is Psoriasis?

Psoriasis is an immune-mediated disease. This means that your immune system causes your skin cells to reproduce in three to four days instead of 28 to 30 days, as is the case for skin without psoriasis.

Whereas normal skin cells are shed from people unnoticed, skin cells affected by psoriasis build up and form raised, scaly lesions.

Skin with psoriasis becomes red from the increased blood supply to the rapidly dividing cells, and the white scale is composed of dead skin cells.

Psoriasis goes through an unpredictable cycle: flares, improvement, remission, and recurrence. It is not contagious.

Severity

The severity of each case depends on how much of your body has psoriasis lesions:

About This Chapter: Text in this chapter is from "Facts About Psoriasis," and "Coping with Psoriasis," © National Psoriasis Foundation (www.psoriasis.org). Reprinted with permission. The National Psoriasis Foundation helps people with psoriasis get support, information, and encouragement, both online and in the community. For information about the National Psoriasis Foundation online message board and chat room, or to find local support groups and events, visit www.psoriasis.org.

- Mild cases involve only a few spots.

- Moderate cases cover three to 10 percent of the body. (The palm of your hand represents one percent of the body's skin surface.)

- Severe cases involve more than 10 percent of the skin surface and may include all of a person's skin.

Onset And Flaring

Ordinarily, people have their first outbreak of psoriasis between the ages of 15 and 35, but it can appear at any age. Thirty percent of those who get psoriasis are less than 20 years old when the disease first surfaces.

Though psoriasis is believed to be an immune-mediated disease, heredity seems to play a part and so do environmental factors. About 25 percent of young people report the onset of their psoriasis followed an infection, particularly strep throat. One-third to one-half of all young people with psoriasis may experience a flare-up two to six weeks after an earache, strep throat, bronchitis, tonsillitis or a respiratory infection.

Stress is thought to play a role in psoriasis, but stress alone is not a cause. Some studies have linked stress to psoriasis outbreaks and more severe progression of the disease, but other studies have found no connection between stress and psoriasis.

Areas of the skin that have been injured or traumatized are sometimes the sites of psoriasis; this is called the "Koebner phenomenon." However, not everyone with psoriasis develops it at the site of an injury.

Treatments

Psoriasis treatments (and there are many) work by slowing skin cell reproduction. Some work to remove scales. Some help soothe itchy or uncomfortable skin. All prescription psoriasis medications can be effective in improving lesions, but not all people with psoriasis react the same way to different medications. It may require experimentation to see which treatments, or combination of treatments, work for you.

There are three basic categories of psoriasis treatments:

1. Topical treatments like creams and ointments are used on the areas of skin that exhibit psoriasis plaques and lesions.

2. Ultraviolet light therapies (UVB and UVA) work by exposing the skin to light waves, sometimes over the whole body and sometimes only affected areas, like hands or feet.

3. Systemic medications are taken by mouth or injected into the body.

Dermatologists and other doctors prescribe treatments according to the type and severity of the psoriasis, the areas of the skin affected, and your age and past medical history. Some of the treatments available for adults are used less often for teenagers because of the possibility of long-term or delayed side effects.

Coping With Psoriasis

Psoriasis creates a mixed bag of emotional reactions. Some people show little emotion over having psoriasis, while others react intensely. You may think this is related to the extent of someone's psoriasis, but in reality that doesn't seem to be the case. Whether someone has a few lesions or many, the emotional response is not always the same.

What's important, then, is to simply know you may experience difficult feelings about having psoriasis. This is helpful in determining how successfully you'll cope. Once you understand the extent of your emotions, you can deal with them constructively. Here are some common questions teens ask about coping with psoriasis.

I feel depressed and fear my psoriasis is affecting my self-esteem. Is this normal?

It's not uncommon to experience a sense of shock, confusion, exasperation and anger about what's happening to your skin. These feelings may give way to profound sadness or depression. Accepting your skin's condition is possible, but it takes time, sometimes a long time, to achieve. Therapy or support groups may be of benefit. Or, you can discuss these issues with your doctor or an adult.

What can I do to help myself cope with psoriasis?

Talking about psoriasis can help. It helps to talk to others who have psoriasis because they can relate to specific issues that you may run into on a day-to-day basis, such as wearing swimsuits or shorts in public.

It's important to find someone, whether they have psoriasis or not, who will listen and recognize the strong feelings that accompany psoriasis. Your feelings are real. Don't dismiss them or trivialize them. The power of the emotions that come from having psoriasis should not be underestimated. Find a dermatologist you can talk to about your feelings. He or she may suggest how to deal with the emotional aspects of psoriasis.

☞ Remember!!

What Guiding Principles Are There To Help Me Cope With Psoriasis?

There are some practical things that you can do:

- Ask for support, or no one will know that you need it.

- The more people know about and understand psoriasis, the better and easier it will be for you. Be willing to discuss your psoriasis with others, to the extent that you feel comfortable.

- Real friends will want to know about you and will want to help. They won't be put off by psoriasis.

- There is nothing to be ashamed of or embarrassed about. You didn't do anything wrong. Skin disease has no meaning other than what it is, even if other people attribute odd things to it.

- It is natural to feel anxious, angry, and depressed. Friends can help.

- People around you can be very supportive. You can help your friends support you by letting them know that psoriasis is not contagious and that it's the result of skin cells rapidly reproducing.

Once I come to terms with my psoriasis, what's next?

One of the hardest things about living with psoriasis is that you go through cycles of strong emotions, usually when the psoriasis goes into remission or reappears. The disease is unpredictable, and the emotions it triggers may occur repeatedly. Common reactions are embarrassment, anger and guilt. You may fear psoriasis returning or getting worse, or being rejected by others. It is important to respect your feelings as they occur and to learn to cope with them, so they do not hold your life hostage.

Will I have to deal with others' reactions to my skin all the time?

Not necessarily—psoriasis is a reality that you have to live with, but it doesn't have to control you. You can avoid dealing directly with others about your psoriasis when you don't have the emotional energy to answer questions. Wearing long sleeves, for example, can make coping in public a lot easier on "low-energy" days.

People are curious when they see something different. You have many choices about how to react to their curiosity. You may choose to ignore their attention, or you can explain that psoriasis is a skin disease that is not contagious.

What about my future?

Your skin doesn't have to be the determining factor in life's important decisions, like your choice of work, whether to attend college, responsibilities for being on your own, and the kind of person you want to be. People who have psoriasis have normal lives.

Chapter 42

Rashes

Alternative Names

- Skin redness or inflammation
- Skin lesion
- Rubor
- Skin rash
- Erythema

Definition

Rashes involve changes in the color or texture of your skin.

Considerations

Often, the cause of a rash can be determined from its visible characteristics and other symptoms.

Causes

A simple rash is called *dermatitis*, meaning inflammation of the skin. Contact dermatitis is caused by things your skin touches, such as:

✔ **Quick Tip**

Home Care

Most simple rashes will improve with gentle skin care and avoiding irritating substances. Follow these general guidelines:

- Avoid scrubbing your skin.

- Use as little soap as possible. Use gentle cleansers instead.

- Avoid applying cosmetic lotions or ointments directly on the rash.

- Use warm (not hot) water for cleaning. Pat dry, don't rub.

- Eliminate any newly added cosmetics or lotions.

- Leave the affected area exposed to the air as much as possible.

- Try calamine medicated lotion for poison ivy, oak, or sumac as well as other types of contact dermatitis.

Hydrocortisone cream (1%) is available without a prescription and may soothe many rashes. If you have eczema, apply moisturizers over your skin. Try oatmeal bath products, available at drugstores, to relieve symptoms of eczema, psoriasis, or shingles.

For *psoriasis*, you may need a prescription. You could also talk to your doctor about ultraviolet (UV) light therapy. It is safest to have such treatment under medical supervision. However, not all clinics or hospitals offer light therapy. Home units are available, but the cost is not always covered by insurance. If you do purchase a home unit, look for a device that delivers narrow band UVB light.

For *seborrheic dermatitis*, try applying small amounts of antidandruff shampoo to patches of this scaly rash on your skin, especially near hairy areas like your eyebrows. Leave on for 10 minutes and then carefully rinse off. If the shampoo feels irritating or your skin becomes redder, stop use.

For *impetigo*, an antibacterial cream or oral antibiotic is generally prescribed.

- Chemicals in elastic, latex, and rubber products

- Cosmetics, soaps, and detergents

- Dyes and other chemicals in clothing

- Poison ivy, oak, or sumac

Seborrheic dermatitis is a rash that appears in patches of redness and scaling around the eyebrows, eyelids, mouth, nose, the trunk, and behind the ears. If it happens on your scalp, it is called *dandruff* in adults and *cradle cap* in infants.

Age, stress, fatigue, weather extremes, oily skin, infrequent shampooing, and alcohol-based lotions aggravate this harmless but bothersome condition.

Other common causes of a rash include:

Eczema (Atopic Dermatitis): Tends to happen in people with allergies or asthma. The rash is generally red, itchy, and scaly.

Psoriasis: Tends to occur as red, scaly, itchy patches over joints and along the scalp. Fingernails may be affected.

Impetigo: Common in children, this infection is from bacteria that live in the top layers of the skin. Appears as red sores that turn into blisters, ooze, then crust over.

Shingles: A painful blistered skin condition caused by the same virus as chicken pox. The virus can lie dormant in your body for many years and re-emerge as shingles.

Childhood Illnesses: Such as chicken pox, measles, roseola, rubella, hand-foot-mouth disease, fifth disease, and scarlet fever.

Medications: Medications and insect bites or stings.

Many medical conditions can cause a rash as well. For example:

- lupus erythematosus;

- rheumatoid arthritis, especially the juvenile type;

- Kawasaki disease.

> **☞ Remember!!**
> ## When To Contact A Medical Professional
>
> Call 911 if:
>
> - you are short of breath, your throat is tight, or your face is swollen;
>
> - child has a purple rash that looks like a bruise.
>
> Call your health care provider if:
>
> - you have joint pain, fever, or a sore throat;
>
> - you have streaks of redness, swelling, or very tender areas as these may indicate an infection;
>
> - you are taking a new medication—do *not* change or stop any of your medications without talking to your doctor;
>
> - you may have a tick bite;
>
> - home treatment doesn't work, or your symptoms get worse.

What To Expect At Your Office Visit

Your doctor will perform a physical examination. He or she will ask questions about your medical conditions, medications, health problems that run in your family, and recent illnesses or exposures. Questions may include:

- When did the rash begin?

- What parts of your body are affected?

- Does anything make the rash better? Worse?

- Have you used any new soaps, detergents, lotions, or cosmetics recently?

- Have you been in any wooded areas recently?

- Have you had any change in your medications?

- Have you noticed a tick or insect bite?

- Have you eaten anything unusual lately?

- Do you have any other symptoms like itching or scaling?

- What are your underlying medical problems? Do you have, for example, asthma or allergies?

Tests may include:

- allergy testing;

- blood tests;

- skin biopsy;

- skin scrapings.

Depending on the cause of your rash, treatments may include medicated creams or lotions, medications taken by mouth, or skin surgery.

Many primary care doctors are comfortable dealing with common rashes, but for more complicated skin disorders, a referral to a dermatologist may be necessary.

Prevention

- Identify and then stay away from products that irritate your skin. If allergies are suspected, your doctor may want to consider skin testing.

- Receive appropriate vaccines for childhood illnesses, like the varicella vaccine for chicken pox and MMR immunization (a combination vaccine that protects against measles, mumps, and rubella).

- Get strep throat treated right away to prevent scarlet fever.

- Wash your hands frequently to prevent spreading viruses like roseola, hand-foot-mouth disease, and fifth disease.

- Learn relaxation methods like yoga, meditation, or tai chi. Stress aggravates many rashes, including eczema, psoriasis, and seborrheic dermatitis.

Chapter 43

Rosacea

Rosacea: An Overview

Rosacea is a long-term disease that affects the skin and sometimes the eyes. Its symptoms include redness, pimples, and, in later stages, thicker skin. In most cases, rosacea only affects the face.

About 14 million people in the United States have rosacea. This disease is most common in the following groups:

- Women (especially during menopause)

- People with fair skin

- Adults between the ages of 30 and 60

What does rosacea look like?

Rosacea has many symptoms, including the following:

- Frequent redness (flushing) of the face. Most redness is at the center of the face (forehead, nose, cheeks, and chin). There may also be a burning feeling and slight swelling.

About This Chapter: This chapter begins with text from "Rosacea," National Institute of Arthritis and Musculoskeletal and Skin Diseases, March 2005. Additional information about rosacea research is cited separately within the chapter.

- Small red lines under the skin. These lines show up when blood vessels under the skin get larger. This area of the skin may be somewhat swollen, warm, and red.

- Constant redness along with bumps on the skin. Sometimes the bumps have pus inside (pimples), but not always. Solid bumps on the skin may later become painful.

- Inflamed eyes or eyelids.

- A swollen nose. In some people (mostly men), the nose becomes red, larger, and bumpy.

- Thicker skin. The skin on the forehead, chin, cheeks, or other areas can become thicker because of rosacea.

How are the eyes affected?

Up to 50 percent of people who have rosacea get eye problems. Eyes can have redness, dryness, itching, burning, excess tears, and the feeling of having sand in the eye. The eyelids may become inflamed and swollen. The eyes may become sensitive to light, and the person may have blurred vision or some other kind of vision problem.

What causes rosacea?

Doctors don't know the exact cause of rosacea. Some doctors think rosacea happens when blood vessels expand too easily, causing flushing. People who blush a lot may be more likely to get rosacea. It is also thought that people inherit the likelihood of getting the disease.

Though not well-researched, some people say that one or more of these factors make their rosacea worse:

- Heat (including hot baths)

- Heavy exercise

- Sunlight

- Winds

- Very cold temperatures

- Hot or spicy foods and drinks
- Drinking alcohol
- Menopause
- Emotional stress
- Long-term use of steroids on the face

♣ It's A Fact!!

People with rosacea and pimples may think the pimples are caused by bacteria. But no one has found a clear link between rosacea and bacteria.

Source: NIAMS, 2005.

Can rosacea be cured?

There is no cure for rosacea, but it can be treated and controlled. In time the skin may look better. A dermatologist (a doctor who works with diseases of the skin) often treats rosacea. There are several ways to treat rosacea.

For skin, the following treatments may be used:

- Sometimes antibiotics can be put right on the skin. Other times, oral antibiotics can be used. The skin bumps may get better quickly, but redness and flushing are less likely to improve.

- Small red lines can be treated with electrosurgery and laser surgery. For some people, laser surgery improves the skin without much scarring or damage.

- Patients with a swollen, bumpy nose can have extra skin tissue taken off to make it smaller. Usually patients feel this process helps their appearance.

- Some people find that green-tinted makeup is good for hiding the skin's redness.

For the eyes, the following treatments may be used:

- Most eye problems are treated with oral antibiotics.

- People who get infections of the eyelids must clean them a lot. The doctor may say to scrub the eyelids gently with watered-down baby shampoo or an over-the-counter eyelid cleaner. After scrubbing, you should apply a warm (but not hot) compress a few times a day.

- If needed, the doctor may prescribe steroid eye drops.

What can people with rosacea do to help themselves?

You play a key role in taking care of your rosacea. Here are a few steps to take:

• Keep a written record of when flare-ups happen. This can give you clues about what bothers your skin.

• Use a sunscreen every day that protects against UVA and UVB rays. Make sure it has a sun-protecting factor (SPF) of 15 or higher.

• Use a mild moisturizer if it helps. Don't put irritating products on the face.

• If your eyes have problems, follow your doctor's treatment plan, and clean your eyelids as told.

• Talk with a doctor if you feel sad or have other signs of depression. Some people with rosacea feel bad because of the way their skin looks.

What research is being conducted to help people with rosacea?

Research is being done on the following issues:

• Ways to stop dry eyes and help other eye problems

• Drugs that can help treat rosacea

• Ways to reduce scarring after extra skin on the nose is removed

Common Skin Ailment May Be Caused By Immune Response

From "Spotlight on Research 2007," National Institute of Arthritis and Musculo-skeletal and Skin Diseases, December 2007.

Researchers funded in part by the National Institute of Arthritis and Musculoskeletal and Skin Diseases have uncovered clues related to the cause of rosacea, a common inflammatory skin condition that causes redness of the face, bumps, and visible blood vessels. Their discovery could trigger the development of novel therapies for prevention or treatment, offering new hope for individuals affected by the disease.

In the absence of solid evidence, rosacea has been believed to be caused by the bacteria responsible for causing acne. However, research conducted by Richard L. Gallo, M.D., Ph.D., of the University of California, San Diego, and the VA San Diego Healthcare System, along with an international team of investigators, has uncovered a possible flaw in the immune system that contributes to the disease. Their findings were reported in *Nature Medicine*.

Through skin biopsies, Gallo and his team found that people with rosacea had high levels of cathelicidins, peptides with antimicrobial and pro-inflammatory properties that protect the skin against infection. (Cathelicidins are secreted in an inactive form and undergo a cleaving process to take on their active form.) Investigators also discovered that levels of stratum corneum tryptic enzyme or SCTE—the enzyme responsible for cleaving the inactive cathelicidins into their active form—were also elevated in people with the disease.

In separate experiments, Gallo's team then injected mice with cathelicidins found in rosacea, added SCTE, and increased SCTE by turning off the gene that inhibits its activity. Each of these actions produced the inflammatory characteristics of rosacea in the skin of the mice. However, these responses were absent in mice with a deleted cathelicidin gene. Says Gallo, "Our findings help to show that antimicrobial peptides such as the cathelicidins, which are evolutionarily ancient elements of immune defense, play a critical role in inflammation."

Other support for this research came from the National Rosacea Society, the Veterans Administration and the Association for Preventive Medicine of Japan.

Chapter 44

Scabies

What is scabies?

Scabies is an infestation of the skin with the microscopic mite *Sarcoptes scabei*. Infestation is common, found worldwide, and affects people of all races and social classes. Scabies spreads rapidly under crowded conditions where there is frequent skin-to-skin contact between people, such as in hospitals, institutions, child-care facilities, and nursing homes.

What are the signs and symptoms of scabies infestation?

- Pimple-like irritations, burrows or rash of the skin, especially the webbing between the fingers; the skin folds on the wrist, elbow, or knee; the penis, the breast, or shoulder blades.

- Intense itching, especially at night and over most of the body.

- Sores on the body caused by scratching. These sores can sometimes become infected with bacteria.

How does a person get scabies?

Scabies is contracted by direct, prolonged, skin-to-skin contact with a person who is already infested by it. Contact generally must be prolonged (a

About This Chapter: Text in this chapter is from the fact sheet "Scabies," Centers for Disease Control and Prevention, Division of Parasitic Diseases, February 2008.

quick handshake or hug will usually not spread infestation). Infestation is easily spread to sexual partners and household members. Infestation may also occur by sharing clothing, towels, and bedding.

Who is at risk for severe infestation?

People with weakened immune systems and the elderly are at risk for a more severe form of scabies, called Norwegian or crusted scabies. Scabies is spread more easily by persons who have Norwegian, or crusted, scabies than by persons with other types of scabies.

Did my pet spread scabies to me?

No. Pets become infested with a different kind of scabies mite. If your pet is infested with scabies, (also called mange) and they have close contact with you, the mite can get under your skin and cause itching and skin irritation. However, the mite dies in a couple of days and does not reproduce. The mites may cause you to itch for several days, but you do not need to be treated with special medication to kill the mites. Until your pet is successfully treated, mites can continue to burrow into your skin and cause you to have symptoms.

> ♣ **It's A Fact!!**
> **How long will mites live?**
> Once away from the human body, mites usually do not survive more than 48 to 72 hours. When living on a person, an adult female mite can live up to a month.

How soon after infestation will symptoms begin?

For a person who has never been infested with scabies, symptoms may take four to six weeks to begin. For a person who has had scabies before, symptoms appear within several days.

How is scabies infestation diagnosed?

Diagnosis is most commonly made by looking at the burrows or rash. A skin scraping may be taken to look for mites, eggs, or mite fecal matter (scybala) to confirm the diagnosis. Even if a skin scraping or biopsy is taken and returns negative, it is still possible that you may be infested. Typically, there are fewer than 10 mites on the entire body of an infested person; this makes it easy for an infestation to be missed. However, persons with Norwegian, or crusted, scabies can be infested with thousands of mites and should be considered highly infectious.

Can scabies be treated?

Yes. Several creams or lotions that are available by prescription are approved by the U.S. Food and Drug Administration (FDA) to treat scabies. Always follow the directions provided by your physician or the directions on the package label or insert. Apply the medication to a clean body from the neck down to the toes. After leaving the medication on the body for the recommended time, take a bath or shower to wash off the cream or lotion. Put on clean clothes. All clothes, bedding, and towels used by the infested person during the three days before treatment should be washed in hot water and dried in a hot dryer. A second treatment of the body with the same cream or lotion may be necessary. Pregnant women and children are often treated with milder scabies medications such as 5% permethrin cream.

Who should be treated for scabies?

Anyone who is diagnosed with scabies, as well as his or her sex partners and persons who have close, prolonged contact to the infested person should also be treated. If your health care provider has instructed family members to be treated, everyone should receive treatment at the same time to prevent reinfestation.

How soon after treatment will I feel better?

Itching may continue for two to three weeks, and does not mean that you are still infested. Your health care provider may prescribe additional medication to relieve itching if it is severe.

Chapter 45

Scleroderma

What Is Scleroderma?

Derived from the Greek words *sklerosis*, meaning hardness, and *derma*, meaning skin, scleroderma literally means hard skin. Although it is often referred to as if it were a single disease, scleroderma is really a symptom of a group of diseases that involve the abnormal growth of connective tissue, which supports the skin and internal organs. It is sometimes used, therefore, as an umbrella term for these disorders. In some forms of scleroderma, hard, tight skin is the extent of this abnormal process. In other forms, however, the problem goes much deeper, affecting blood vessels and internal organs, such as the heart, lungs, and kidneys.

Scleroderma is called both a rheumatic (roo-MA-tik) disease and a connective tissue disease. The term *rheumatic disease* refers to a group of conditions characterized by inflammation or pain in the muscles, joints, or fibrous tissue. A connective tissue disease is one that affects tissues such as skin, tendons, and cartilage.

About This Chapter: Text in this chapter is from "Scleroderma," National Institute of Arthritis and Musculoskeletal and Skin Diseases, July 2006. Brand names included in this chapter are provided as examples only, and their inclusion does not mean that these products are endorsed by the National Institutes of Health or any other government agency. Also, if a particular brand name is not mentioned, this does not mean or imply that the product is unsatisfactory.

What Are The Different Types Of Scleroderma?

The group of diseases we call scleroderma fall into two main classes: localized scleroderma and systemic sclerosis. (Localized diseases affect only certain parts of the body; systemic diseases can affect the whole body.) Both groups include subgroups. Although there are different ways these groups and subgroups may be broken down or referred to (and your doctor may use different terms from what you see here), the following is a common way of classifying these diseases:

Localized Scleroderma: Localized scleroderma has two subgroups: morphea and linea.

Systemic Scleroderma: Systemic scleroderma has three subgroups: limited, diffuse, and sine.

Localized Scleroderma

Localized types of scleroderma are those limited to the skin and related tissues and, in some cases, the muscle below. Internal organs are not affected by localized scleroderma, and localized scleroderma can never progress to the systemic form of the disease. Often, localized conditions improve or go away on their own over time, but the skin changes and damage that occur when the disease is active can be permanent. For some people, localized scleroderma is serious and disabling.

There are two generally recognized types of localized scleroderma:

Morphea: Morphea (mor-FEE-ah) comes from a Greek word that means "form" or "structure." The word refers to local patches of scleroderma. The first signs of the disease are reddish patches of skin that thicken into firm, oval-shaped areas. The center of each patch becomes ivory colored with violet borders. These patches sweat very little and have little hair growth. Patches appear most often on the chest, stomach, and back. Sometimes they appear on the face, arms, and legs.

Morphea can be either localized or generalized. Localized morphea limits itself to one or several patches, ranging in size from a half-inch to 12 inches in diameter. The condition sometimes appears on areas treated by radiation therapy. Some people have both morphea and linear scleroderma. The disease is referred to as generalized morphea when the skin patches become very hard and dark and spread over larger areas of the body. Regardless of the type, morphea generally fades out in three to five years; however, people are often left with darkened skin patches and, in rare cases, muscle weakness.

Linear Scleroderma: As suggested by its name, the disease is characterized by a single line or band of thickened or abnormally colored skin. Usually, the line runs down an arm or leg, but in some people it runs down the forehead. People sometimes use the French term *en coup de sabre*, or "sword stroke," to describe this highly visible line.

Systemic Scleroderma (Also Known As Systemic Sclerosis)

This is the term for the form of the disease that not only includes the skin, but also involves the tissues beneath, the blood vessels, and the major organs. Systemic sclerosis is typically broken down into limited cutaneous scleroderma and diffuse cutaneous scleroderma. Some doctors break systemic sclerosis down into a third subset called systemic sclerosis sine (SEEN-ay, Latin for "without") scleroderma. This means that patients have other manifestations of scleroderma but they do not have any overt skin thickening.

Limited Cutaneous Scleroderma: Limited cutaneous scleroderma typically comes on gradually and affects the skin only in certain areas: the fingers, hands, face, lower arms, and legs. Most people with limited disease have Raynaud's phenomenon for years before skin thickening starts. Telangiectasia and calcinosis often follow. Gastrointestinal involvement occurs commonly, and some patients have severe lung problems, even though the skin thickening remains limited. People with limited disease often have all or some of the symptoms that some doctors call CREST, which stands for the following:

- **Calcinosis (KAL-sin-OH-sis):** The formation of calcium deposits in the connective tissues, which can be detected by x-ray. These deposits are typically found on the fingers, hands, face, and trunk and on the skin above elbows and knees. When the deposits break through the skin, painful ulcers can result.

- **Raynaud's (ray-NOHZ) Phenomenon:** A condition in which the small blood vessels of the hands or feet contract in response to cold or anxiety. As the vessels contract, the hands or feet turn white and cold, then blue. As blood flow returns, they become red. Fingertip tissues may suffer damage, leading to ulcers, scars, or gangrene.

- **Esophageal (eh-SOFF-uh-GEE-ul) Dysfunction:** Impaired function of the esophagus (the tube connecting the throat and the stomach) that occurs when smooth muscles in the esophagus lose normal movement. In the upper and lower esophagus, the result can be swallowing difficulties. In the lower esophagus, the result can be chronic heartburn or inflammation.

- **Sclerodactyly (SKLER-oh-DAK-till-ee):** Thick and tight skin on the fingers, resulting from deposits of excess collagen within skin layers. The condition makes it harder to bend or straighten the fingers. The skin may also appear shiny and darkened, with hair loss.

- **Telangiectasia (tel-AN-jee-ek-TAY-zee-uhs):** A condition caused by the swelling of tiny blood vessels, in which small red spots appear on the hands and face. Although not painful, these red spots can create cosmetic problems.

Diffuse Cutaneous Scleroderma: This condition typically comes on suddenly. Skin thickening begins in the hands and spreads quickly and over much of the body, affecting the hands, face, upper arms, upper legs, chest, and stomach in a symmetrical fashion (for example, if one arm or one side of the trunk is affected, the other is also affected). Some people may have more area of their skin affected than others. Internally, this condition can damage key organs such as the intestines, lungs, heart, and kidneys.

People with diffuse disease often are tired, lose appetite and weight, and have joint swelling or pain. Skin changes can cause the skin to swell, appear shiny, and feel tight and itchy.

The damage of diffuse scleroderma typically occurs over a few years. After the first three to five years, people with diffuse disease often enter a stable phase lasting for varying lengths of time. During this phase, symptoms subside:

joint pain eases, fatigue lessens, and appetite returns. Progressive skin thickening and organ damage decrease.

Gradually, however, the skin may begin to soften, which tends to occur in reverse order of the thickening process: the last areas thickened are the first to begin softening. Some patients' skin returns to a somewhat normal state, while other patients are left with thin, fragile skin without hair or sweat glands. Serious new damage to the heart, lungs, or kidneys is unlikely to occur, although patients are left with whatever damage they have in specific organs.

People with diffuse scleroderma face the most serious long-term outlook if they develop severe kidney, lung, digestive, or heart problems. Fortunately, less than one-third of patients with diffuse disease develop these severe problems. Early diagnosis and continual and careful monitoring are important.

Who Gets Scleroderma?

Although scleroderma is more common in women, the disease also occurs in men and children. It affects people of all races and ethnic groups. However, there are some patterns by disease type. For example:

- Localized forms of scleroderma are more common in people of European descent than in African Americans. Morphea usually appears between the ages of 20 and 40, and linear scleroderma usually occurs in children or teenagers.

- Systemic scleroderma, whether limited or diffuse, typically occurs in people from 30 to 50 years old. It affects more women of African American than European descent.

Because scleroderma can be hard to diagnose and it overlaps with or resembles other diseases, scientists can only estimate how many cases there actually are. Estimates for the number of people in the United States with systemic sclerosis range from 40,000 to 165,000. By contrast, a survey that included all scleroderma-related disorders, including Raynaud's phenomenon, suggested a number between 250,000 and 992,500.

✤ **It's A Fact!!**

What causes scleroderma?

Although scientists don't know exactly what causes scleroderma, they are certain that people cannot catch it from or transmit it to others. Studies of twins suggest it is also not inherited.

Scientists suspect that scleroderma comes from several factors that may include:

- **Abnormal Immune Or Inflammatory Activity:** Like many other rheumatic disorders, scleroderma is believed to be an autoimmune disease. An autoimmune disease is one in which the immune system, for unknown reasons, turns against one's own body.

  In scleroderma, the immune system is thought to stimulate cells called fibroblasts so they produce too much collagen. The collagen forms thick connective tissue that builds up within the skin and internal organs and can interfere with their functioning. Blood vessels and joints can also be affected.

- **Genetic Makeup:** Although genes seem to put certain people at risk for scleroderma and play a role in its course, the disease is not passed from parent to child like some genetic diseases.

- **Environmental Triggers:** Research suggests that exposure to some environmental factors may trigger scleroderma-like disease (which is not actually scleroderma) in people who are genetically predisposed to it. Suspected triggers include viral infections, certain adhesive and coating materials, and organic solvents such as vinyl chloride or trichloroethylene. But no environmental agent has been shown to cause scleroderma. In the past, some people believed that silicone breast implants might have been a factor in developing connective tissue diseases such as scleroderma. But several studies have not shown evidence of a connection.

- **Hormones:** By the middle to late childbearing years (age 30 to 55), women develop scleroderma seven to 12 times more often than men. Because of female predominance at these and all ages, scientists suspect that hormonal differences between women and men play a part in the disease. However, the role of estrogen or other female hormones has not been proven.

For some people, scleroderma (particularly the localized forms) is fairly mild and resolves with time. But for others, living with the disease and its effects day to day has a significant impact on their quality of life.

How Is Scleroderma Diagnosed?

Depending on your particular symptoms, a diagnosis of scleroderma may be made by a general internist, a dermatologist (a doctor who specializes in treating diseases of the skin, hair, and nails), an orthopedist (a doctor who treats bone and joint disorders), a pulmonologist (a lung specialist), or a rheumatologist (a doctor specializing in treatment of musculoskeletal disorders and rheumatic diseases). A diagnosis of scleroderma is based largely on the medical history and findings from the physical exam. To make a diagnosis, your doctor will ask you a lot of questions about what has happened to you over time and about any symptoms you may be experiencing. Are you having a problem with heartburn or swallowing? Are you often tired or achy? Do your hands turn white in response to anxiety or cold temperatures?

Once your doctor has taken a thorough medical history, he or she will perform a physical exam. Finding one or more of the following factors can help the doctor diagnose a certain form of scleroderma:

- Changed skin appearance and texture, including swollen fingers and hands and tight skin around the hands, face, mouth, or elsewhere
- Calcium deposits developing under the skin
- Changes in the tiny blood vessels (capillaries) at the base of the fingernails
- Thickened skin patches

Finally, your doctor may order lab tests to help confirm a suspected diagnosis. In some cases, your doctor may order a skin biopsy (the surgical removal of a small sample of skin for microscopic examination) to aid in or help confirm a diagnosis. However, skin biopsies also have their limitations: biopsy results cannot distinguish between localized and systemic disease, for example.

Diagnosing scleroderma is easiest when a person has typical symptoms and rapid skin thickening. In other cases, a diagnosis may take months, or even years, as the disease unfolds and reveals itself and as the doctor is able to rule out some other potential causes of the symptoms. In some cases, a diagnosis is never made, because the symptoms that prompted the visit to the doctor go away on their own.

Some patients have some symptoms related to scleroderma and may fit into one of the following groups:

Undifferentiated Connective Tissue Disease (UCTD): This is a term for patients who have some signs and symptoms of various related diseases, but not enough symptoms of any one disease to make a definitive diagnosis. In other words, their condition hasn't "differentiated" into a particular connective tissue disease. In time, UCTD can go in one of three directions: it can change into a systemic disease such as systemic sclerosis, systemic lupus erythematosus, or rheumatoid arthritis; it can remain undifferentiated; or it can improve spontaneously.

Overlap Syndromes: This is a disease combination in which patients have symptoms and lab findings characteristic of two or more conditions.

What Other Conditions Can Look Like Scleroderma?

A number of other diseases have symptoms similar to those seen in scleroderma. Here are some of the most common scleroderma "look-alikes."

Eosinophilic Fasciitis (EF): This disease involves the fascia (FA-shuh), the thin connective tissue around the muscles, particularly those of the forearms, arms, legs, and trunk. EF causes the muscles to become encased in collagen, the fibrous protein that makes up tissue such as the skin and tendons. Permanent shortening of the muscles and tendons, called contractures, may develop, sometimes

☞ Remember!!

An explanation of most of these other diseases is beyond the scope of this chapter. What's important to understand, however, is that diagnosing scleroderma isn't always easy, and it may take time for you and your doctor to do this. While having a definite diagnosis may be helpful, you do not need to know the precise form of your disease to receive proper treatment.

causing disfigurement and problems with joint motion and function. EF may begin after hard physical exertion. The disease usually fades away after several years, but people sometimes have relapses. Although the upper layers of the skin are not thickened in EF, the thickened fascia may cause the skin to look somewhat like the tight, hard skin of scleroderma. A skin biopsy easily distinguishes between the two diseases.

Skin Thickening On The Fingers And Hands: This also appears with diabetes, mycosis fungoides, amyloidosis, and adult celiac disease. It can also result from hand trauma.

Generalized Scleroderma-Like Skin Thickening: This may occur with scleromyxedema, graft-versus-host disease, porphyria cutanea tarda, and human adjuvant disease.

Internal Organ Damage: Similar to that seen in systemic sclerosis, this may instead be related to primary pulmonary hypertension, idiopathic pulmonary fibrosis, or collagenous colitis.

Raynaud's Phenomenon: This condition also appears with atherosclerosis or systemic lupus erythematosus or in the absence of underlying disease.

How Is Scleroderma Treated?

Because scleroderma can affect many different organs and organ systems, you may have several different doctors involved in your care. Typically, care will be managed by a rheumatologist (a doctor specializing in treatment of musculoskeletal disorders and rheumatic diseases). Your rheumatologist may refer you to other specialists, depending on the specific problems you are having. For example, you may see a dermatologist for the treatment of skin symptoms, a nephrologist for kidney complications, a cardiologist for heart complications, a gastroenterologist for problems of the digestive tract, and a pulmonary specialist for lung involvement.

In addition to doctors, professionals such as nurse practitioners, physician assistants, physical or occupational therapists, psychologists, and social workers may play a role in your care. Dentists, orthodontists, and even speech therapists can treat oral complications that arise from thickening of tissues in and around the mouth and on the face.

Currently, there is no treatment that controls or stops the underlying problem—the overproduction of collagen—in all forms of scleroderma. Thus, treatment and management focus on relieving symptoms and limiting damage. Your treatment will depend on the particular problems you are having. Some treatments will be prescribed or given by your doctor. Others are things you can do on your own.

Here is a listing of the potential problems that can occur in systemic scleroderma and the medical and nonmedical treatments for them. These problems do not occur as a result or complication of localized scleroderma. This listing is not complete because different people experience different problems with scleroderma and not all treatments work equally well for all people. Work with your doctor to find the best treatment for your specific symptoms.

Raynaud's Phenomenon: More than 90 percent of people with scleroderma have this condition, in which the fingers and sometimes other extremities change color in response to cold temperature or anxiety. For many, Raynaud's phenomenon precedes other manifestations of the disease. In other people, however, Raynaud's phenomenon is unrelated to scleroderma, but may signal damage to the blood vessels supplying the hands arising from occupational injuries (from using jackhammers, for example), trauma, excessive smoking, circulatory problems, drug use, or exposure to toxic substances. For some people, cold fingers and toes are the extent of the problem and are little more than a nuisance. For others, the condition can worsen and lead to puffy fingers, finger ulcers, and other complications that require aggressive treatment.

If you have Raynaud's phenomenon, the following measures may make you more comfortable and help prevent problems:

- Don't smoke. Smoking narrows the blood vessels even more and makes Raynaud's phenomenon worse.
- Dress warmly, with special attention to hands and feet. Dress in layers and try to stay indoors during cold weather.

- Use biofeedback, which governs various body processes that are not normally thought of as being under conscious control, and relaxation exercises.

- For severe cases, speak to your doctor about prescribing drugs called calcium channel blockers, such as nifedipine (Procardia), which can open up small blood vessels and improve circulation. Other drugs are in development and may become available.

- If Raynaud's phenomenon leads to skin sores or ulcers, increasing your dose of calcium channel blockers (under the direction of your doctor **only**) may help. You can also protect skin ulcers from further injury or infection by applying nitroglycerin paste or antibiotic cream. Severe ulcerations on the fingertips can be treated with bioengineered skin.

Stiff, Painful Joints: In diffuse systemic sclerosis, hand joints can stiffen due to hardened skin around the joints or inflammation within them. Other joints can also become stiff and swollen.

- Stretching exercises under the direction of a physical or occupational therapist are extremely important to prevent loss of joint motion. These should be started as soon as scleroderma is diagnosed.

- Exercise regularly. Ask your doctor or physical therapist about an exercise plan that will help you increase and maintain range of motion in affected joints. Swimming can help maintain muscle strength, flexibility, and joint mobility.

- Use acetaminophen or an over-the-counter or prescription nonsteroidal anti-inflammatory drug, as recommended by your doctor, to help relieve joint or muscle pain. If pain is severe, speak to a rheumatologist about the possibility of prescription-strength drugs to ease pain and inflammation.

- Learn to do things in a new way. A physical or occupational therapist can help you learn to perform daily tasks, such as lifting and carrying objects or opening doors, in ways that will put less stress on tender joints.

Skin Problems: When too much collagen builds up in the skin, it crowds out sweat and oil glands, causing the skin to become dry and stiff. If your skin is affected, try the following:

- Apply oil-based creams and lotions frequently, and always right after bathing.

- Apply sunscreen before you venture outdoors to protect against further damage from the sun's rays.

- Use humidifiers to moisten the air in your home in colder winter climates. Clean humidifiers often to stop bacteria from growing in the water.

- Avoid very hot baths and showers, as hot water dries the skin.

- Avoid harsh soaps, household cleaners, and caustic chemicals, if at all possible. Otherwise, be sure to wear rubber gloves when you use such products.

- Exercise regularly. Exercise, especially swimming, stimulates blood circulation to affected areas.

Dry Mouth And Dental Problems: Dental problems are common in people with scleroderma for a number of reasons. Tightening facial skin can make the mouth opening smaller and narrower, which makes it hard to care for teeth; dry mouth due to salivary gland damage speeds up tooth decay; and damage to connective tissues in the mouth can lead to loose teeth. You can avoid tooth and gum problems in several ways:

- Brush and floss your teeth regularly. If hand pain and stiffness make this difficult, consult your doctor or an occupational therapist about specially made toothbrush handles and devices to make flossing easier.

- Have regular dental checkups. Contact your dentist immediately if you experience mouth sores, mouth pain, or loose teeth.

- If decay is a problem, ask your dentist about fluoride rinses or prescription toothpastes that remineralize and harden tooth enamel.

- Consult a physical therapist about facial exercises to help keep your mouth and face more flexible.

- Keep your mouth moist by drinking plenty of water, sucking ice chips, using sugarless gum and hard candy, and avoiding mouthwashes with alcohol. If dry mouth still bothers you, ask your doctor about a saliva substitute—or prescription medications such as pilocarpine hydrochloride (Salagen) or cevimeline hydrochloride (Evoxac)—that can stimulate the flow of saliva.

Gastrointestinal (GI) Problems: Systemic sclerosis can affect any part of the digestive system. As a result, you may experience problems such as heartburn, difficulty swallowing, early satiety (the feeling of being full after you've barely started eating), or intestinal complaints such as diarrhea, constipation, and gas. In cases where the intestines are damaged, your body may have difficulty absorbing nutrients from food. Although gastrointestinal problems are diverse, here are some things that might help at least some of the problems you have:

- Eat small, frequent meals.

- To keep stomach contents from backing up into the esophagus, stand or sit for at least an hour (preferably two or three hours) after eating. When it is time to sleep, keep the head of your bed raised using blocks.

- Avoid late-night meals, spicy or fatty foods, alcohol, and caffeine, which can aggravate gastrointestinal distress.

- Eat moist, soft foods, and chew them well. If you have difficulty swallowing or if your body doesn't absorb nutrients properly, your doctor may prescribe a special diet.

- Ask your doctor about prescription medications for problems such as diarrhea, constipation, and heartburn. Some drugs called proton pump inhibitors are highly effective against heartburn. Oral antibiotics may stop bacterial overgrowth in the bowel, which can be a cause of diarrhea in some people with systemic sclerosis.

Lung Damage: Virtually all people with systemic sclerosis have some loss of lung function. Some develop severe lung disease, which comes in two forms: pulmonary fibrosis (hardening or scarring of lung tissue because of excess collagen) and pulmonary hypertension (high blood pressure in the artery that carries blood from the heart to the lungs). Treatment for the two conditions is different:

- Pulmonary fibrosis may be treated with drugs that suppress the immune system, such as cyclophosphamide (Cytoxan) or azathioprine (Imuran), along with low doses of corticosteroids.

- Pulmonary hypertension may be treated with drugs that dilate the blood vessels, such as prostacyclin (Iloprost), or with newer medications that are prescribed specifically for treating pulmonary hypertension.

Regardless of your particular lung problem or its medical treatment, your role in the treatment process is essentially the same. To minimize lung complications, work closely with your medical team. Do the following:

- Watch for signs of lung disease, including fatigue, shortness of breath or difficulty breathing, and swollen feet. Report these symptoms to your doctor.

- Have your lungs closely checked, using standard lung-function tests, during the early stages of skin thickening. These tests, which can find problems at the earliest and most treatable stages, are needed because lung damage can occur even before you notice any symptoms.

- Get regular flu and pneumonia vaccines as recommended by your doctor. Contracting either illness could be dangerous for a person with lung disease.

Heart Problems: Common among people with scleroderma, heart problems include scarring and weakening of the heart (cardiomyopathy), inflamed heart muscle (myocarditis), and abnormal heartbeat (arrhythmia). All of these problems can be treated. Treatment ranges from drugs to surgery and varies depending on the nature of the condition.

Kidney Problems: Renal crisis occurs in about 10 percent of all patients with scleroderma, primarily those with early diffuse scleroderma. Renal crisis results in severe uncontrolled high blood pressure, which can quickly lead to kidney failure. It's very important that you take measures to identify and treat the hypertension as soon as it occurs. These are things you can do:

- Check your blood pressure regularly. You should also check it if you have any new or different symptoms such as a headache or shortness of breath. If your blood pressure is higher than usual, call your doctor right away.

- If you have kidney problems, take your prescribed medications faithfully. In the past two decades, drugs known as ACE (angiotensin-converting enzyme) inhibitors, including captopril (Capoten), enalapril (Vasotec), and lisinopril, have made scleroderma-related kidney failure a less threatening problem than it used to be. But for these drugs to work, you must take them as soon as the hypertension is present.

Cosmetic Problems: Even if scleroderma doesn't cause any lasting physical disability, its effects on the skin's appearance—particularly on the face—can take their toll on your self-esteem. Fortunately, there are procedures to correct some of the cosmetic problems scleroderma causes:

- The appearance of telangiectasias—small red spots on the hands and face caused by swelling of tiny blood vessels beneath the skin—may be reduced or even eliminated with the use of guided lasers.

- Facial changes of localized scleroderma—such as the *en coup de sabre* that may run down the forehead in people with linear scleroderma—may be corrected through cosmetic surgery. (However, such surgery is not appropriate for areas of the skin where the disease is active.)

How Can Scleroderma Affect My Life?

Having a chronic disease can affect almost every aspect of your life, from family relationships to holding a job. For people with scleroderma, there may be other concerns about appearance or even the ability to dress, bathe, or handle the most basic daily tasks. Here are some areas in which scleroderma could intrude.

Appearance And Self-Esteem: Aside from the initial concerns about health and longevity, people with scleroderma quickly become concerned with how the disease will affect their appearance. Thick, hardened skin can be difficult to accept, particularly on the face. Systemic scleroderma may result in facial changes that eventually cause the opening to the mouth to become smaller and the upper lip to virtually disappear. Linear scleroderma may leave its mark on the forehead. Although these problems can't always be prevented, their effects may be minimized with proper treatment. Also, special cosmetics—and in some cases plastic surgery—can help conceal scleroderma's damage.

Caring For Yourself: Tight, hard connective tissue in the hands can make it difficult to do what were once simple tasks, such as brushing your teeth and hair, pouring a cup of coffee, using a knife and fork, unlocking a door, or buttoning a jacket. If you have trouble using your hands, consult an occupational therapist, who can recommend new ways of doing things or devices to make tasks easier. Devices as simple as Velcro fasteners and built-up brush handles can help you be more independent.

Family Relationships: Spouses, children, parents, and siblings may have trouble understanding why you don't have the energy to keep house, drive to soccer practice, prepare meals, or hold a job the way you used to. If your condition isn't that visible, they may even suggest you are just being lazy. On the other hand, they may be overly concerned and eager to help you, not allowing you to do the things you are able to do or giving up their own interests and activities to be with you. It's important to learn as much about your form of the disease as you can and to share any information you have with your family. Involving them in counseling or a support group may also help them better understand the disease and how they can help you.

Sexual Relations: Sexual relationships can be affected when systemic scleroderma enters the picture. For men, the disease's effects on the blood vessels can lead to problems achieving an erection. For women, damage to the moisture-producing glands can cause vaginal dryness that makes intercourse painful. People of either sex may find they have difficulty moving the way they once did. They may be self-conscious about their appearance or afraid that their sexual partner will no longer find them attractive. With communication between partners, good medical care, and perhaps counseling, many of these changes can be overcome or at least worked around.

Pregnancy And Childbearing: In the past, women with systemic scleroderma were often advised not to have children. But thanks to better medical treatments and a better understanding of the disease itself, that advice is changing. (Pregnancy, for example, is not likely to be a problem for women with localized scleroderma.) Although blood vessel involvement in the placenta may cause babies of women with systemic scleroderma to be born early, many women with the disease can have safe pregnancies and healthy babies if they follow some precautions.

One of the most important pieces of advice is to wait a few years after the disease starts before attempting a pregnancy. During the first three years, you are at the highest risk of developing severe problems of the heart, lungs, or kidneys that could be harmful to you and your unborn baby.

If you haven't developed severe organ problems within three years of the disease's onset, your chances of such problems are less and pregnancy would be safer. But it is important to have both your disease and your pregnancy monitored regularly. You'll probably need to stay in close touch with both the doctor you typically see for your scleroderma and an obstetrician who is experienced in guiding high-risk pregnancies.

Chapter 46

Shingles

Shingles, also known as *herpes zoster*, is a disease that affects an estimated two in every 10 people in their lifetime. This year, more than 500,000 people will develop shingles.

Although it is most common in people over age 50, if you have had chicken pox, you are at risk for developing shingles. Shingles is also more common in people with weakened immune systems from HIV infection, chemotherapy or radiation treatment, transplant operations, and stress.

Symptoms: Early signs of shingles include burning or shooting pain and tingling or itching generally located on one side of the body or face. The pain can be severe. Rash or blisters are present anywhere from one to 14 days.

Diagnosis: You should go to your health care provider if you develop a rash. By looking at the rash, your health care provider can tell whether you have shingles and start you on treatment if you do.

Treatment: There is no cure for shingles, but the severity and duration of an attack of shingles can be significantly reduced if you are treated immediately with antiviral medicines. These medicines include acyclovir, valacyclovir, or famciclovir.

About This Chapter: Text in this chapter is from "Shingles," National Institute of Allergy and Infectious Diseases, October 2007.

Prevention: The Centers for Disease Control and Prevention recommends that adults 60 years of age and older get a single dose of the shingles vaccine (called Zostavax) even if they have had a prior episode of shingles.

> ♣ **It's A Fact!!**
> **What Causes Shingles?**
>
> Shingles is a disease caused by the varicella-zoster virus, the same virus that causes chicken pox. After an attack of chicken pox, the virus lies dormant in the nerve tissue. As we get older, it is possible for the virus to reappear in the form of shingles.

Health experts estimate the vaccine could prevent 250,000 cases of shingles that occur in the United States each year and significantly reduce the severity of the disease in another 250,000 cases annually.

Complications: According to the Centers for Disease Control and Prevention, among those who get shingles, more than one-third will develop serious complications. The risk of complications rises after 60 years of age.

If shingles appears on your face, it can lead to complications in your hearing and vision. For instance, if shingles affects your eye, the cornea can become infected and lead to temporary or permanent blindness.

Another complication of the virus is postherpetic neuralgia (PHN), a condition where the pain from shingles persists for months, sometimes years, after the shingles rash has healed.

Research: The National Institute of Allergy and Infectious Diseases, National Institute of Neurological Disorders and Stroke, and other institutes of the National Institutes of Health (NIH) conduct shingles research in NIH laboratories and support additional research through grants to major medical institutions across the country. Currently, researchers are trying to find new methods for treating shingles and its complications.

Chapter 47

Swimmer's Itch

What is swimmer's itch?

Swimmer's itch, also called *cercarial dermatitis*, appears as a skin rash caused by an allergic reaction to certain parasites that infect some birds and mammals. These microscopic parasites are released from infected snails into fresh and salt water (such as lakes, ponds, and oceans). While the parasite's preferred host is the specific bird or mammal, if the parasite comes into contact with a swimmer, it burrows into the skin causing an allergic reaction and rash. Swimmer's itch is found throughout the world and is more frequent during summer months.

How does water become infested with the parasite?

The adult parasite lives in the blood of infected animals such as ducks, geese, gulls, swans, and certain aquatic mammals such as muskrats and beavers. The parasites produce eggs that are passed in the feces of infected birds or mammals.

If the eggs land in or are washed into the water, the eggs hatch, releasing small, free-swimming larvae. These larvae swim in the water in search of a certain species of aquatic snail.

About This Chapter: Text in this chapter is from "Swimmer's Itch (Cercarial Dermatitis)," Centers for Disease Control and Prevention, Division of Parasitic Diseases, September 2008. The use of trade names is for identification only and does not imply endorsement by the Public Health Service or by the U.S. Department of Health and Human Services.

If the larvae find one of these snails, they infect the snail, multiply and undergo further development. Infected snails release a different type of larvae (or cercariae, hence the name cercarial dermatitis) into the water. This larval form then swims about searching for a suitable host (bird, muskrat) to continue the life cycle. Although humans are not suitable hosts, the larvae burrow into the swimmer's skin, and may cause an allergic reaction and rash. Because these larvae cannot develop inside a human, they soon die.

What are the signs and symptoms of swimmer's itch?

Within minutes to days after swimming in contaminated water, you may experience tingling, burning, or itching of the skin. Small reddish pimples appear within twelve hours. Pimples may develop into small blisters. Scratching the areas may result in secondary bacterial infections. Itching may last up to a week or more, but will gradually go away.

☞ **Remember!!**

Symptoms of swimmer's itch may include the following:

- Tingling, burning, or itching of the skin
- Small reddish pimples
- Small blisters

Because swimmer's itch is caused by an allergic reaction to infection, the more often you swim or wade in contaminated water, the more likely you are to develop more serious symptoms. The greater the number of exposures to contaminated water, the more intense and immediate symptoms of swimmer's itch will be.

Be aware that swimmer's itch is not the only rash that may occur after swimming in fresh or salt water.

Do I need to see my health care provider for treatment?

Most cases of swimmer's itch do not require medical attention. If you have a rash, you may try the following remedies for relief:

- Use corticosteroid cream

- Apply cool compresses to the affected areas

- Bathe in Epson salts or baking soda

- Soak in colloidal oatmeal baths or use of lotions such as Aveeno

- Apply baking soda paste to the rash (made by stirring water into baking soda until it reaches a paste-like consistency)

- Use an anti-itch lotion, such as Calamine lotion

Though difficult, try not to scratch. Scratching may cause the rash to become infected. If itching is severe, your health care provider may suggest prescription-strength lotions or creams to lessen your symptoms.

Who is at risk for swimmer's itch?

Anyone who swims or wades in infested water may be at risk. Larvae are more likely to be present in shallow water by the shoreline. Children are most often affected because they tend to swim, wade, and play in the shallow water more than adults. Also, they are less likely to towel dry themselves when leaving the water.

Once an outbreak of swimmer's itch has occurred in water, will the water be unsafe?

No. Many factors must be present for swimmer's itch to become a problem in water. Since these factors change (sometimes within a swim season), swimmer's itch will not always be a problem. However, there is no way to know how long water may be unsafe. Larvae generally survive for 24 hours

♣ **It's A Fact!!**
Can swimmer's itch be spread from person-to-person?

Swimmer's itch is not contagious and cannot be spread from one person to another.

✔ **Quick Tip**

Try these tips to reduce the likelihood of developing swimmer's itch:

1. Do not swim in areas where swimmer's itch is a known problem or where signs have been posted warning of unsafe water.

2. Do not swim near or wade in marshy areas where snails are commonly found.

3. Towel dry or shower immediately after leaving the water.

4. Do not attract birds (e.g., by feeding them) to areas where people are swimming.

5. Encourage health officials to post signs on shorelines where swimmer's itch is a current problem.

For further information on protecting yourself from recreational water illnesses, please visit http://www.cdc.gov/healthyswimming/index.htm

once they are released from the snail. However, an infected snail will continue to produce cercariae throughout the remainder of its life. For future snails to become infected, migratory birds or mammals in the area must also be infected so the life cycle can continue.

Is it safe to swim in my swimming pool?

Yes. As long as your swimming pool is well maintained and chlorinated, there is no risk of swimmer's itch. The appropriate snails must be present in order for swimmer's itch to occur.

Chapter 48

Tinea Infections: Athlete's Foot, Jock Itch, And Ringworm

What is tinea?

Tinea is a fungus that can grow on your skin, hair, or nails. As it grows, it spreads out in a circle, leaving normal-looking skin in the middle. This makes it look like a ring. At the edge of the ring, the skin is lifted up by the irritation and looks red and scaly. To some people, the infection looks like a worm is under the skin. Because of the way it looks, tinea infection is often called *ringworm*. However, there really isn't a worm under the skin.

How did I get a fungal infection?

You can get a fungal infection by touching a person who has one. Some kinds of fungi live on damp surfaces, like the floors in public showers or locker rooms. You can easily pick up a fungus there. You can even catch a fungal infection from your pets. Dogs and cats, as well as farm animals, can be infected with a fungus. Often this infection looks like a patch of skin where fur is missing.

What areas of the body are affected by tinea infections?

Fungal infections are named for the part of the body they infect. *Tinea corporis* is a fungal infection of the skin on the body. (*Corporis* is the Latin word for body.) If you have this infection, you may see small, red spots that grow into large rings almost anywhere on your arms, legs, or chest.

Tinea pedis is usually called "athlete's foot." (*Pedis* is the Latin word for foot.) The moist skin between your toes is a perfect place for a fungus to grow. The skin may become itchy and red, with a white, wet surface. The infection may spread to the toenails. (This is called *tinea unguium—unguium* comes from the Latin word for nail.) Here it causes the toenails to become thick and crumbly. It can also spread to your hands and fingernails.

When a fungus grows in the moist, warm area of the groin, the rash is called *tinea cruris*. (*Cruris* comes from the Latin for leg.) The common name for this infection is "jock itch." *Tinea cruris* generally occurs in men, especially if they often wear athletic equipment.

Tinea capitis, which is called "ringworm," causes itchy, red areas, usually on the head. (*Capitis* comes from the Latin for head.) The hair is destroyed, leaving bald patches. This tinea infection is most common in children.

How do I know if I have a fungal infection?

The best way to know for sure is to ask your doctor. Other skin problems can look just like a fungal infection but have very different treatments. To find out what is causing your rash, your doctor may scrape a small amount of the irritated skin onto a glass slide (or clip off a piece of nail or hair). Then he or she will

✎ What's It Mean?

Tinea Capitis: A fungal infection of the head. Also called ringworm.

Tinea Corporis: A fungal infection of the skin on the body.

Tinea Cruris: A fungal infection of the groin or leg. Also called jock itch.

Tinea Pedis: A fungal infection of the foot. Usually called athlete's foot.

Tinea Unguium: A fungal infection of the toenail or fingernail.

—KW

✔ **Quick Tip**

What can I do to prevent tinea infections?

Skin that is kept clean and dry is your best defense. However, you're also less likely to get a tinea infection if you do the following things:

- When you're at home, take your shoes off and expose your feet to the air.

- Change your socks and underwear every day, especially in warm weather.

- Dry your feet carefully (especially between the toes) after using a locker room or public shower.

- Avoid walking barefoot in public areas. Instead, wear flip-flops, sandals or water shoes.

- Don't wear thick clothing for long periods of time in warm weather. It will make you sweat more.

- Throw away worn-out exercise shoes. Never borrow other people's shoes.

- Check your pets for areas of hair loss. Ask your veterinarian to check them too. It's important to check pets carefully, because if you don't find out whether they're causing your fungal infection, you may get it again from them, even after treatment.

---

look at the skin, nail, or hair under a microscope. After doing this, your doctor will usually be able to tell if your skin problem is caused by a fungus.

Sometimes a piece of your skin, hair or nail will be sent to a lab to grow the fungus in a test tube. This is another way the lab can tell if your skin problem is caused by a fungus. They can also find out the exact type of fungus. This process takes a while because a fungus grows slowly.

How do I get rid of a tinea infection?

Once your doctor decides that you have a tinea infection, medicine can be used to get rid of it. You may only need to put a special cream on the rash for a few weeks. This is especially true for jock itch.

It can be harder to get rid of fungal infections on other parts of the body. Sometimes you have to take medicine by mouth. This medicine usually has to be taken for a long time, maybe even for months. Irritated skin takes time to heal. New hair or nails will have to grow back.

Some medicines can have unpleasant effects on the rest of your body, especially if you're also taking other medicines. There are some newer medicines that seem to work better with fewer side effects. You may need to have blood tests to make sure that your body is not having a bad reaction to the medicine.

Can tinea cause serious illness?

A fungus rarely spreads below the surface of the body to cause serious illness. Your body usually prevents this. However, people with weak immune systems, such as people with AIDS, may have a hard time getting well from a fungal infection.

Tinea infections usually don't leave scars after the fungus is gone. Sometimes, people don't even know they have a fungal infection and get better without any treatment.

Chapter 49

Vitiligo

What Is Vitiligo?

Vitiligo (pronounced vit-ill-EYE-go) is a pigmentation disorder in which melanocytes (the cells that make pigment) in the skin are destroyed. As a result, white patches appear on the skin in different parts of the body. Similar patches also appear on both the mucous membranes (tissues that line the inside of the mouth and nose), and the retina (inner layer of the eyeball). The hair that grows on areas affected by vitiligo sometimes turns white.

The cause of vitiligo is not known, but doctors and researchers have several different theories. There is strong evidence that people with vitiligo inherit a group of three genes that make them susceptible to depigmentation. The most widely accepted view is that the depigmentation occurs because vitiligo is an autoimmune disease—a disease in which a person's immune system reacts against the body's own organs or tissues. As such, people's bodies produce proteins called cytokines that alter their pigment-producing cells and

About This Chapter: Adapted from "Questions and Answers About Vitiligo," National Institute of Arthritis and Musculoskeletal and Skin Diseases (NIAMS), National Institutes of Health, Department of Health and Human Services, October 2006. Note: Brand names included in this chapter are provided as examples only, and their inclusion does not mean that these products are endorsed by the National Institutes of Health or any other government agency. Also, if a particular brand name is not mentioned, this does not mean or imply that the product is unsatisfactory.

cause these cells to die. Another theory is that melanocytes destroy themselves. Finally, some people have reported that a single event such as sunburn or emotional distress triggered vitiligo; however, these events have not been scientifically proven as causes of vitiligo.

Who Is Affected By Vitiligo?

About 0.5 to one percent of the world's population, or as many as 65 million people, have vitiligo. In the United States, one to two million people have the disorder. Half the people who have vitiligo develop it before age 20; most develop it before their 40th birthday. The disorder affects both sexes and all races equally; however, it is more noticeable in people with dark skin.

Vitiligo seems to be somewhat more common in people with certain autoimmune diseases. These autoimmune diseases include hyperthyroidism (an overactive thyroid gland), adrenocortical insufficiency (the adrenal gland does not produce enough of the hormone called corticosteroid), alopecia areata (patches of baldness), and pernicious anemia (a low level of red blood cells caused by the failure of the body to absorb vitamin B12). Scientists do not know the reason for the association between vitiligo and these autoimmune diseases. However, most people with vitiligo have no other autoimmune disease.

Vitiligo may also be hereditary; that is, it can run in families. Children whose parents have the disorder are more likely to develop vitiligo. In fact, 30 percent of people with vitiligo have a family member with the disease.

What's It Mean?

Antibodies: Protective proteins produced by the body's immune system to fight infectious agents (such as bacteria or viruses) or other "foreign" substances. Occasionally, antibodies develop that can attack a part of the body and cause an "autoimmune" disease. These antibodies are called autoantibodies.

Depigmentation: Loss of color in the skin, hair, mucous membranes, or retina of the eye.

Melanin: A yellow, brown, or black pigment that determines skin color. Melanin also acts as a sunscreen and protects the skin from ultraviolet light.

Pigmentation: Coloring of the skin, hair, mucous membranes, and retina of the eye.

—KW

However, only five to seven percent of children will get vitiligo even if a parent has it, and most people with vitiligo do not have a family history of the disorder.

What Are The Symptoms Of Vitiligo?

People who develop vitiligo usually first notice white patches (depigmentation) on their skin. These patches are more commonly found on sun-exposed areas of the body, including the hands, feet, arms, face, and lips. Other common areas for white patches to appear are the armpits and groin, and around the mouth, eyes, nostrils, navel, genitals, and rectal areas.

Vitiligo generally appears in one of three patterns:

- **Focal Pattern:** The depigmentation is limited to one or only a few areas

- **Segmental Pattern:** Depigmented patches develop on only one side of the body

- **Generalized Pattern:** Depigmentation occurs symmetrically on both sides of the body. This is the most common pattern.

In addition to white patches on the skin, people with vitiligo may have premature graying of the scalp hair, eyelashes, eyebrows, and beard. People with dark skin may notice a loss of color inside their mouths.

Will The Depigmented Patches Spread?

Focal pattern vitiligo and segmental vitiligo remain localized to one part of the body and do not spread. There is no way to predict if generalized vitiligo will spread. For some people, the depigmented patches do not spread. The disorder is usually progressive, however, and over time the white patches will spread to other areas of the body. For some people, vitiligo spreads slowly, over many years. For other people, spreading occurs rapidly. Some people have reported additional depigmentation following periods of physical or emotional stress.

How Is Vitiligo Diagnosed?

The diagnosis of vitiligo is made based on a physical examination, medical history, and laboratory tests.

A doctor will likely suspect vitiligo if the patient reports (or the physical examination reveals) white patches of skin on the body—particularly on sun-exposed areas, including the hands, feet, arms, face, and lips. If vitiligo is suspected, the doctor will ask about the patient's medical history. Important factors in the diagnosis include a family history of vitiligo; a rash, sunburn, or other skin trauma at the site of vitiligo two to three months before depigmentation started; stress or physical illness; and premature (before age 35) graying of the hair. In addition, the doctor will ask whether the patient or anyone in the patient's family has had any autoimmune diseases, and whether the patient is very sensitive to the sun.

To help confirm the diagnosis, the doctor may take a small sample (biopsy) of the affected skin to examine under a microscope. In vitiligo, the skin sample will usually show a complete absence of pigment-producing melanocytes. On the other hand, the presence of inflamed cells in the sample may suggest that another condition is responsible for the loss of pigmentation.

Because vitiligo may be associated with pernicious anemia (a condition in which an insufficient amount of vitamin B12 is absorbed from the gastrointestinal tract) or hyperthyroidism (an overactive thyroid gland), the doctor may also take a blood sample to check the blood-cell count and thyroid function. For some patients, the doctor may recommend an eye examination to check for uveitis (inflammation of part of the eye), which sometimes occurs with vitiligo. A blood test to look for the presence of antinuclear antibodies (a type of autoantibody) may also be done. This test helps determine if the patient has another autoimmune disease.

How Can People Cope With The Emotional And Psychological Aspects Of Vitiligo?

While vitiligo is usually not harmful medically, its emotional and psychological effects can be devastating. In fact, in India, women with the disease are sometimes discriminated against in marriage. Developing vitiligo after marriage can be grounds for divorce.

Regardless of a person's race and culture, white patches of vitiligo can affect emotional and psychological well-being and self-esteem. People with vitiligo can experience emotional stress, particularly if the condition develops on visible areas of the body, such as the face, hands, arms, and feet; or on the genitals. Adolescents, who are often particularly concerned about their appearance, can be devastated by widespread vitiligo. Some people who have vitiligo feel embarrassed, ashamed, depressed, or worried about how others will react.

Fortunately, there are several strategies to help people cope with vitiligo. Also, various treatments—which we will discuss a bit later—can minimize, camouflage, or, in some cases, even eliminate white patches. First, it is important to find a doctor who is knowledgeable about the disorder and takes it seriously. The doctor should also be a good listener and be able to provide emotional support. Patients must let their doctor know if they are feeling depressed, because doctors and other mental health professionals can help people deal with depression. Patients should also learn as much as possible about the disorder and treatment choices so that they can participate in making important decisions about medical care.

Talking with other people who have vitiligo may also help. The National Vitiligo Foundation can provide information about vitiligo and refer people to local chapters that have support groups of patients, families, and physicians. Family and friends are another source of support.

Some people with vitiligo have found that cosmetics that cover the white patches improve their appearance and help them feel better about themselves. A person may need to experiment with several brands of concealing cosmetics before finding the product that works best.

What Treatment Options Are Available?

The main goal of treating vitiligo is to improve appearance. Therapy for vitiligo takes a long time—it usually must be continued for six to 18 months. The choice of therapy depends on the number of white patches; their location, sizes, and how widespread they are; and what the patient prefers in terms of treatment. Each patient responds differently to therapy, and a particular treatment may not work for everyone. Current treatment options for vitiligo include medical, surgical, and adjunctive therapies (therapies that can be used along with surgical or medical treatments).

Medical Therapies

A number of medical therapies, most of which are applied topically, can reduce the appearance of white patches with vitiligo. The following are some of the most commonly used ones.

Topical Steroid Therapy: Steroid creams may be helpful in repigmenting (returning the color to) white patches, particularly if they are applied in the initial stages of the disease. Corticosteroids are a group of drugs similar to hormones such as cortisone, which are produced by the adrenal glands. Doctors often prescribe a mild topical corticosteroid cream for children under 10 years old and a stronger one for adults. Patients must apply the cream to the white patches on the skin for at least three months before seeing any results. Corticosteroid creams are the simplest and safest treatment for vitiligo, but are not as effective as psoralen photochemotherapy. Yet, like any medication, these creams can cause side effects. For this reason, the doctor will monitor the patient closely for skin shrinkage and skin striae (streaks or lines on the skin). These side effects are more likely to occur in areas where the skin is thin, such as on the face and armpits, or in the genital region. They can be minimized by using weaker formulations of steroid creams in these areas.

Psoralen Photochemotherapy: Psoralen photochemotherapy (also known as psoralen and ultraviolet A therapy, or PUVA therapy), is probably the most effective treatment for vitiligo available in the United States. The goal of PUVA therapy is to repigment the white patches. However, it is time-consuming, and care must be taken to avoid side effects, which can sometimes be severe. Psoralen is a drug that contains chemicals that react with ultraviolet light to cause darkening of the skin. The treatment involves taking psoralen by mouth (orally) or applying it to the skin (topically). This is followed by carefully timed exposure to sunlight or to ultraviolet A (UVA) light that comes from a special lamp. Typically, the patient will receive treatments in the doctor's office so they can be carefully watched for any side effects. Patients must minimize exposure to sunlight at other times.

Topical Psoralen Photochemotherapy: Topical psoralen photochemotherapy is often used for people with a small number of depigmented patches affecting a limited part of the body. It is also used for children two years old and older who have localized patches of vitiligo. Treatments are done in a doctor's office under artificial UVA light once or twice a week. The doctor or nurse applies a thin coat of psoralen to the patient's depigmented patches about 30 minutes before exposing them to enough UVA light to turn the affected area pink. The doctor usually increases the dose of UVA light slowly over many weeks. Eventually, the pink areas fade and a more normal skin color appears. After each treatment, the patient washes their skin with soap and water and applies a sunscreen before leaving the doctor's office.

There are two major potential side effects of topical PUVA therapy: severe sunburn and blistering, and too much repigmentation or darkening (hyperpigmentation) of the treated patches or the normal skin surrounding the vitiligo. Patients can minimize their chances of sunburn if they avoid exposure to direct sunlight after each treatment. Usually, hyperpigmentation is a temporary problem that eventually disappears when treatment is stopped.

Oral Psoralen Photochemotherapy: Oral PUVA therapy is used for people with extensive vitiligo (affecting more than 20 percent of the body) or for people who do not respond to topical PUVA therapy. Oral psoralen is not recommended for children under 10 years of age because it increases the risk of damage to the eyes caused by conditions such as cataracts. For oral PUVA therapy, the patient takes a prescribed dose of psoralen by mouth about two hours before exposure to artificial UVA light or sunlight. If artificial light is used, the doctor adjusts the dose of light until the skin in the areas being treated becomes pink. Treatments are usually given two or three times a week, but never two days in a row.

For patients who cannot go to a facility to receive PUVA therapy, the doctor may prescribe psoralen that can be used with natural sunlight exposure. The doctor will give you careful instructions on carrying out treatment at home and monitor you during scheduled checkups.

Known side effects of oral psoralen include sunburn, nausea and vomiting, itching, abnormal hair growth, and hyperpigmentation. Oral psoralen photochemotherapy may also increase the risk of skin cancer, although the risk is minimal at doses used for vitiligo. Patients undergoing oral PUVA therapy should apply sunscreen and avoid direct sunlight for 24 to 48 hours after each treatment to avoid sunburn and reduce the risk of skin cancer. To avoid eye damage, particularly cataracts, patients should also wear protective UVA sunglasses for 18 to 24 hours after each treatment.

Depigmentation: Depigmentation involves fading the rest of the skin on the body to match the areas that are already white. For people who have vitiligo on more than 50 percent of their bodies, depigmentation may be the best treatment option. Patients apply the drug monobenzylether of hydroquinone (monobenzone or Benoquin) twice a day to pigmented areas until they match the already-depigmented areas. Patients must avoid direct skin-to-skin contact with other people for at least two hours after applying the drug, as transfer of the drug may cause depigmentation of the other person's skin.

The major side effect of depigmentation therapy is inflammation (redness and swelling) of the skin. Patients may experience itching or dry skin. Depigmentation tends to be permanent and is not easily reversed. In addition, a person who undergoes depigmentation will always be unusually sensitive to sunlight.

Surgical Therapies

All surgical therapies must be considered only after proper medical therapy is provided. Surgical techniques are time-consuming and expensive and usually not paid for by insurance carriers. They are appropriate only for carefully selected patients who have vitiligo that has been stable for at least three years.

Autologous Skin Grafts: In an autologous (use of a person's own tissues) skin graft, the doctor removes skin from one area of your body and attaches it to another area. This type of skin grafting is sometimes used for patients with small patches of vitiligo. The doctor removes sections of the normal, pigmented skin (donor sites) and places them on the depigmented areas (recipient sites).

There are several possible complications of autologous skin grafting. Infections may occur at the donor or recipient sites. The recipient and donor sites may develop scarring, a cobblestone appearance, or a spotty pigmentation, or may fail to repigment at all. Treatment with grafting takes time and is costly, and many people find it neither acceptable nor affordable.

Skin Grafts Using Blisters: In this procedure, the doctor creates blisters on the patient's pigmented skin by using heat, suction, or freezing cold. The tops of the blisters are then cut out and transplanted to a depigmented skin area. The risks of blister grafting include scarring and lack of repigmentation. However, there is less risk of scarring with this procedure than with other types of grafting.

Micropigmentation (Tattooing): This procedure involves implanting pigment into the skin with a special surgical instrument. This procedure works best for the lip area, particularly in people with dark skin. However, it is difficult for the doctor to match perfectly the color of the skin of the surrounding area.

The tattooed area will not change in color when exposed to sun, while the surrounding normal skin will. So even if the tattooed area matches the surrounding skin perfectly at first, it may not later on. Tattooing tends to fade over time. In addition, tattooing of the lips may lead to episodes of blister outbreaks caused by the herpes simplex virus.

Autologous Melanocyte Transplants: In this procedure, the doctor takes a sample of the patient's normal pigmented skin and places it in a laboratory dish containing a special cell-culture solution to grow melanocytes. When the melanocytes in the culture solution have multiplied, the doctor transplants them to the patient's depigmented skin patches. This procedure is currently experimental and is impractical for the routine care of people with vitiligo. It is also very expensive, and its side effects are not known.

Additional Therapies

Sunscreens: People who have vitiligo, particularly those with fair skin, should minimize sun exposure and use a sunscreen that provides protection from both the UVA and UVB forms of ultraviolet light. Sunscreen helps protect the skin from sunburn and long-term damage. Sunscreen also minimizes tanning, which makes the contrast between normal and depigmented skin less noticeable.

Cosmetics: Some patients with vitiligo cover depigmented patches with stains, makeup, or self-tanning lotions. These cosmetic products can be particularly effective for people whose vitiligo is limited to exposed areas of the body.

Self-tanning lotions have an advantage over makeup in that the color will last for several days and will not come off with washing.

Counseling And Support Groups: Many people with vitiligo find it helpful to get counseling from a mental health professional. People often find they can talk to their counselor about issues that are difficult to discuss with anyone else. A mental health counselor can also offer support and help in coping with vitiligo. In addition, it may be helpful to attend a vitiligo support group.

What Research Is Being Done On Vitiligo?

In the past two decades, research on the role that melanocytes play in vitiligo has greatly increased. A variety of technical advances, such as gene mapping and cloning, have permitted relatively rapid advances in knowledge of melanocytes at the cellular and molecular levels.

Much of the research that holds promise for understanding, treating, and possibly preventing vitiligo is supported by the National Institute of Arthritis and Musculoskeletal and Skin Diseases. NIAMS is currently supporting research that includes the following areas:

- Examination of the mechanism by which trauma or stress to the skin can trigger vitiligo or the development of new lesions

- Development of a mouse model of vitiligo that not only would help scientists better understand the disease but also would allow them to test treatments for it

- Identification of genes that play a role in and predispose people to vitiligo

At the University of Colorado, the National Institute of Arthritis and Musculoskeletal and Skin Diseases supports a large collaborative project involving families with vitiligo in the United States and the United Kingdom. Researchers have found evidence of a link between vitiligo and variants of a gene called FOXD3. It is hoped that further genetic analyses of these and other families will enable them to identify one or more additional vitiligo susceptibility genes. This work may lead to development of specific approaches to disease therapy and prevention for patients at high genetic risk.

Chapter 50

Warts

Viral Warts

Warts are tumors or growths of the skin caused by infection with human papillomavirus (HPV). More than 70 HPV subtypes are known.

Warts are particularly common in childhood and are spread by direct contact or autoinoculation. This means if a wart is scratched, the viral particles may be spread to another area of skin. It may take as long as twelve months for the wart to first appear.

What Do They Look Like?

Warts have a hard 'warty' or 'verrucous' surface. You can often see a tiny black dot in the middle of each scaly spot, due to a thrombosed capillary blood vessel. There are various types of viral wart.

- Common warts arise most often on the backs of fingers or toes, and on the knees.

- Plantar warts (verrucas) include one or more tender inwardly growing 'myrmecia' on the sole of the foot.

About This Chapter: This information, from "Viral Warts," is reprinted with permission from DermNet, the web site of the New Zealand Dermatological Society. Visit www.dermnetnz.org for patient information on numerous skin conditions and their treatment. © 2009 New Zealand Dermatological Society.

- Mosaic warts on the sole of the foot are in clusters over an area sometimes several centimeters in diameter.

- Plane, or flat, warts can be very numerous and may be inoculated by shaving.

- Periungual warts prefer to grow at the sides or under the nails and can distort nail growth.

- Filiform warts are on a long stalk.

- Oral warts can affect the lips and even inside the cheeks. They include squamous cell papillomas.

- Genital warts are often transmitted sexually and predispose to cervical, penile and vulval cancer.

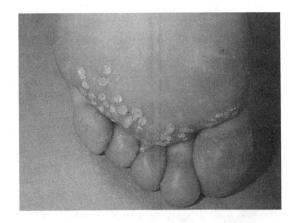

Figure 50.1. Plantar warts (foot)

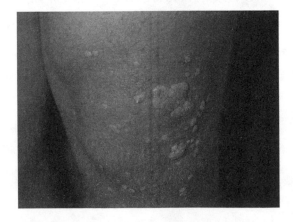

Figure 50.2. Common warts (leg)

In children, even without treatment, 50 percent of warts disappear within six months; 90 percent are gone in two years. They are more persistent in adults but they clear up eventually.

Warts are particularly numerous and troublesome in patients who are immunosuppressed, most often due to medications such as azathioprine or ciclosporin. In these patients, the warts almost never disappear despite treatment.

Treatment

Many people don't bother to treat them because treatment can be more uncomfortable and troublesome than the warts—they are hardly ever a serious problem. However, warts may be painful and they often look ugly and cause embarrassment.

To get rid of them, we have to stimulate the body's own immune system to attack the wart virus. Persistence with the treatment and patience is essential.

Chemical Treatment

Chemical treatment includes wart paints containing salicylic acid or similar compounds, which work by removing the dead surface skin cells. Podophyllin is a cytotoxic agent, and must not be used in pregnancy or in women considering pregnancy.

The paint is normally applied once daily. Perseverance is essential—although 70 percent of warts will go away with wart paints, it may take twelve weeks to work. Even if the wart doesn't go away completely, the wart paint usually makes it smaller and less uncomfortable.

First, the skin should be softened in a bath or bowl of hot soapy water. The hard skin should be rubbed away from the wart surface with a piece of pumice stone or emery board. The wart paint or gel should be applied accurately, allowing it to dry. It works better if covered with plaster or duct tape (particularly recommended when the wart is on the foot).

Stronger preparations such as Upton's paste are used for thick verrucas, applied every few days. It is important to protect the surrounding skin with adhesive plaster before applying Upton's paste, and to apply a plaster over the paste to keep it in place.

If the chemical makes the skin sore, stop treatment until the discomfort has settled, then recommence as above. Take care to keep the chemical off normal skin.

A 3% formalin solution can be used to soak multiple mosaic plantar warts several times a week. Protect unaffected skin with Vaseline, and apply cotton wool soaked in the solution, left in place for about ten minutes before rinsing off.

> ✔ **Quick Tip**
>
> **Occlusion:** Just keeping the wart covered 24 hours of the day may result in clearance. Duct tape is convenient and inexpensive.

Cryotherapy

The wart is frozen with liquid nitrogen repeatedly, at one- to three-week intervals. This is uncomfortable for a few minutes and may result in blistering for several days. Success is in the order of 70 percent after three to four months of regular freezing. Dermatologists debate whether a light freeze to stimulate immunity is sufficient, or whether a harder freeze is necessary to destroy all the infected skin. A hard freeze might cause a permanent white mark or scar.

Electrosurgery

Electrosurgery (curettage and cautery) is used for particularly large and annoying warts. Under local anesthetic, the growth is pared away and the base burned by diathermy or cautery. The wound heals in about two weeks; even then 20 percent of warts can be expected to recur within a few months.

Other Treatments

There are numerous treatments for warts and none offer a guarantee of cure. They include bleomycin injections, laser vaporization, pulse dye laser, oral acitretin, and immune modulators such as imiquimod cream.

Chapter 51

Hair Loss And Its Causes

What is the normal cycle of hair growth and loss?

The normal cycle of hair growth lasts for two to six years. Each hair grows approximately one centimeter (less than half an inch) per month during this phase. About 90 percent of the hair on your scalp is growing at any one time. About 10 percent of the hair on your scalp, at any one time, is in a resting phase. After two to three months, the resting hair falls out and new hair starts to grow in its place.

It is normal to shed some hair each day as part of this cycle. However, some people may experience excessive (more than normal) hair loss. Hair loss of this type can affect men, women, and children.

What causes excessive hair loss?

A number of things can cause excessive hair loss. For example, about three or four months after an illness or a major surgery, you may suddenly lose a large amount of hair. This hair loss is related to the stress of the illness and is temporary.

Hormonal problems may cause hair loss. If your thyroid gland is over-active or underactive, your hair may fall out. This hair loss usually can be helped by the treatment of thyroid disease. Hair loss may occur if male or female hormones, known as androgens and estrogens, are out of balance. Correcting the hormone imbalance may stop your hair loss.

Many women notice hair loss about three months after they've had a baby. This loss is also related to hormones. During pregnancy, high levels of certain hormones cause the body to keep hair that would normally fall out. When the hormones return to pre-pregnancy levels, that hair falls out and the normal cycle of growth and loss starts again.

Some medicines can cause hair loss. This type of hair loss improves when you stop taking the medicine. Medicines that can cause hair loss include blood thinners (also called anticoagulants), medicines used for gout, medicines used in chemotherapy to treat cancer, vitamin A (if too much is taken), birth control pills, and antidepressants.

Certain infections can cause hair loss. Fungal infections of the scalp can cause hair loss in children. The infection is easily treated with antifungal medicines.

♣ **It's A Fact!!**
Can improper care
of my hair cause hair loss?

Yes. If you wear pigtails or cornrows or use tight hair rollers, the pull on your hair can cause a type of hair loss called traction alopecia (say: al-oh-pee-sha). If the pulling is stopped before scarring of the scalp develops, your hair will grow back normally. However, scarring can cause permanent hair loss. Hot oil hair treatments or chemicals used in permanents (also called "perms") may cause inflammation (swelling) of the hair follicle, which can result in scarring and hair loss.

Finally, hair loss may occur as part of an underlying disease, such as lupus or diabetes. Since hair loss may be an early sign of a disease, it is important to find the cause so that it can be treated.

What is common baldness?

The term "common baldness" usually means male pattern baldness, or permanent-pattern baldness. Male pattern baldness is the most common cause of hair loss in men. Men who have this type of hair loss usually have inherited the trait. Men who start losing their hair at an early age tend to develop more extensive baldness. In male pattern baldness, hair loss typically results in a receding hair line and baldness on the top of the head.

Women may develop female pattern baldness. In this form of hair loss, the hair can become thin over the entire scalp.

Can my doctor do something to stop hair loss?

Perhaps. Your doctor will probably ask you some questions about your diet, any medicines you're taking, whether you've had a recent illness, and how you take care of your hair. If you're a woman, your doctor may ask questions about your menstrual cycle, pregnancies, and menopause. Your doctor may want to do a physical exam to look for other causes of hair loss. Finally, blood tests or a biopsy (taking a small sample of cells to examine under a microscope) of your scalp may be needed.

Is there any treatment for hair loss?

Depending on your type of hair loss, treatments are available. If a medicine is causing your hair loss, your doctor may be able to prescribe a different medicine. Recognizing and treating an infection may help stop the hair loss. Correcting a hormone imbalance may prevent further hair loss.

Medicines may also help slow or prevent the development of common baldness. One medicine, minoxidil (brand name: Rogaine), is available without a prescription. It is applied to the scalp. Both men and women can use it. Another medicine, finasteride (brand name: Propecia) is available with a prescription. It comes in pills and is only for men. It may take up to six months before you can tell if one of these medicines is working.

If adequate treatment is not available for your type of hair loss, you may consider trying different hairstyles or wigs, hairpieces, hair weaves, or artificial hair replacement.

Chapter 52

Alopecia Areata

Alopecia areata is a condition that causes a person's hair to fall out. *Alopecia* is the medical term for baldness; there are various types of alopecia, including alopecia areata. Alopecia areata is an autoimmune disease; that is, the person's immune system attacks their body, in this case, their hair follicles. When this happens, the person's hair begins to fall out, often in clumps the size and shape of a quarter. The extent of the hair loss varies; in some cases, it is only in a few spots. In others, the hair loss can be greater. On rare occasions, the person loses all of the hair on his or her head (alopecia areata totalis) or entire body (alopecia areata universalis).

It is believed that the person's genetic makeup may trigger the autoimmune reaction of alopecia areata, along with a virus or a substance the person comes into contact with.

Alopecia areata is an unpredictable disease. In some people, hair grows back but falls out again later. In others, hair grows back and remains. Each case is unique. Even if someone loses all of his or her hair, there is a chance that it will grow back.

About This Chapter: Text in this chapter is from "Alopecia Areata," © 2009 The Cleveland Clinic Foundation, 9500 Euclid Avenue, Cleveland, OH 44195, http://my.clevelandclinic.org. Additional information is available from the Cleveland Clinic Health Information Center, 216-444-3771, toll-free 800-223-2273 extension 43771, or at http://my.clevelandclinic.org/health.

Who Gets Alopecia Areata?

Anyone can develop alopecia; however, your chances of having alopecia areata are slightly greater if you have a relative with the disease. In addition, alopecia areata occurs more often among people who have family members with autoimmune disorders such as diabetes, lupus, or thyroid disease.

Can Alopecia Areata Be Cured?

Alopecia areata cannot be cured; however, it can be treated and the hair can grow back.

In many cases, alopecia is treated with drugs that are used for other conditions. Treatment options for alopecia areata include:

- **Corticosteroids:** Anti-inflammatory drugs that are prescribed for autoimmune diseases. Corticosteroids can be given as an injection into the scalp or other areas, orally (as a pill), or applied topically (rubbed into the skin) as an ointment, cream, or foam. Response to therapy may be gradual.

- **Rogaine:** This topical drug is already used as a treatment for pattern baldness. It usually takes about 12 weeks of treatment with Rogaine before hair begins to grow.

- **Psoriatec:** This treatment, commonly used for eczema, is applied to the skin for short periods. As with Rogaine, hair growth takes approximately 12 weeks.

Other drugs that are used for alopecia with varying degrees of effectiveness include medications used to treat psoriasis and topical sensitizers (drugs that are applied to the skin and cause an allergic reaction that can cause hair growth).

Other Tips

Apart from drug treatments, there are various cosmetic and protective techniques that people with alopecia can try. These include:

- Using makeup to hide or minimize hair loss

- Wearing sunglasses to protect the eyes from the sun and the environment, if there is loss of eyelashes

- Wearing coverings (wigs, hats, or scarves) to protect the head from the elements

- Eating a well-balanced diet. Hair growth is a vitamin- and mineral-dependent process. People on fad diets often have problems with hair loss (although not specifically related to alopecia areata.)

☞ **Remember!!**

While the disease is not medically serious, it can impact people psychologically. Support groups are available to help people with alopecia areata deal with the psychological effects of the condition. Further information may be found at the National Alopecia Areata Foundation (www.naaf.org).

- Reducing stress. Although never proven through large trials and investigations, many people with new onset alopecia areata have had recent stresses in life, such as work, family, deaths, surgeries, or accidents.

Chapter 53

Head Lice

Facts About Head Lice

What are head lice?

The head louse, or *Pediculus humanus capitis* (peh-DICK-you-lus HUE-man-us CAP-ih-TUS), is a parasitic insect that can be found on the head, eyebrows, and eyelashes of people. Head lice feed on human blood several time a day and live close to the human scalp. Head lice are not known to spread disease.

Who is at risk for getting head lice?

Head lice are found worldwide. In the United States, infestation with head lice is most common among preschool children attending child care, elementary school children, and the household members of infested children. Although reliable data on how many people in the United States get head lice each year are not available, an estimated six million to 12 million infestations occur each year in the United States among children three to 11 years of age. In the United States, infestation with head lice is much less

About This Chapter: This chapter begins with excerpts from "Head Lice: Fact Sheet," and "Head Lice: Treatment," Centers for Disease Control and Prevention (www.cdc.gov), 2008. The use of trade names is for identification purposes only and does not imply endorsement by the Public Health Service or by the U.S. Department of Health and Human Services.

common among African Americans than among persons of other races, possibly because the claws of the of the head louse found most frequently in the United States are better adapted for grasping the shape and width of the hair shaft of other races.

Head lice move by crawling; they cannot hop or fly. Head lice are spread by direct contact with the hair of an infested person. Anyone who comes in head-to-head contact with someone who already has head lice is at greatest risk. Spread by contact with clothing (such as hats, scarves, coats) or other personal items (such as combs, brushes, or towels) used by an infested person is uncommon. Personal hygiene or cleanliness in the home or school has nothing to do with getting head lice.

What do head lice look like?

Head lice have three forms: the egg (also called a nit), the nymph, and the adult.

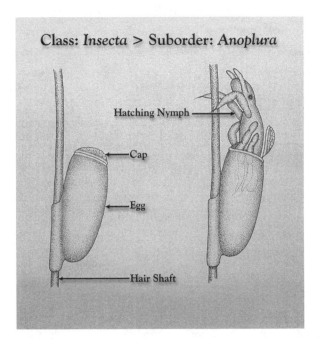

Figure 53.1. Illustration of a lice egg on a hair shaft and a hatching nymph. Source: Centers for Disease Control and Prevention, Public Health Image Library (PHIL).

Egg/Nit: Nits are lice eggs laid by the adult female head louse at the base of the hair shaft nearest the scalp. Nits are firmly attached to the hair shaft and are oval-shaped and very small (about the size of a knot in thread) and hard to see. Nits often appear yellow or white although live nits sometimes appear to be the same color as the hair of the infested person. Nits are often confused with dandruff, scabs, or hair spray droplets. Head lice nits usually take about eight to nine days to hatch. Eggs that are likely to hatch are usually located no more than 1/4 inch (or one centimeter) from the base of the hair shaft.

Nymph: A nymph is an immature louse that hatches from the nit. A nymph looks like an adult head louse, but is smaller. To live, a nymph must feed on blood. Nymphs mature into adults about nine to 12 days after hatching from the nit.

> ✔ **Quick Tip**
>
> These are the signs and symptoms of head lice infestation:
>
> - Tickling feeling of something moving in the hair
> - Itching, caused by an allergic reaction to the bites of the head louse
> - Irritability and difficulty sleeping; head lice are most active in the dark
> - Sores on the head caused by scratching. These sores can sometimes become infected with bacteria found on the person's skin.

Adult: The fully grown and developed adult louse is about the size of a sesame seed, has six legs, and is tan to grayish-white in color. Adult head lice may look darker in persons with dark hair than in persons with light hair. To survive, adult head lice must feed on blood. An adult head louse can live about 30 days on a person's head but will die within one or two days if it falls off a person. Adult female head lice are usually larger than males and can lay about six eggs each day.

Where are head lice most commonly found?

Head lice and head lice nits are found almost exclusively on the scalp, particularly around and behind the ears and near the neckline at the back of the head. Head lice or head lice nits sometimes are found on the eyelashes or eyebrows but this is uncommon. Head lice hold tightly to hair with hook-like claws at the end of each of their six legs; head lice nits are cemented firmly to the hair shaft and can be difficult to remove.

How does a person get head lice?

Head-to-head contact with an already infested person is the most common way to get head lice. Head-to-head contact is common during play at school, at home, and elsewhere (sports activities, playground, slumber parties, camp).

Though more uncommon, head lice may be spread by sharing clothing or belongings onto which lice or nits may have crawled or fallen. Some examples include:

> ♣ **It's A Fact!!**
> Dogs, cats, and other pets do not play a role in the spread of human lice.

- sharing clothing (hats, scarves, coats, sports uniforms) or articles (hair ribbons, barrettes, combs, brushes, towels, stuffed animals) recently worn or used by an infested person

- lying on a bed, couch, pillow, or carpet that has recently been in contact with an infested person. The risk of getting an infestation by a louse or nit that has fallen onto a carpet or furniture is very small.

How is head lice infestation diagnosed?

The diagnosis of a head lice infestation is best made by finding a live nymph or adult louse on the scalp or hair of a person. Because nymphs and adult lice are very small, move quickly, and avoid light, they can be difficult to find. Use of a magnifying lens and a fine-toothed comb may be helpful to find live lice. If crawling lice are not seen, finding nits firmly attached within a 1/4 inch of the base of the hair shafts strongly suggests, but does not confirm, that a person is infested and should be treated. Nits that are attached more than 1/4 inch from the base of the hair shaft are almost always dead or already hatched. Nits are often confused with other things found in the hair such as dandruff, hair spray droplets, and dirt particles. If no live nymphs or adult lice are seen, and the only nits found are more than 1/4 inch from the scalp, the infestation is probably old and no longer active and does not need to be treated.

If a person is not sure they have head lice, the diagnosis should be made by their health care provider, local health department, or other person trained to identify live head lice.

Treatment For Head Lice

Treatment for head lice is recommended for persons diagnosed with an active infestation. All household members and other close contacts should be checked; those persons with evidence of an active infestation should be treated. Some experts believe prophylactic treatment is prudent for persons who share the same bed with actively-infested individuals. All infested persons (household members and close contacts) and their bedmates should be treated at the same time.

Retreatment of head lice usually is recommended because no approved pediculicide (peh-DICK-you-luh-side) is completely ovicidal. To be most effective, retreatment should occur after all eggs have hatched but before new eggs are produced. The retreatment schedule can vary depending on the pediculicide used.

When treating head lice, supplemental measures can be combined with recommended medicine, however, such additional measures generally are not required to eliminate a head lice infestation. For example, hats, scarves, pillow cases, bedding, clothing, and towels worn or used by the infested person in the two-day period just before treatment is started can be machine washed and dried using the hot water and hot air cycles because lice and eggs are killed by exposure for five minutes to temperatures greater than 53.5° C (128.3° F). Items that cannot be laundered may be dry-cleaned or sealed in a plastic bag for two weeks. Items such as hats, grooming aids,

🖎 What's It Mean?

Ovicidal: Causing death of the ovum [egg].

Pediculicide: An agent used to destroy lice.

Source: Stedman's Online Dictionary, 2009.

and towels that come in contact with the hair of an infested person should not be shared. Vacuuming furniture and floors can remove an infested person's hairs that might have viable nits attached.

Treatment Of The Infested Person(s): Treatment requires using an over-the-counter (OTC) or prescription medication. Follow these treatment steps:

1. Before applying treatment, it may be helpful to remove clothing that can become wet or stained during treatment.

2. Apply lice medicine according to the instructions contained in the box or printed on the label. If the infested person has very long hair (longer than shoulder length), it may be necessary to use a second bottle. Pay special attention to instructions on the label or in the box regarding how long the medication should be left on the hair and how it should be washed off.

3. Have the infested person put on clean clothing after treatment.

4. If a few live lice are still found eight to 12 hours after treatment, but are moving more slowly than before, do not retreat. The medicine may take longer to kill all the lice. Comb dead and any remaining live lice out of the hair using a fine-toothed nit comb.

5. If, after eight to 12 hours of treatment, no dead lice are found and lice seem as active as before, the medicine may not be working. Do not retreat until speaking with your health care provider; a different lice medicine may be necessary.

6. Nit (head lice egg) combs, often found in lice medicine packages, should be used to comb nits and lice from the hair shaft. Many flea combs made for cats and dogs are also effective.

7. After each treatment, checking the hair and combing with a nit comb to remove nits and lice every two to three days may decrease the chance of self-reinfestation. Continue to check for two to three weeks to be sure all lice and nits are gone.

8. Retreatment generally is recommended for most prescription and non-prescription drugs after nine to 10 days in order to kill any surviving

hatched lice before they produce new eggs. However, if using the prescription drug malathion, retreatment is recommended after seven to nine days *only* if crawling bugs are found.

Remember!! Warning

Do not use a creme rinse, combination shampoo and conditioner, or condition hair before using lice medicine. Do not re-wash the hair for one to two days after the lice medicine is removed.

Supplemental Measures: Head lice do not survive long if they fall off a person and cannot feed. You don't need to spend a lot of time or money on housecleaning activities. Follow these steps to help avoid reinfestation by lice that have recently fallen off the hair or crawled onto clothing or furniture.

1. Machine wash and dry clothing, bed linens, and other items that the infested person wore or used during the two days before treatment using the hot water (130° F) laundry cycle and the high heat drying cycle. Clothing and items that are not washable can be dry-cleaned or sealed in a plastic bag and stored for two weeks.

2. Soak combs and brushes in hot water (at least 130° F) for five to 10 minutes.

3. Vacuum the floor and furniture, particularly where the infested person sat or lay. However, the risk of getting infested by a louse that has fallen onto a rug or carpet or furniture is very small. Head lice survive less than one to two days if they fall off a person and cannot feed; nits cannot hatch and usually die within a week if they are not kept at the same temperature as that found close to the human scalp. Spending much time and money on housecleaning activities is not necessary to avoid reinfestation by lice or nits that may have fallen off the head or crawled onto furniture or clothing.

4. Do not use fumigant sprays; they can be toxic if inhaled or absorbed through the skin.

Prevent Reinfestation: Prevent reinfestation by taking the following precautions:

- Avoid head-to-head (hair-to-hair) contact during play and other activities at home, school, and elsewhere (sports activities, playground, slumber parties, camp). Lice are spread most commonly by direct head-to-head contact and much less frequently by sharing clothing or belongings onto which lice or nits may have crawled or fallen.

- Do not share clothing such as hats, scarves, coats, sports uniforms, hair ribbons, or barrettes.

- Do not share infested combs, brushes, or towels.

- Do not lie on beds, couches, pillows, rugs, carpets, or stuffed animals that have recently been in contact with an infested person.

- To help control a head lice outbreak in a community, school, or camp, children can be taught to avoid activities that may spread head lice.

Over-The-Counter Medications

Many head lice medications are available "over-the-counter" without a prescription at a local drug store or pharmacy. Each over-the-counter product approved for the treatment of head lice contains one of the following active ingredients.

1. Pyrethrins (pie-WREATH-rins) combined with piperonyl butoxide (pie-PER-a-nil beu-TOX-side). Brand name products: A-200, Pronto, R&C, Rid, Triple X. Pyrethrins are naturally occurring pyrethroid extracts from the chrysanthemum flower. Pyrethrins are safe and effective when used as directed. Pyrethrins can only kill live lice, not unhatched eggs (nits). A second treatment is recommended in nine to 10 days to kill any newly hatched lice before they can produce new eggs. Treatment failures can be common depending on whether lice are resistant to pyrethrins in the patient's geographic location. Pyrethrins generally should not be used by persons who are allergic to chrysanthemums or ragweed.

2. Permethrin lotion 1% (per-meth-rin). Brand name product: Nix. Permethrin is a synthetic pyrethroid similar to naturally occurring pyrethrins. Permethrin lotion 1% is approved by the FDA for the treatment

of head lice. Permethrin is safe and effective when used as directed. Permethrin kills live lice but not unhatched eggs. Permethrin may continue to kill newly hatched lice for several days after treatment. A second treatment often is necessary in nine to 10 days to kill any newly hatched lice before they can produce new eggs. Treatment failures can be common depending whether lice are resistant to permethrin in the patient's geographic location. Permethrin is not approved for use in children under two years old.

Prescription Medications

The following medications approved by the U.S. Food and Drug Administration (FDA) for the treatment of head lice are available only by prescription.

1. Malathion lotion 0.5%. Brand name product: Ovide. Malathion is an organophosphate. Malathion lotion 0.5% is approved by the FDA for the treatment of head lice. The formulation of malathion approved in the United States for the treatment of head lice is a lotion that is safe and effective when used as directed. Malathion is pediculicidal (kills live lice) and partially ovicidal (kills some lice eggs). A second treatment is recommended if live lice still are present seven to nine days after treatment. Malathion is intended for use on persons six years of age and older. Malathion can be irritating to the skin and scalp; contact with the eyes should be avoided. Malathion lotion is flammable; do not smoke or use electrical heat sources, including hair dryers, curlers, and curling or flat irons, when applying malathion lotion and while the hair is wet.

2. Lindane shampoo 1%. Brand name products: None available. Lindane is an organochloride. Although lindane shampoo 1% is approved by the FDA for the treatment of head lice, it is not recommended as a first-line therapy. Overuse, misuse, or accidentally swallowing lindane can be toxic to the brain and other parts of the nervous system; its use should be restricted to patients who have failed treatment with or cannot tolerate other medications that pose less risk. Lindane should not be used to treat premature infants, persons with a seizure disorder, women who are pregnant or breast-feeding, persons who have very irritated skin or sores

where the lindane will be applied, infants, children, the elderly, and persons who weigh less than 110 pounds.

Which Medicine Is Best?

If you aren't sure which medicine to use or how to use a particular medicine, always ask your physician, pharmacist, or other health care provider. When using a medicine, always carefully follow the instructions contained in the package or written on the label, unless the physician and pharmacist direct otherwise.

☞ **Remember!!**
When Treating Head Lice

• Do not use extra amounts of any lice medication unless instructed to do so by your physician and pharmacist. The drugs used to treat lice are insecticides and can be dangerous if they are misused or overused.

• Do not treat an infested person more than two to three times with the same medication if it does not seem to be working. This may be caused by using the medicine incorrectly or by resistance to the medicine. Always seek the advice of your health care provider if this should happen. He or she may recommend an alternative medication.

• Do not use different head lice drugs at the same time unless instructed to do so by your physician and pharmacist.

Part Six

Caring For Injuries To The Skin

Chapter 54

Skin Injury: Cuts, Scrapes, And Bruises

Skin Injury

Definitions

Cuts And Scratches: Superficial cuts (scratches) only extend partially through the skin and rarely become infected. Deep cuts (lacerations) go through the skin (dermis).

Abrasions Or Scrapes: An area of superficial skin that has been scraped off. Commonly occurs on the knees, elbows and palms.

Bruises: Bruises (contusions) result from a direct blow or a crushing injury; there is bleeding into the skin from damaged blood vessels without an overlying cut or abrasion.

Liquid Skin Bandage For Minor Cuts And Scrapes

Liquid skin bandage has several benefits when compared to a regular bandage (e.g., a dressing or a Band-Aid). Liquid Bandage only needs to be applied once to minor cuts and scrapes. It helps stop minor bleeding. It seals the wound and may promote faster healing and lower infection rates. However, it is also more expensive.

After the wound is washed and dried, the liquid is applied by spray or with a swab. It dries in less than a minute and usually lasts a week. It's resistant to bathing.

Examples include:

• Band-Aid Liquid Bandage;

• New-Skin;

• Curad Spray Bandage;

• 3M No Sting Liquid Bandage Spray.

♣ It's A Fact!!
When Are Stitches Needed?

• Any cut that is split open or gaping probably needs sutures (stitches). Cuts longer than 1/2 inch (12 mm) usually need sutures. On the face, cuts longer than 1/4 inch (6 mm) usually need sutures.

• A physician should evaluate any open wound that may need sutures regardless of the time that has passed since the initial injury.

Source: Self Care Decisions, 2006.

What Is Tetanus?

Tetanus is a rare infection caused by bacteria that are found in many places, especially in dirt and soil. The tetanus bacteria enter through a break in the skin and then spread through the body.

Tetanus is commonly called "lock jaw" because the first symptom is a tightening of the muscles of the face. However, the final stage of the infection is much more serious. All of the muscles of the body go into severe spasm, including the muscles that control breathing. Eventually a person with a tetanus infection loses the ability to breathe, and may die in spite of intensive treatment in the hospital.

A tetanus booster protects you from getting a tetanus infection. It does not prevent other kinds of wound infection.

When Does An Adult Need A Tetanus Booster Shot?

Clean Cuts And Scrapes—Booster Needed Every 10 Years: Patients with clean *minor* wounds *and* who have previously had three or more tetanus shots (full series), need a booster every 10 years. Examples of minor wounds include a superficial abrasion or a cut sustained while washing dishes. Obtain booster within 72 hours.

Dirty Cuts And Scrapes—Booster Needed Every 5 Years: Patients with dirty wounds need a booster every five years. Examples of dirty wounds include those contaminated with soil, feces, saliva and more serious wounds from deep punctures, crushing, and burns. Obtain booster within 72 hours. When in doubt, assume that it is a dirty wound.

When To Call Your Doctor

Call 911 now (you may need an ambulance) for:

• major bleeding (actively bleeding or spurting) that can't be stopped;

• knife wound (or other possibly deep cut) to the chest, abdomen, back, neck, or head.

Call your doctor now (night or day) if:

• you think you have a serious injury;

• you have severe pain;

• bleeding hasn't stopped after 10 minutes of direct pressure;

• cut causes numbness (i.e., loss of sensation);

• cut causes weakness (i.e., decreased ability to move hand, finger, toe);

• cut is very deep (e.g., can see bone or tendons);

• cut is split open or gaping and may need stitches;

• dirt or grime in the wound is not removed after 15 minutes of scrubbing;

- skin loss from bad scrape goes very deep;

- skin loss involves greater than 10 percent of body surface (Note: the hand's surface equals one percent);

✔ Quick Tip

First Aid Advice

First aid advice for bleeding:

- Apply direct pressure to the entire wound with a clean cloth.

First aid advice for severe bleeding:

- Place two or three sterile dressings (or a clean towel or washcloth) over the wound immediately.

- Apply direct pressure to the wound, using your entire hand.

- If bleeding continues, apply pressure more forcefully or move the pressure to a slightly different spot.

- Act quickly because ongoing blood loss can cause shock.

- Do not use a tourniquet.

First aid advice for penetrating object:

- If penetrating object still in place, don't remove it (Reason: removal could increase bleeding).

First aid advice for shock:

- Lie down with feet elevated.

First aid advice for transport of an amputated finger or toe:

- Briefly rinse amputated part with water (to remove any dirt).

- Place amputated part in plastic bag (to protect and keep clean).

- Place plastic bag containing part in a container of ice (to keep cool and preserve tissue).

Source: Self Care Decisions, 2006.

- high pressure injection injury (e.g. from paint gun, usually work-related);

- cut or scrape looks infected (redness, red streak, or pus).

Call your doctor within 24 hours (between 9 a.m. and 4 p.m.) if:

- you think you need to be seen;

- several bruises occur without any known injury;

- very large bruise follows a minor injury (wider than 2 inches);

- diabetic with any cut or scrape on foot.

Call your doctor during weekday office hours if:

- you have other questions or concerns;

- you haven't had a tetanus booster in more than 10 years (five years for dirty cuts and scrapes).

Use self care at home if:

- injury is a minor cut, scrape or bruise, and you don't think you need to be seen.

Home Care Advice For Minor Cut, Scrape, Or Bruise

- Treatment of minor cuts, scratches and scrapes (abrasions)

  1. Apply direct pressure for 10 minutes to stop any bleeding

  2. Wash the wound with soap and water for five minutes

  3. Gently scrub out any dirt with a washcloth

  4. Cut off any pieces of dead loose skin using a fine scissors (cleaned with rubbing alcohol before and after use)

  5. Apply an antibiotic ointment, covered by a Band-Aid or dressing. Change daily. Another option is to use a Liquid Skin Bandage that only needs to be applied once. Avoid using ointments with this.

- Treatment of minor bruise

  1. Apply a cold pack or an ice bag wrapped in a towel for 20 minutes each hour for four consecutive hours (20 minutes of cold followed by 40 minutes of rest for four hours in a row).

  2. 48 hours after the injury, use local heat for 10 minutes three times each day to help reabsorb the blood

  3. Rest the injured part as much as possible for 48 hours.

- Pain medication

  1. For pain and fever relief, take acetaminophen or ibuprofen

  2. Acetaminophen (e.g., Tylenol): The dose is 650 mg by mouth every four hours or 1,000 mg by mouth every six hours. Maximum dose per day is 4,000 mg.

  3. Ibuprofen (e.g., Motrin, Advil): The dose is 400 mg by mouth every six hours or 600 mg by mouth every eight hours.

  4. People who are over 65 years of age: Acetaminophen is generally considered safer than ibuprofen. Acetaminophen dosing interval should be increased to every eight hours because of reduced liver metabolism. Maximum dose per day is 3,000 mg.

  5. Caution: Do not take ibuprofen if you have stomach problems, kidney disease, are pregnant, or have been told by your doctor to avoid this type of anti-inflammatory drug. Do not take ibuprofen for more than seven days without consulting your doctor.

  6. Caution: Do not take acetaminophen if you have liver disease.

  7. Read the package instructions thoroughly on all medications that you take.

- **Expected Course:** Pain and swelling usually begin to improve two or three days after an injury. Swelling is usually gone in seven days. Pain may take two weeks to completely resolve.

- Call your doctor if injury looks infected (pus, redness, increasing tenderness), doesn't heal within 10 days, or you become worse.

Keloids And Hypertrophic Scars

This information is reprinted with permission from DermNet, the web site of the New Zealand Dermatological Society. Visit www.dermnetnz.org for patient information on numerous skin conditions and their treatment. © 2008 New Zealand Dermatological Society.

Keloid Scars

Occasionally scars enlarge spontaneously to form firm, smooth, hard growths called keloids. Keloids may be uncomfortable or itchy, and may be much larger than the original wound. They can arise soon after the injury, or develop months later.

> ✤ **It's A Fact!!**
>
> Keloid scars are usually just a cosmetic problem. They never become malignant.
>
> Source: New Zealand Dermatological Society, 2008.

It is not known why keloids appear. While most people never form keloids, others develop them after minor injuries, even insect bites or pimples. Keloids may form on any part of the body, although the upper chest and shoulders are especially prone to them. Dark skinned people form keloids more easily than Caucasians.

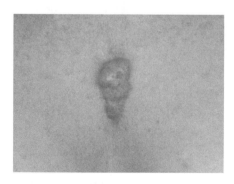

Figure 54.1. A keloid scar (Source: DermNet).

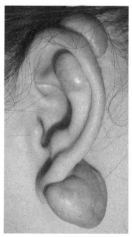

Figure 54.2. Keloid scars behind the ear (Source: DermNet).

Hypertrophic Scars

As wounds heal, scar tissue forms, which at first is often red and somewhat prominent. Over several months, a scar usually becomes flat and pale. If there is a lot of tension on a healing wound, the healing area is thicker than usual. This is known as a hypertrophic scar.

Treatment

Hypertrophic scars generally settle in time but keloids may prove resistant to treatment. The following measures are helpful.

Dressings should be worn for 12 to 24 hours per day, for at least eight to 12 weeks, and perhaps for much longer.

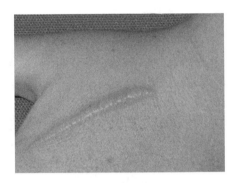

Figure 54.3. A hypertrophic scar on the hand (Source: DermNet).

Some types of dressings for hypertrophic scars include the following:

- Polyurethane or silicone scar reduction patches

- Silicone gel

- Pressure dressings

- Surgical excision (but this may result in a second keloid even larger than the original one)

- Corticosteroid injection, repeated every few weeks

- Cryotherapy

- Superficial x-ray treatment soon after surgery

- Pulsed dye laser

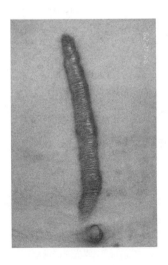

Figure 54.4. Vertical hypertrophic scar (Source: DermNet).

Chapter 55

Stitches

How should I clean a wound?

The best way to clean a cut, scrape, or puncture wound (such as from a nail) is with cool water. You can hold the wound under running water or fill a tub with cool water and pour it from a cup over the wound.

Use soap and a soft washcloth to clean the skin around the wound. Try to keep soap out of the wound itself because soap can cause irritation. Use tweezers that have been cleaned in isopropyl alcohol to remove any dirt that remains in the wound after washing.

Even though it may seem that you should use a stronger cleansing solution (such as hydrogen peroxide or an antiseptic), these things may irritate wounds. Ask your family doctor if you feel you must use something other than water.

What about bleeding?

Bleeding helps clean out wounds. Most small cuts or scrapes will stop bleeding in a short time. Wounds on the face, head, or mouth will sometimes bleed a lot because these areas are rich in blood vessels.

About This Chapter: Reprinted with permission from "Cuts, Scrapes and Stitches: Caring for Wounds," December 2006, http://familydoctor.org/online/famdocen/home/healthy/firstaid/after-injury/041.html. Copyright © 2006 American Academy of Family Physicians. All Rights Reserved.

To stop the bleeding, apply firm but gentle pressure on the cut with a clean cloth, tissue or piece of gauze. If the blood soaks through the gauze or cloth you're holding over the cut, don't take it off. Just put more gauze or another cloth on top of what you already have in place and apply more pressure.

✔ **Quick Tip**
If your wound is on an arm or leg, raising it above your heart will also help slow the bleeding.

Should I use a bandage?

Leaving a wound uncovered helps it stay dry and helps it heal. If the wound isn't in an area that will get dirty or be rubbed by clothing, you don't have to cover it.

If it's in an area that will get dirty (such as your hand) or be irritated by clothing (such as your knee), cover it with an adhesive strip (Band-Aid) or with sterile gauze and adhesive tape. Change the bandage each day to keep the wound clean and dry.

Certain wounds, such as scrapes that cover a large area of the body, should be kept moist and clean to help reduce scarring and speed healing. Bandages used for this purpose are called occlusive or semiocclusive bandages. You can buy them in drug stores without a prescription. Your family doctor will tell you if he or she thinks this type of bandage is best for you.

Should I use an antibiotic ointment?

Antibiotic ointments (such as Bacitracin) help healing by keeping out infection and by keeping the wound clean and moist. A bandage does pretty much the same thing. If you have stitches, your doctor will tell you whether he or she wants you to use an antibiotic ointment. Most minor cuts and scrapes will heal just fine without antibiotic ointment, but it can speed healing and help reduce scarring.

What should I do about scabs?

Nothing. Scabs are the body's way of bandaging itself. They form to protect wounds from dirt. It's best to leave them alone and not pick at them. They will fall off by themselves when the time is right.

When should I call my doctor?

Call your doctor if your wound is deep, if you can't get the edges to stay together or if the edges are jagged. Your doctor may want to close your wound with stitches or skin adhesive. These things can help reduce the amount of scarring.

You can close small cuts yourself with special tape, called butterfly tape, or special adhesive strips, such as Steri-Strips.

How do I take care of stitches?

You can usually wash an area that has been stitched in one to three days. Washing off dirt and the crust that may form around the stitches helps reduce scarring. If the wound drains clear yellow fluid, you may need to cover it.

Your doctor may suggest that you rinse the wound with water and re-bandage it in 24 hours. Be sure to dry it well after washing. You may want to keep the wound elevated above your heart for the first day or two to help lessen swelling, reduce pain, and speed healing.

Your doctor may also suggest using a small amount of antibiotic ointment to prevent infection. The ointment also keeps a heavy scab from forming and may reduce the size of a scar.

Stitches are usually removed in three to 14 days, depending on where the cut is located. Areas that move, such as over or around the joints, require more time to heal.

What is skin adhesive?

Skin adhesive (such as Dermabond) is a new way to close small wounds. Your doctor will apply a liquid film to your wound and let it dry. The film holds the edges of your wound together. You can leave the film on your skin until it falls off (usually in five to 10 days).

It's important not to scratch or pick at the adhesive on your wound. If your doctor puts a bandage over the adhesive, you should be careful to keep the bandage dry. Your doctor will probably ask you to change the bandage every day.

Don't put any ointment, including antibiotic ointment, on your wound when the skin adhesive is in place. This could cause the adhesive to loosen and fall off too soon. You should also keep your wound out of direct light (such as sunlight or tanning booth lamps).

Keep an eye on your wound. If the skin around your wound becomes very red and warm to touch, or if the wound reopens, call your doctor.

Do I need a tetanus shot?

Tetanus is a serious infection you can get after a wound. The infection is also called "lockjaw," because stiffness of the jaw is the most frequent symptom.

To prevent tetanus infection when the wound is clean and minor, you'll need a tetanus shot if you haven't had at least three doses before or haven't had a dose in the last 10 years.

When the wound is more serious, you'll need a tetanus shot if you haven't had at least three doses before or if you haven't had a shot in the last five years. The best way to avoid tetanus infection is to talk to your family doctor to make sure your shots are up to date.

☞ Remember!!

Call your family doctor if any of the following things occur:

- The wound is jagged
- The wound is on your face
- The edges of the cut gape open
- The cut has dirt in it that won't come out
- The cut becomes tender or inflamed
- The cut drains a thick, creamy, grayish fluid
- You start to run a temperature over 100° F
- The area around the wound feels numb
- You can't move comfortably
- Red streaks form near the wound
- It's a puncture wound or a deep cut and you haven't had a tetanus shot in the past five years
- The cut bleeds in spurts, blood soaks through the bandage or the bleeding doesn't stop after 10 minutes of firm, direct pressure

Chapter 56

Corns and Calluses

What Is It?

Corns and calluses are similar, and indeed, the terms are often used interchangeably, although they are not the exactly the same. They do, however, share a common cause in that both are a thickening of the skin in an area that receives extra pressure. They are actually an interesting example of the way our body protects itself; in this case, it builds up hard, dead skin to toughen up an area and prevent it from developing a blister, which can lead to infection.

What Is The Difference?

Generally speaking, the location differentiates the two. The disorder is called a corn when it applies to a small, specific area of the foot. Many corns form on the sides of toes, particularly where the knuckle joints of one toe press or rub against the knuckle joints of another. A podiatric physician will probably be able to examine a corn and show you where the center, (or "seed") of it lies.

Calluses, on the other hand, can be caused by many things, but mostly by incorrectly fitting or improperly padded shoes, flat feet, bone spurs or hammertoes. Calluses may also be seen on the hands of anyone who works hard,

About This Chapter: Text in this chapter is from "Corns and Callouses," © American College of Foot and Ankle Orthopedics and Medicine. Reprinted with permission. Reviewed by David A. Cooke, MD, FACP, March 11, 2009.

or without gloves. The bottom of the foot or the ball of the foot are common locations for calluses.

What To Look For

If you see a hardened area of skin, particularly in an area that receives pressure, such as the heel, ball of the foot, or areas on the sides or tops of toes, suspect corns and calluses. The area may or may not be painful. Corns and calluses generally look like other skin around them, but they may feel rough or somewhat less sensitive to the casual touch.

What It Means To You

Corns and calluses can be annoying and sometimes painful, but they're not life-threatening. However, it is important to note that there are various lesions of the skin on the foot, including moles, warts—and even a few rare cancerous growths—that have similar or identical characteristics. It's best to have a podiatric physician examine any growth on your foot to ascertain that it is indeed a corn or callus. Many corns and calluses can be addressed with over-the-counter treatments; however, it depends on the specific condition, the cause, the patient, and how far the problem has progressed.

> ✔ **Quick Tip**
> **Important**
> If you have diabetes, you should see your podiatric physician at the first sign of any problems with the skin of your feet or toes, no matter how minor you may think they are. Patients with diabetes who develop podiatric problems often require special attention. The precautions and steps in this chapter may be recommended by your podiatric physician, but should not be undertaken without his or her supervision and consent.

What Causes It?

As previously mentioned, you develop corns and calluses through continued, sustained pressure on a particular area (or areas) of your foot. They're not contagious, and generally speaking, they're not dangerous. If, however, you have diabetes, have your feet checked by a doctor before you attempt any

type of self-treatment, self-medication or home remedy. An incorrectly treated problem can lead to infection with serious and lasting consequences.

Some of the causes of corns and calluses include shoes that fit incorrectly, are incorrectly padded, or that have an area that rubs or irritates part of the foot continually. Flat feet, a bone spur, or hammertoes are also contributing factors to some corns and/or calluses. Occasionally, a blocked sweat gland on the foot can have symptoms that mimic a corn or callus.

What Cures It?

Of all the podiatric problems out there, corns and calluses have given rise to a veritable cottage industry of home remedies, do-it-yourself fixes and all-natural cures. Before you go trying your grandma's favorite corn remover made out of who-knows-what that came out of the refrigerator, try the scientific approach.

A corn or callus is caused by constant pressure to a specific area. Your goal, logically, is to remove the pressure. If improperly fitted shoes are the source of the pressure, then obviously choosing properly fitted shoes will help. At a minimum, shoes should have ½ inch of space between the toes and the end of the shoe, along with a large, square toe box. It is equally important that the widest part of the foot fits in the widest part of the shoe.

Pads made of silicone, foam, or cotton are available in the healthcare sections of many stores. These can be considered the first line of attack (or defense, as it were) in treatment.

Some patients report success with the use of a callus file or a pumice stone; however, this tends to leave a rough skin surface, and some patients tend to be overzealous and damage their skin while pursuing this course of action. Should the low-key, at-home forms of treatment not be successful in treating your disorder, a podiatric physician has a greater array of tools at his or her disposal, and can treat the problem with greater precision and usually better results.

If the corn or callus is the offshoot of a bone spur or hammertoe condition, your podiatric physician may recommend further treatment.

✔ **Quick Tip**
Who Can Help Me?

The American College of Foot & Ankle Orthopedics & Medicine (ACFAOM) stands ready to help you find a podiatric physician in your area. Visit ACFAOM.org to find a professional who can help you find the most effective treatment.

How Can Corns And Calluses Be Prevented?

Wearing properly fitted shoes and paying special attention to your feet is your best bet for avoiding corns and calluses. Do not wear shoes that cause blisters, redness or sore spots on your feet; over time, your body develops corns and calluses to prevent further injury. Corns and calluses aren't contagious (the way plantar warts are), but they can be hard to get rid of if the patient persists in wearing shoes or performing activities that cause injury to his or her feet.

Outside of these precautions, follow common sense rules regarding foot health. Do examine your feet (and indeed, all of your skin) regularly. Note any unusual growths or lumps. Pay special attention to the soles of your feet, the tops of feet or toes, and the skin between the toes. Call anything unusual to the attention of your doctor immediately.

Do These Symptoms Always Mean Corns Or Calluses?

No—as mentioned before, several other problems, including plantar warts, blocked sweat glands and other lesions can have symptoms that are similar to those of corns and calluses. Therefore, it's essential to get a professional's diagnosis of the problem. If you assume that bump on your foot is a corn, and begin treatment with some kind of an over-the-counter medication—and it isn't a corn after all—the true problem could get far worse because of the delay in getting the correct treatment, not to mention the additional trauma you have inflicted on the foot, particularly if an infection is already present.

Chapter 57

Types Of Burns And Treatments

What Causes Burns?

You can get burned by heat and fire, radiation, sunlight, electricity, or chemicals. There are three degrees of burns:

- First-degree burns are red and painful. They swell a little. They turn white when you press on the skin. The skin over the burn may peel off after one or two days.

- Thicker burns, called second-degree burns, have blisters and are painful. The skin is very red or splotchy, and it may swell a lot.

- Third-degree burns cause damage to all layers of the skin. The burned skin looks white or charred. These burns may cause little or no pain because the nerves in the skin are damaged.

How Long Does It Take For Burns To Heal?

- First-degree burns usually heal in three to six days.

- Second-degree burns usually heal in two to three weeks.

- Third-degree burns usually take a very long time to heal.

About This Chapter: Reprinted with permission from "Burns: Taking Care of Burns," December 2006, http://familydoctor.org/online/famdocen/home/healthy/firstaid/after-injury/638.html. Copyright © 2006 American Academy of Family Physicians. All Rights Reserved.

How Are Burns Treated?

The treatment depends on what kind of burn you have. If a first- or second-degree burn covers an area larger than two to three inches in diameter, or is on your face, hands, feet or genitals, you should see a doctor right away. Third-degree burns require emergency medical attention.

☞ **Remember!!**
Do not put butter, oil, ice, or ice water on burns. This can cause more damage to the skin.

First-Degree Burn: Soak the burn in cool water. Then treat it with a skin-care product like aloe vera cream or an antibiotic ointment. To protect the burned area, you can put a dry gauze bandage over the burn. Take an over-the-counter pain reliever, such as acetaminophen (one brand name: Tylenol), ibuprofen (some brand names: Advil, Motrin) or naproxen (brand name: Aleve), to help with the pain.

Second-Degree Burn: Soak the burn in cool water for 15 minutes. If the burned area is small, put cool, clean, wet cloths on the burn for a few minutes every day. Then put on an antibiotic cream, or other creams or ointments prescribed by your doctor. Cover the burn with a dry nonstick dressing (for example, Telfa) held in place with gauze or tape. Check with your doctor's office to make sure you are up to date on tetanus shots.

Change the dressing every day. First, wash your hands with soap and water. Then gently wash the burn and put antibiotic ointment on it. If the burn area is small, a dressing may not be needed during the day. Check the burn every day for signs of infection, such as increased pain, redness, swelling or pus. If you see any of these signs, see your doctor right away. To prevent infection, avoid breaking any blisters that form.

Burned skin itches as it heals. Keep your fingernails cut short and don't scratch the burned skin. The burned area will be sensitive to sunlight for up to one year.

Third-Degree Burn: For third-degree burns, go to the hospital right away. Don't take off any clothing that is stuck to the burn. Don't soak the burn in water or apply any ointment. You can cover the burn with a sterile bandage or clean cloth until you receive medical assistance.

What Do I Need To Know About Electrical And Chemical Burns?

A person with an electrical burn (for example, from a power line) should go to the hospital right away. Electrical burns often cause serious injury inside the body. This injury may not show on the skin.

A chemical burn should be washed with large amounts of water. Take off any clothing that has the chemical on it. Don't put anything on the burned area. This might start a chemical reaction that could make the burn worse. If you don't know what to do, call 911 or your local poison control center, or see your doctor right away.

Chapter 58

What You Should Know About Animal Bites

Animal bites can sometimes result in severe infections and some people are at higher risk than others. Are you at risk? And do you know what to do if you are bitten?

The information and recommendations in this chapter will help you avoid serious problems.

I've always heard that dogs' mouths are cleaner than humans. Is this true?

Neither dogs nor cats nor humans have mouths that can even remotely be considered clean. All are filled with bacteria, many of which can cause disease if they enter broken skin. Over 130 disease-causing microbes have been isolated from dog and cat bite wounds. Animals' saliva is also heavily contaminated with bacteria, so a bite may not even be necessary to cause infection; if you have a cut or scratch and allow a pet to lick it, you could be setting yourself up for trouble.

What are the particular dangers from animal bites?

Bites to the hand, whether from cats or dogs, are potentially dangerous because of the structure of the hand. There are many bones, tendons, and joints in the hand and there is less blood circulation in these areas. This makes it harder for the body to fight infection in the hand. Infections that develop in the hand may lead to severe complications, such as osteomyelitis or septic arthritis.

In small children, bites to the face, neck, or head are extremely hazardous. Because their small stature often puts their heads near dogs' mouths, children are often bitten in these areas. Dog bites can cause fractures of the face and skull and lead to brain and nervous system infections. Dog bites cause, on average, about 15 to 20 fatalities a year in the United States. Most of these victims are infants and young children.

☞ **Remember!!**

If you have any of the risk factors listed here, particularly if you have had your spleen removed, it is very important that you take proper immediate care of any animal bite wound and promptly seek medical advice.

How do I know if I am at risk for infection?

Anyone who is bitten by a cat or a dog and who does not take proper care of the wound is at risk of developing infection. But some people are at increased risk.

- Are you over 50 years of age?

- Do you have diabetes, circulatory problems, liver disease, alcoholism, or HIV/AIDS?

- Have you had a mastectomy or organ transplant?

- Are you taking chemotherapy or long-term steroids?

- Have you had your spleen removed?

If you answered "yes" to any of these questions, you may be more likely to develop a serious infection than other people. You should take special care to avoid being bitten or scratched by any animal.

Which is worse, dog bites or cat bites?

Dogs have strong jaws—large dogs can exert more than 450 pounds of pressure per square inch—and their teeth are relatively dull. So the wounds caused by dogs are usually crushing of the tissue bitten and lacerations or tearing of the skin rather than puncture wounds. Most dog bites do not penetrate deeply enough to get bacteria into bones, tendons, or joints, but they often do a lot of damage just from the trauma of the bite. Tissue that has been crushed, however, such as may occur with a bite to the hand, is particularly susceptible to infection.

Cats' teeth are thin and sharp, so the wounds they cause are more likely to be puncture wounds. These wounds can reach into joints and bones and introduce bacteria deeply into the tissue. Puncture wounds are very difficult to clean, so a lot of bacteria may be left in the wound. Also, most cat bites are to the hand, which makes infection more likely.

Dog bites often do more outright damage, but only three to 18 percent become infected. In contrast, cat bites may appear more trivial, but up to 80 percent of cat bites may become infected if proper care is not taken.

What kinds of infections can develop?

Many infection-causing bacteria have been isolated from dog and cat bite wounds. The four we discuss here are probably the most significant.

Pasteurellosis: The most common bite-associated infection is caused by a bacterium called *Pasteurella*. Most cats and dogs—even healthy ones—naturally carry this organism in their mouths. When an animal bites a person (or another animal), these bacteria can enter the wound and start an infection. The first signs of pasteurellosis usually occur within two to 12 hours of the bite and include pain, reddening, and swelling of the area around the site of the bite. Pasteurellosis can progress quickly, spreading toward the body from the bitten area. It is important that you seek medical care immediately if these symptoms occur. Untreated, this infection can lead to severe complications. Bites to the hand need special attention; if pasteurellosis develops in the tissues of the hand, the bacteria can infect tendons or even bones and sometimes cause permanent damage if appropriate medical care is not administered promptly.

Streptococcal And Staphylococcal Infections: These bacteria can cause infections similar to those caused by *Pasteurella*. Redness and painful swelling occur at or near the site of the bite and progress toward the body. As with pasteurellosis, you should seek prompt medical care if these symptoms develop.

Capnocytophaga Infection: This is a very rare infection, but we mention it here because it is so dangerous if it develops. There is no common name for this infection, which is caused by the bacterium *Capnocytophaga canimorsus*. Most of the people who have become infected were bitten by dogs; in many instances the bite wounds themselves were tiny and would not have ordinarily called for any special medical care. But *Capnocytophaga* can cause septicemia, or blood poisoning, particularly in people whose immune systems are compromised by some underlying condition. Up to 30 percent of people who have developed septicemia have died. People who have had their spleens removed are at special risk for this infection. Early symptoms may include nausea, headache, muscle aches, and tiny reddened patches on the skin.

What should I do if I am bitten?

Immediately and thoroughly wash the wound with plenty of soap and warm water. The idea is to remove as much dirt and saliva—and therefore, bacteria—as possible. It may hurt to scrub a wound, but an infection will hurt a lot more. Scrub it well and run water over it for several minutes to make sure it is clean and all soap is rinsed out. It is a good idea to follow the washing with an antiseptic solution, such as iodine or other disinfectant, but always wash with soap and water first. Apply antibiotic ointment and cover the wound with gauze or a bandage. If the wound is severe, or if you have any of the risk factors listed in this chapter, seek medical advice at once. Your doctor may want you to take antibiotics to prevent infection from developing. If you have not had a recent tetanus booster, you may be advised to take one. And if you are bitten by a wild or stray animal that could have rabies, you may need to begin anti-rabies treatment.

If you have had your spleen removed, you should be aware that the potential for fatal infection exists, even from seemingly minor wounds. Some experts recommend that people without spleens should completely avoid contact with cats and dogs. This is an issue you and your doctor should discuss in detail.

For most people, however, the benefits of companion animals outweigh the risk. If you have any of the risk factors listed in this chapter, you should do everything possible to avoid being bitten or scratched by dogs or cats. If wounds do occur, you should clean them promptly and thoroughly and seek medical advice. A little care and common sense can go a long way in preventing bite-associated infections.

If you are bitten by any animal, always consult your physician for his or her recommendations.

Chapter 59

Bug Bites And Stings

Hey! A Bedbug Bit Me!

What A Bedbug Is

A bedbug is a small (about the size of a pencil eraser), flat, reddish-brown bug that can be found in homes all over the world. It hides during the day and comes out during the night to look for blood. A bedbug has a special ingredient in its saliva (spit) that keeps blood from clotting while it's eating.

What A Bedbug Bite Looks And Feels Like

If a person gets bitten by a bedbug, the bite will feel itchy. Bedbug bites look like little red bumps (similar to mosquito bites) and they can sometimes occur in a line on the body.

About This Chapter: The text in this chapter is from the following articles: "Hey! A Bed Bug Bit Me!," "Hey! A Bee Stung Me!," "Hey! A Black Widow Spider Bit Me!," "Hey! A Brown Recluse Spider Bit Me!," "Hey! A Chigger Bit Me!," "Hey! A Fire Ant Stung Me!," "Hey! A Flea Bit Me!," "Hey! A Gnat Bit Me!," "Hey! A Louse Bit Me!," "Hey! A Mosquito Bit Me!," "Hey! A Scorpion Stung Me!," "Hey! A Tarantula Bit Me!," and "Hey! A Tick Bit Me!," September 2007, reprinted with permission from www.kidshealth.org. Copyright © 2007 The Nemours Foundation. This information was provided by KidsHealth, one of the largest resources online for medically reviewed health information written for parents, kids, and teens. For more articles like this one, visit www.KidsHealth.org, or www.TeensHealth.org.

What You Should Do

If you think you've been bitten by a bedbug, wash the bites with soap and water. Put on some calamine lotion to help with the itching. An adult can find an anti-itch cream at the drugstore for you. Try not to scratch the bites too much because this can make them become infected.

> **✔ Quick Tip**
> **How To Avoid Getting Bitten**
>
> The best way to avoid getting bitten by bedbugs is to keep your room uncluttered so bedbugs won't have places to hide. Changing your sheets once a week and vacuuming the floor often are also important things to do. If you think you have bedbugs, ask an adult about the best way to get rid of the bugs.

What A Doctor Will Do

If you get an infection from scratching bedbug bites, a doctor will need to prescribe medication to clear up the infection.

Hey! A Bee Stung Me!

Bee, or honeybee, is the word many people use to describe any flying insect that has wings and a stinger. But honeybees are really only one of a group of insects that includes other bees, wasps, and ants.

Bees are fuzzy insects that feed on flowers. There are thousands of different types of bees worldwide, and they can be many different colors. The most familiar kind of bee is the honeybee. These bees build nests out of wax in old trees and manmade hives (like the ones that beekeepers take care of) and spend a lot of their time collecting nectar and pollen from flowers. Then they turn the nectar into honey for food.

Wasps are closely related to bees, but instead of only feeding on pollen and honey, wasps eat animal food, other insects, or spiders. They are not fuzzy like bees, but seem kind of smooth and shiny, and they have skinnier bodies. There are also thousands of different types of wasps in the world. Two common types of wasps are bald-faced hornets and yellow jackets. Bald-faced hornets are black with white markings, and they build papery nests shaped like footballs in trees and shrubs. Yellow jackets have yellow and black stripes on their bodies and are smaller than hornets and honeybees. They make their nests in the ground or in old tree stumps.

Ants are small insects that can be brown, black, or red. Some have wings and others don't. Some ants can sting, like the fire ant. Fire ants are tiny and reddish-brown and live in nests under the ground.

What A Bee Sting Looks And Feels Like

Honeybees, wasps, hornets, fire ants, and yellow jackets may look different and have different homes, but they all sting when they are upset. If a person is stung by any of these insects, the sting will feel a lot like a shot at the doctor's office.

The site of the sting will feel hot and it may itch. A red bump surrounded by white skin will develop around the sting, except for the sting of the fire ant, which turns into an itchy blister.

Wasps and many bees can sting more than once because they are able to pull out their stinger without injuring themselves. Only honeybees have special hooks on their stinger that keep the stinger in the skin after a person is stung. The stinger gets torn out of the bee's body as it tries to fly away. As a result, the honeybee dies after stinging.

What You Should Do

If you think you have been stung by one of these insects, tell an adult immediately. Some people are allergic to stings from insects. The symptoms of an allergic reaction include hives (red patches on the skin that sting and itch), nausea, dizziness, a tight feeling in the throat, or difficulty breathing. If these symptoms occur, the person needs medical attention right away.

But more often, you can follow these steps after getting stung:

- Have an adult help you remove the stinger, if one is left behind after a honeybee sting. (It doesn't really matter how it's removed. What is important is that it's removed as quickly as possible.)

- Wash the area with soap and water.

- Apply some ice to the area.

- Ask your mom or dad for a pain reliever.

What A Doctor Will Do

You'll want to check with the doctor if you have redness, swelling, or itching. Sometimes, the doctor will suggest giving a medicine

> ### ✔ Quick Tip
> ### How To Avoid Getting Stung
>
> The best way to keep from getting stung by bees is to avoid places where they spend time, like gardens or orchards in bloom. If you are going to be outside in summertime, keep your shoes on and don't wear sweet-smelling perfume. Dress in long pants and a lightweight, long-sleeved shirt. Avoid bright-colored clothing and clothing with flowery prints. Cover food at picnics and don't drink soda from open cans at a summer picnic or barbecue—yellow jackets like to climb inside for a sip.
>
> Stay away from garbage cans in summer that are swarming with bees. If you suddenly see a bee flying around you, don't swat at it or run around. This makes bees angry and upset, and they may sting. Just move slowly or stand still instead, and the bee will be more likely to move on.

called an antihistamine to control these symptoms. If a person has an allergic reaction to a bee sting, it's necessary for a doctor to immediately give a shot that fights the reaction. People who know that they are allergic to bee stings also sometimes carry emergency medicine that they can give to themselves to prevent a severe reaction from happening.

Hey! A Black Widow Spider Bit Me!

What A Black Widow Spider Is

The black widow spider is one of a few poisonous kinds of spiders in the United States. It is part of the arachnid family, which includes not just spiders, but ticks, mites, and scorpions, too. Its body is about one-half inch long (smaller than a dime), and it has long legs. The black widow spider is shiny and black with a red-orange or yellow mark in the shape of an hourglass on its stomach.

Black widow spiders and their relatives can be found almost anywhere in the Western hemisphere of the world in damp and dark places. Their favorite places are wood piles, tree stumps, trash piles, storage sheds, fruit and vegetable gardens, in stone walls, and under rocks. If they come inside, they will go to dark places like corners of closets, garages, or behind furniture. They are shy by nature and bite only when trapped, sat on, or accidentally touched.

What A Black Widow Spider Bite Looks And Feels Like

A person who gets bitten by a black widow spider might not know it right away, since the bite can sometimes feel like a little pinprick. After 30 to 40 minutes, though, the area of the bite will swell and hurt a lot, and sometimes a person can get achy all over. Other symptoms can include weakness, nausea, vomiting, sweating, and headache.

What You Should Do

If you ever think that you've been bitten by a black widow spider, tell an adult immediately. Black widow spider bites rarely kill people, but it's important to get medical attention as soon as you can because they can make you very sick. With an adult's help, wash the bite well with soap and water. Then apply an ice pack to the bite, and try to elevate the area and keep it still to help prevent the spread of venom (poison).

If it's possible, have an adult catch and bring the spider to the doctor's office with you. Even though it's usually easy to identify black widows, you'll want to make sure that's the kind of spider that bit you. The spider can be killed first before you bring it with you; just be sure not to squish it so much that no one can tell what it is.

What A Doctor Will Do

Doctors treat people who have been bitten by black widow spiders with medications to help relax the muscles and reduce pain. They sometimes give

✔ **Quick Tip**

How To Avoid Getting Bitten

The best way to avoid getting bitten by black widow spiders is to be careful in areas where they like to spend time. Don't play around in rock piles or wood piles. If you are working outside in the yard in big piles of logs or leaves, wear gloves. Be sure to shake out blankets and clothing that have been stored in the attic or the basement, or if they have been in a closet but not used for a long time. If you are cleaning behind furniture, look carefully behind it before reaching around. If you keep your shoes in a mudroom or garage, shake them out before putting them on.

antivenin, a medication that fights the venom in the spider's bite, if someone who has been bitten has underlying medical problems or doesn't get better from the other medications.

Hey! A Brown Recluse Spider Bit Me!

What A Brown Recluse Spider Is

The brown recluse spider is one of a few poisonous kinds of spiders in the United States. It is part of the arachnid family, which includes not just spiders, but ticks, mites, and scorpions, too. It has long, skinny legs and is about ½ to 1 inch long overall. Its entire body is brown, except for a dark mark in the shape of a violin on its head.

Brown recluse spiders are most commonly found in midwestern and southern states of the United States, and they usually hang out in dark places. When they are outside, they like to spend time in piles of rocks, wood, or leaves. If they come inside, brown recluse spiders will go to dark closets, attics, or basements. They aren't aggressive, and they bite only when disturbed.

What A Brown Recluse Spider Bite Looks And Feels Like

A person who gets bitten by a brown recluse spider may not notice anything at first or only feel a little sting at first. After about four to eight hours, the sting will start to hurt a little more. It might look like a bruise or might form a blister surrounded by a bluish-purple area that turns black or brown and becomes crusty after a few days.

What You Should Do

If you ever think that you've been bitten by a brown recluse spider, tell an adult immediately. Brown recluse spider bites rarely kill people, but it's important to get medical attention as soon as you can because they can make you pretty sick. With an adult's help, wash the bite well with soap and water. You can also apply ice to the area, elevate it, and keep it still.

If it's possible, have an adult catch and bring the spider to the doctor's office with you—this is important because it can sometimes be hard to diagnose a spider bite correctly. The spider can be killed first before you bring it with you; just be sure not to squish it so much that no one can tell what it is.

What A Doctor Will Do

Doctors treat people who have been bitten by a brown recluse spider with different types of medications like antibiotics, antihistamines, or pain medicines. Rarely, a skin graft might be needed if the skin is really damaged at the area of the bite. (A skin graft is when a small amount of skin is removed from some part of the body and put in a place where skin is damaged to create new skin.)

> ✔ **Quick Tip**
> **How To**
> **Avoid Getting Bitten**
>
> The best way to avoid getting bitten by brown recluse spiders is to be careful in areas where they like to spend time. Don't play around in rock piles or wood piles. If you are working outside in the yard in big piles of logs or leaves, wear gloves. Be sure to shake out blankets and clothing that have been stored in the attic or the basement, or if they have been in a closet but not used for a long time. If you keep your shoes in a mudroom or garage, shake them out before putting them on.

Hey! A Chigger Bit Me!

What A Chigger Is

Chiggers are tiny (most can only be seen with a magnifying glass) and red, and they are a type of mite. Mites aren't insects—they are arachnids and part of the same family as spiders, scorpions, and ticks. Chiggers are found all over the place, including in grassy fields, along lakes and streams, and in forests. There are adult chiggers and baby chiggers (called larvae), but only the baby chiggers bother people and animals.

Chiggers have tiny claws that allow them to attach tightly onto people and animals. Once attached, they are able to pierce the

> ✔ **Quick Tip**
> **How To Avoid Getting Bitten**
> - The best way to avoid getting bitten by a chigger is to wear an insect repellent. Ask your parents to apply one that contains 10 to 30 percent DEET.
> - When it's possible, wear long-sleeved shirts and long pants outside, especially if you'll be hiking or playing in fields.
> - Once you come in from being in an outdoor area that may have chiggers, take a hot shower and use plenty of soap. Also, be sure to wash your clothes in hot water to kill any chiggers that might be living there.

skin and inject their saliva, which contains digestive juices that dissolve skin cells. The chigger then slurps up the dissolved skin cells. To the chigger, this is a tasty meal. Having a chigger do this is very irritating to your skin. After a few days, the chigger will be done feeding and fall off a person's skin, leaving behind a red welt where it had once been.

What A Chigger Bite Looks And Feels Like

If a person gets bitten by a chigger, the bite will be very itchy. A chigger bite will cause a tiny red bump, which will get bigger and itchier as time goes on. The itchy bump can last for days or even a couple of weeks.

What You Should Do

If you think you've been bitten by a chigger, wash the bite with soap and water. Put on some calamine lotion or cool compresses to help with the itching, or an adult can find an anti-itch cream or medicine at the drugstore for you. Try not to scratch the bites too much, because this can make the bites become infected.

What A Doctor Will Do

Because chigger bites are so itchy, many people do get an infection from scratching the bites. If this happens, the doctor will prescribe a medication to help with the itching and a medicine to clear up the infection.

Hey! A Fire Ant Stung Me!

What A Fire Ant Is

There are many different types of fire ants, and they are found all throughout the southeastern and southwestern United States. The most common and aggressive kind is the red imported fire ant, which is reddish-brown and measures about 1/8-inch long (about half the size of a pencil eraser).

Red imported fire ants live in colonies that first nest in the ground, and then create a mound of dirt over the nest. These mounds can grow up to 18 inches high and over two feet wide. Red imported fire ants' nests can be found on lawns, in parks, on playgrounds, in fields, and in pastures. Some red imported fire ants create nests in walls of buildings.

What A Fire Ant Sting Looks And Feels Like

A person who gets stung by a fire ant will feel a sharp pain and burning. A person who steps on a fire ant mound will get a lot of stings at once because the ants have been disturbed where they all live together. Each sting will turn into an itchy white blister over the next day.

What You Should Do

If you ever think that you have been stung by a fire ant, tell an adult immediately. That's because the venom (poison) in the fire ants' stings can cause the area of the sting to swell up quite a bit, and a doctor may want to have a look to make sure you are not having an allergic reaction. The symptoms of an allergic reaction include hives (red patches on the skin that sting and itch), nausea, dizziness, a tight feeling in the throat, or difficulty breathing. If these symptoms occur, the person needs to get medical attention right away.

But more often, you can follow these steps after a fire ant sting:

- Wash the area with soap and water.

- Apply some ice to the area.

- Check with the doctor if you have redness, swelling, or itching.

> ✔ **Quick Tip**
> **How To**
> **Avoid Getting Bitten**
>
> The best way to avoid getting bitten by fire ants is to keep your shoes on when playing near fire ant mounds. If you come across one, don't ever poke at it or try to play with it.

What A Doctor Will Do

A doctor may suggest giving a medicine called an antihistamine to control swelling and itching. If you are having a more severe allergic reaction to a fire ant sting, he or she may give you a shot to fight the reaction. People who know that they are allergic to fire ant stings also sometimes carry emergency medicine that they can give to themselves to prevent a severe reaction from happening.

Hey! A Flea Bit Me!

What A Flea Is

A flea is a small (no bigger than the head of a pin) brown bug with a hard shell. Fleas have tiny claws at the ends of their legs to help them attach to people or other warm-blooded animals and drink their blood.

If you have a dog or cat, chances are pretty good that you've seen a flea. Fleas are often found on the coats of these animals. Once the animal comes inside, the fleas can then jump onto people or carpeting.

What A Flea Bite Looks And Feels Like

If a person gets bitten by a flea, the bite will feel itchy. Flea bites usually occur in groups of three or four bites on the body, and they look like tiny red bumps. A lot of kids end up with flea bites when they play with their dogs or cats.

What You Should Do

If you think you've been bitten by a flea, wash the bite with soap and water. Put on some calamine lotion to help with the itching, or an adult can find an anti-itch cream at the drugstore for you. Try not to scratch the bites too much, because this can make the bites become infected.

What A Doctor Will Do

If you get an infection from scratching flea bites, a doctor will need to prescribe medication to clear up the infection.

> ✔ **Quick Tip**
> ### How To Avoid Getting Bitten
>
> The best way to avoid getting bitten by fleas is to keep the fleas off your pets. Cats and dogs can be bathed in special flea-control shampoo. Your pet can wear a flea collar or take medication once a year which will also help keep fleas away. In addition, a professional exterminator can treat your home or yard with flea-control chemicals to keep the flea population down. Wearing an insect repellent also may help. Ask your parents to apply one that contains 10 to 30 percent DEET.

Hey! A Gnat Bit Me!

What A Gnat Is

A gnat (say: nat) is one of a family of insects that includes flies and mosquitoes. Gnats are actually tiny flies, and can go by different names (like blackflies, or midges). Gnats are found anyplace in the world where there is a river or stream because they lay their eggs in watery places. They need the blood of warm-blooded animals to survive. Unlike mosquitoes, gnats usually don't bite through clothing. But they can crawl into hair or under clothing to get at places such as ankles and belt lines.

What A Gnat Bite Looks And Feels Like

A person who gets bitten by a gnat may not even know it at the time. But soon after, the area around the bite will start to swell up. There may be a little bit of blood coming from the bite. The bite will be very itchy and can be painful.

What You Should Do

If you've been bitten by a gnat, wash the bite with soap and water. Because gnats can pick up bacteria from other things they've landed on (like rotten food or dead animals), it's also a good idea to swab the bite with a little antiseptic. An adult can find an anti-itch cream or anti-itch medicine at the drugstore that you swallow to help you with the itching. If the bite hurts a lot, you can ask an adult if you can take some pain medication. Putting an ice pack on the bite can also make it feel less painful.

> ✔ **Quick Tip**
> **How To Avoid Getting Bitten**
>
> The best way to avoid getting bitten by gnats is to wear an insect repellent. Ask your mom or dad to apply one that contains 10 to 30 percent DEET. When it's possible, wear long-sleeved shirts and long pants if you'll be hiking or playing near rivers and streams.

What A Doctor Will Do

If the area around a gnat bite is very swollen, a doctor might prescribe a special cream or medicine by mouth. If you develop an infection from scratching the bite, he or she may also prescribe an antibiotic to clear up the infection.

While it's very unusual for someone to have an allergic reaction to a gnat bite, you should tell an adult right away if you feel sick, have a hard time breathing, or get hives (red patches on the skin that sting and itch) on your skin. The doctor can treat allergic reactions with medicines.

Hey! A Louse Bit Me!

What A Louse Is

A louse is a parasite (say: par-uh-site), which means it feeds off of other living things. Lice (the word for more than one louse) are about the size of a sesame seed, and are tan to gray in color. Lice need to suck a tiny bit of blood to survive, and they sometimes live on people's heads and lay eggs in the hair, on the back of the neck, or behind the ears. It's very easy for a person with lice to give it to another person when they come into close head-to-head contact with each other. Sometimes, lice can be transmitted by friends sharing things that have touched the hair, such as combs, brushes, hats, and headphones. Lice cannot jump or fly, so a person can't catch lice by simply sitting near someone who has lice.

What A Louse Bite Looks And Feels Like

If a person gets lice, it doesn't feel like anything at first. A louse lays tiny, oval eggs called nits. They are yellow, tan, or brown before the lice hatch. After the lice hatch, nits appear clear or white. They look a little like dandruff flakes but they can't be shaken off. The lice mature within one to two weeks and begin feeding and attaching their tiny claws to the hair shaft. Louse bites look like tiny red spots on the skin, and they are very itchy.

What You Should Do

If your head is very itchy, tell an adult immediately. Getting lice has nothing to do with being dirty, and it's very common among kids who are in school together. It is something that will need to be cleared up as soon as possible.

What A Doctor Will Do

Doctors treat people who have lice by giving them a prescription for a medicated shampoo, cream, or lotion that kills lice, or instructing that they buy one off of the store shelf. An adult will need to use a fine-tooth comb to get rid of the existing nits and follow the instructions for putting

> ### ✔ Quick Tip
> ### How To Avoid Getting Bitten
>
> It can be hard to avoid lice completely, especially if you are like most kids and go to school every day. But there are things you can do to protect yourself:
>
> - If you know kids with lice, avoid touching them—especially their hair.
>
> - Always bring your own pillows, sleeping bags, or sheets to a sleepover.
>
> - Finally, do not share brushes, combs, hats, headphones, or hair accessories — like barrettes and headbands, with anyone else.

the medication in your hair to kill the lice. It's not a good a idea to use a hairdryer to dry a person's hair after using the medication, as some medicines contain flammable ingredients (which means they can catch on fire and burn easily). It may take a few days for the itching to stop and the treatment may need to be repeated in seven to 10 days to make sure any remaining lice eggs are killed.

All the carpets and furniture in the house should be vacuumed, and bedding, clothing, and stuffed animals should be washed in hot water or placed in airtight bags for at least 10 days to kill the lice and eggs. Brushes, combs, and hair accessories should be soaked in hot water, washed with medicated shampoo, or thrown away.

Hey! A Mosquito Bit Me!

What A Mosquito Is

A mosquito (say: mus-kee-toe) is an insect that is found all over the world. There are thousands of different kinds of mosquitoes in many different sizes and colors. The female mosquito needs blood from vertebrates (animals that have a spine) to lay eggs and produce more mosquitoes. She has a special part of her mouth that she uses to suck blood, and her saliva (spit) thins the blood so she can drink it. In fact, it's the mosquito's saliva that makes the bites itch.

What A Mosquito Bite Looks And Feels Like

A person who gets bitten by a mosquito will notice a round pink or red bump that itches a lot.

✔ Quick Tip
How To Avoid Getting Bitten

The best way to avoid mosquito bites is to wear an insect repellent. Repellents that include one of these ingredients are best: DEET, lemon eucalyptus, or picaridin. Ask a parent to help you apply them.

Since mosquitoes lay their eggs in water, it's also a good idea to empty out buckets, flower pots, toys, and other things in your yard that may have collected water during a rainstorm. And when it's possible, wear long-sleeved shirts and long pants to keep mosquitoes away from your skin.

What You Should Do

If you think you've been bitten by a mosquito, wash the bite with soap and water. Put on some calamine lotion to help stop the itching, or an adult can find an anti-itch cream at the drugstore for you. Placing an ice pack on the bite may also help. Tell an adult you've been bitten by a mosquito, especially if you live in the eastern United States.

What A Doctor Will Do

It's very unusual for someone to have an allergic reaction to a mosquito bite. But if you develop an allergic reaction and feel dizzy or sick, tell an adult immediately. A doctor can treat allergic reactions with medicines.

Hey! A Scorpion Stung Me!

What A Scorpion Is

A scorpion is part of the arachnid family, which also includes mites, ticks, and spiders. Scorpions are about three inches long (about the length of a crayon), with eight legs and a small pair of claws that look like crabs' claws. A scorpion's stinger is at the end of its long tail.

There are more than 1,000 species of scorpions all over the world, and at least 70 species are found in United States, mostly in the southwestern states and Florida. Of these species, only one type of scorpion, which usually lives in Arizona, New Mexico, and other southwestern states, can kill people. Scorpions like to live in cool, damp places like basements, wood piles, and junk piles. They are usually nocturnal (they sleep during the day and come out at night) and are usually more active when it rains.

What A Scorpion Sting Looks And Feels Like

If a person gets stung by a scorpion, the area of the sting will hurt and may get swollen or red, depending on the type of scorpion. More severe reactions from the venom (poison) involving other parts of the body also can occur.

What You Should Do

If you ever think you've been stung by a scorpion, tell an adult immediately. Because it's hard to tell a dangerous scorpion from one that is harmless, all scorpion stings must be treated by a doctor. With an adult's help, put an ice pack on the sting immediately to keep down swelling.

What A Doctor Will Do

Doctors treat someone stung by a scorpion with medications if needed that help take pain away and control the body's reactions to the venom. They may give a medicine called antivenin that fights the scorpion's venom to someone who doesn't get better with the other medications.

> ✔ **Quick Tip**
> **How To**
> **Avoid Getting Bitten**
>
> The best way to avoid getting stung by scorpions is to avoid the places where they like to spend time. Don't play in junk piles or wood piles, and if you are working outside with big piles of logs, wear gloves. If you live in the American Southwest and keep your shoes in a garage, basement, or mudroom, shake them out carefully before putting them on.

Hey! A Tarantula Bit Me!

What A Tarantula Is

A tarantula is a hairy spider that is part of the arachnid family, which also includes mites, ticks, and scorpions. Tarantulas are found all over the world and can grow up to five inches long, but those found in the United States are usually about two to three inches long (about the length of a crayon). Tarantulas can be black, brown, gray, or even brightly colored. Most people are afraid of tarantulas because they are so large and weird-looking, but the truth is that these spiders are not dangerous. They live in nests in the ground and are pretty timid, avoiding people whenever they can.

What A Tarantula Bite Looks And Feels Like

If a person gets bitten by a tarantula, the bite will probably feel a lot like a bee sting, with pain in the area of the bite. It will look like a bee sting, too, with redness and some swelling. Because the tarantula's venom (poison) is weak, it's unusual to have more severe reactions involving other parts of the body.

What You Should Do

If you think you've been bitten by a tarantula, wash the bite with soap and water. If the bite hurts a lot, you can ask an adult for some pain medication. Placing an ice pack on the bite can also help.

✔ Quick Tip
How To Avoid Getting Bitten

If you come across a tarantula, don't bother it or try to play with it. These spiders will not bite you unless they feel threatened—if you leave them alone, they will leave you alone.

What A Doctor Will Do

Allergic reactions to a tarantula's bite are unusual. But just like some people have allergic reactions to bee stings (like trouble breathing or feeling sick), some people may have allergic reactions to tarantula bites. If a doctor suspects that someone is allergic to a tarantula bite, he or she will treat the person with medicine to fight this reaction.

Hey! A Tick Bit Me!

A tick is part of the arachnid family, which also includes mites, spiders, and scorpions. A tick attaches itself to the skin of an animal and sucks blood. There are hundreds of kinds of ticks on the planet, and they can be found almost everywhere. The two types of ticks that many people talk about are the deer tick and the dog tick.

The deer tick is about the same size as the head of a pin, and it is found in many parts of the United States. One of the diseases that deer ticks can carry is Lyme disease, especially ticks in New England and parts of the Midwest. (Lyme disease gets its name from the place where it was discovered—Lyme, Connecticut, which is in New England.) The dog tick is very common, and can be up to ½ inch long. If you have a dog, chances are pretty good that you've seen a dog tick on its coat. One disease that this type of tick can carry is called Rocky Mountain spotted fever.

What A Tick Bite Looks And Feels Like

A person who gets bitten by a tick usually won't feel anything at all. There might be a little redness around the area of the bite. If you think you've been bitten by a tick, tell an adult immediately. Some ticks carry diseases (such as Lyme disease or Rocky Mountain spotted fever) and can pass them to people.

What You Should Do

Ask an adult to check you for ticks after you've been playing or hiking in the woods, and have him or her pay special attention to your head (including your scalp), back, neck, armpits, and groin area. If you ever find a tick on you, ask for an adult's help in removing it. Using tweezers, an adult should grab the tick as close as possible to your skin, and pull the tick off in one motion. Don't cover the tick with petroleum jelly, rubbing alcohol, or fingernail polish, since these don't help the tick come out and can make things more complicated. If any of the tick parts are left behind, they should be removed using a sterile needle or pin. Once the tick is removed, your parent may want to put the tick in a jar to save it to show to your doctor.

> ✔ **Quick Tip**
> ## How To Avoid Getting Bitten
>
> Ticks like spending time in shrubbery, where they can remain close to the ground in order to jump on people or animals that pass by. If you are hiking in the woods, wear long sleeves and long pants, and tuck your pants into your socks. Wearing an insect repellent also might help. Have your parents apply one that contains 10 to 30 percent DEET.
>
> Dogs are also very good at picking up ticks in their coats, so ask an adult to help you bathe your dog with a tick shampoo and give your dog a tick collar.

What A Doctor Will Do

Doctors don't need to treat most tick bites. But if the tick was carrying Lyme disease or Rocky Mountain spotted fever and passed it on, any symptoms that might mean you are sick will be treated with antibiotics. Your doctor may ask to see the tick to help make a diagnosis. If these diseases are treated early on, it's rare for there to be any lasting changes to a person's health.

Chapter 60

Ticks And Lyme Disease

Stop Ticks

Gardening, camping, hiking, just playing outdoors—these are all great spring and summertime activities, but don't forget about the ticks that may be in the same environment. Fortunately there are several tactics you can use to prevent tick bites and reduce your risk of tick-borne disease.

Some of the more common diseases that you can get from a tick bite include:

- Babesiosis

- Ehrlichiosis

- Lyme disease

- Rocky Mountain spotted fever

- Southern tick-associated rash illness

- Tick-borne relapsing fever

- Tularemia

About This Chapter: Text in this chapter is from "Stop Ticks," Centers for Disease Control and Prevention, August 2008; and "Learn About Lyme Disease," and "Tick Removal," from Centers for Disease Control and Prevention, October 2008.

✎ What's It Mean?

Babesiosis: A disease caused by infection with a species of the protozoan Babesia, transmitted by ticks. In animals, the disease is characterized by fever, malaise, listlessness, severe anemia, and hemoglobinuria (the presence of free hemoglobin in the urine). The death rate frequently is higher in adult than in young animals.

Colorado Tick Fever: An infection caused by Colorado tick fever virus and transmitted to humans by *Dermacentor andersoni*. The symptoms are mild, there is no rash, the temperature is not excessive, and the disease is rarely, if ever, fatal.

Ehrlichiosis: Infection with *leukocytic rickettsiae* of the genus *Ehrlichia*. In humans, the infection produces manifestations similar to those of Rocky Mountain spotted fever.

Lyme Disease: A subacute inflammatory disorder caused by infection with *Borrelia burgdorferi*, and transmitted by the deer tick (*Ixodes scapularis*), in the eastern United States and the western black-legged tick (*I. pacificus*), in the western United States. The characteristic skin lesion, *erythema chronicum migrans,* is usually preceded or accompanied by fever, malaise, fatigue, headache, and stiff neck; neurologic, cardiac, or articular manifestations may occur weeks to months later.

Powassan Encephalitis: An acute disease of children varying clinically from undifferentiated febrile illness to encephalitis. The disease is caused by the Powassan virus, a member of the *Flaviviridae* family, and transmitted by ixodid ticks. Most frequently seen in Canada.

Rocky Mountain Spotted Fever: An acute infectious disease of high mortality, characterized by frontal and occipital headache, intense lumbar pain, malaise, a moderately high continuous fever, and a rash on the wrists, palms, ankles, and soles from the second to the fifth day, later spreading to all parts of the body. It occurs in the spring of the year primarily in the southeastern United States and the Rocky Mountain region, although it is also endemic elsewhere in the United States, in parts of Canada, in Mexico, and in South America.

Tularemia: A disease transmitted to humans from rodents through the bite of a deer fly and other bloodsucking insects. The disease can also be acquired directly through the bite of an infected animal or through handling of an infected animal carcass. Symptoms, similar to those of undulant fever and plague, are a prolonged intermittent or remittent fever and often swelling and suppuration of the lymph nodes draining the site of infection. Rabbits are an important reservoir host.

Source: Stedman's Online Medical Dictionary, 2008.

Other diseases that you can get from a tick in the United States include anaplasmosis (a tick-borne disease of cattle and sheep), Colorado tick fever, and Powassan encephalitis.

Some species and some life stages of ticks are so small that they can be difficult to see, but all hungrily look for animals and people to bite. Depending on the species, ticks may be found in a variety of environments, often in or near wooded areas. You may come into contact with ticks when walking through infested areas or by brushing up against infested vegetation (such as leaf litter or shrubs). Ticks also feed on mammals and birds, which play a role in maintaining ticks and the pathogens they carry.

Tick-borne diseases can occur worldwide. Fortunately, there are some simple steps you can take to protect yourself.

Protect Yourself From Tick Bites

Know Where To Expect Ticks: Ticks live in moist and humid environments, particularly in or near wooded or grassy areas. You may come into contact with ticks during outdoor activities around your home or when walking through vegetation such as leaf litter or shrubs. Always walk in the center of trails, in order to avoid ticks.

Use A Repellent With DEET: Use a repellent with DEET (on skin or clothing) or permethrin (on clothing) and wear long sleeves, long pants and socks. Products containing permethrin can be used to treat boots, clothing and camping gear and can remain protective through several washings. Repellents containing 20 percent or more DEET can be applied to the skin, and they can protect up to several hours. Always follow product instructions for application. Parents should apply this product to their children, avoiding contact with the hands, eyes, and mouth.

Wear Light-Colored Clothing: Wearing light-colored clothing allows you to see ticks crawling on your clothing.

Tuck Your Pant Legs Into Your Socks: Tuck your pants legs into your socks so that ticks cannot crawl up inside of your pant legs. Some ticks can crawl down into shoes and are small enough to crawl through most socks. When traveling in areas with lone star ticks (which are associated with Southern tick-associated rash illness, ehrlichiosis, and possibly Rocky Mountain spotted fever) you should examine your feet and ankles to ensure that ticks are not attached.

Perform Daily Tick Checks

Check your body for ticks after being outdoors, even in your own yard. Conduct a body check upon return from potentially tick-infested areas by searching your entire body for ticks. Use a hand-held or full-length mirror to view all parts of your body and remove any tick you find.

Check Children For Ticks

Children should be checked for ticks, especially in the hair, when returning from potentially tick-infested areas. Remove any tick you find on a child's body.

> ✔ **Quick Tip**
> **Where To Check Your Body For Ticks**
>
> • Under the arms
> • In and around the ears
> • Inside belly button
> • Back of the knees
> • In and around the hair
> • Between the legs
> • Around the waist
>
> Source: "Stop Ticks," CDC, August 2008.

Check Your Clothing And Pets For Ticks

Ticks may be carried into the house on clothing and pets. Both should be examined carefully, and any ticks that are found should be removed. Placing clothes into a dryer on high heat effectively kills ticks.

Reduce Ticks In Your Yard

• **Modify Your Landscape To Create Tick-Safe Zones:** To do this, keep play areas and playground equipment away from shrubs, bushes, and other vegetation. Also, regularly remove leaf litter and clear tall grasses and brush around homes, and place wood chips or gravel between lawns and wooded areas to keep ticks away from recreational areas.

• **Provide A Vegetation-Free Play Area:** Keep play areas and playground equipment away from shrubs, bushes, and other vegetation.

- **Use A Chemical Control Agent:** Effective tick control chemicals are available for use by the homeowner, or they can be applied by a professional pest control expert, and even limited applications can greatly reduce the number of ticks. A single springtime application of acaricide can reduce the population of ticks that cause Lyme disease by 68 to 100 percent.

- **Discourage Deer:** Removing plants that attract deer and constructing physical barriers may help discourage deer from entering your yard and bringing ticks with them.

Prevent Ticks On Animals

Prevent family pets from bringing ticks into the home. Maintain your family pet under a veterinarian's care. Two ways to get rid of ticks on dogs and cats are applying tick medicine and using a tick collar. Be sure to use these products according to the package instructions.

Lyme Disease

Lyme disease is caused by the bacterium *Borrelia burgdorferi* and is transmitted to humans by the bite of infected black-legged ticks. Typical symptoms include fever, headache, fatigue, and a characteristic skin rash called

☞ **Remember!!**
What To Do If You Are Bitten By A Tick

Remove an attached tick as soon as you notice it. Watch for signs of illness such as rash or fever, and see a health care provider if these develop.

Your risk of acquiring a tick-borne illness depends on many factors, including where you live, what type of tick bit you, and how long the tick was attached. If you become ill after a tick bite, see a health care provider.

Source: "Stop Ticks," CDC, August 2008.

erythema migrans. If left untreated, infection can spread to joints, the heart, and the nervous system.

Lyme disease is diagnosed based on symptoms, physical findings (e.g., rash), and the possibility of exposure to infected ticks; laboratory testing is helpful in the later stages of disease.

Most cases of Lyme disease can be treated successfully with a few weeks of antibiotics. Steps to prevent Lyme disease include using insect repellent, removing ticks promptly, landscaping, and integrated pest management. The ticks that transmit Lyme disease can occasionally transmit other tick-borne diseases as well.

✔ Quick Tip
How To Remove A Tick

Remove a tick from your skin as soon as you notice it. Use fine-tipped tweezers to firmly grasp the tick very close to your skin. With a steady motion, pull the tick's body away from your skin. Then clean your skin with soap and warm water. Throw the dead tick away with your household trash.

Avoid crushing the tick's body. Do not be alarmed if the tick's mouthparts remain in the skin. Once the mouthparts are removed from the rest of the tick, it can no longer transmit the Lyme disease bacteria. If you accidentally crush the tick, clean your skin with soap and warm water or alcohol.

Don't use petroleum jelly, a hot match, nail polish, or other products to remove a tick.

Source: "Tick Removal," CDC, October 2008.

Chapter 61

Mosquitoes And West Nile Virus

What is West Nile virus?

West Nile virus is a potentially serious illness. Experts believe West Nile virus is established as a seasonal epidemic in North America that flares up in the summer and continues into the fall. This chapter contains important information that can help you recognize and prevent West Nile virus.

What can I do to prevent West Nile virus?

The easiest and best way to avoid West Nile virus is to prevent mosquito bites.

- When you are outdoors, use insect repellent containing an EPA-registered active ingredient. Follow the directions on the package.

- Many mosquitoes are most active at dusk and dawn. Be sure to use insect repellent and wear long sleeves and pants at these times or consider staying indoors during these hours.

- Make sure you have good screens on your windows and doors to keep mosquitoes out.

About This Chapter: Text in this chapter is from "West Nile Virus: What You Need To Know," Centers for Disease Control and Prevention, September 2006.

What are the symptoms of West Nile virus?

Serious Symptoms In A Few People: About one in 150 people infected with West Nile virus will develop severe illness. The severe symptoms can include high fever, headache, neck stiffness, stupor, disorientation, coma, tremors, convulsions, muscle weakness, vision loss, numbness, and paralysis. These symptoms may last several weeks, and neurological effects may be permanent.

> **✔ Quick Tip**
> **How To Get Rid Of Mosquito Breeding Sites**
> - Empty standing water from flower pots, buckets and barrels
> - Change the water in pet dishes and replace the water in bird baths weekly
> - Drill holes in tire swings so water drains out
> - Keep children's wading pools empty and on their sides when they aren't being used.

Milder Symptoms In Some People: Up to 20 percent of people who become infected have symptoms such as fever, headache, and body aches, nausea, vomiting, and sometimes swollen lymph glands or a skin rash on the chest, stomach, and back. Symptoms can last for as short as a few days, though even healthy people have become sick for several weeks.

No Symptoms In Most People: Approximately 80 percent of people (about four out of five) who are infected with West Nile virus will not show any symptoms at all.

How does West Nile virus spread?

Infected Mosquitoes: Most often, West Nile virus is spread by the bite of an infected mosquito. Mosquitoes become infected when they feed on infected birds. Infected mosquitoes can then spread West Nile virus to humans and other animals when they bite.

Transfusions, Transplants, and Mother-To-Child: In a very small number of cases, West Nile virus also has been spread through blood transfusions, organ transplants, breast-feeding and even during pregnancy from mother to baby.

Not Through Touching: West Nile virus is not spread through casual contact such as touching or kissing a person with the virus.

How soon do infected people get sick?

People typically develop symptoms between three and 14 days after they are bitten by the infected mosquito.

How is West Nile virus infection treated?

There is no specific treatment for West Nile virus infection. In cases with milder symptoms, people experience symptoms such as fever and aches that pass on their own, although even healthy people have become sick for several weeks. In more severe cases, people usually need to go to the hospital where they can receive supportive treatment including intravenous fluids, help with breathing, and nursing care.

✔ Quick Tip
What should I do if I think I have West Nile virus?

Milder West Nile virus illness improves on its own, and people do not necessarily need to seek medical attention for this infection though they may choose to do so. If you develop symptoms of severe West Nile virus illness, such as unusually severe headaches or confusion, seek medical attention immediately. Severe West Nile virus illness usually requires hospitalization. Pregnant women and nursing mothers are encouraged to talk to their doctor if they develop symptoms that could be West Nile virus.

What is the risk of getting sick from West Nile virus?

People Over 50 Are At Higher Risk For Severe Illness: People over the age of 50 are more likely to develop serious symptoms of West Nile virus if they do get sick and should take special care to avoid mosquito bites.

Being Outside Means You're At Risk: The more time you're outdoors, the more time you could be bitten by an infected mosquito. Pay attention to avoiding mosquito bites if you spend a lot of time outside, either working or playing.

Risk Through Medical Procedures Is Very Low: All donated blood is checked for West Nile virus before being used. The risk of getting West Nile virus through blood transfusions and organ transplants is very small, and should not prevent people who need surgery from having it. If you have concerns, talk to your doctor.

Pregnancy And Nursing Do Not Increase Risk Of Becoming Infected With West Nile Virus: The risk that West Nile virus may present to a fetus or an infant infected through breast milk is still being evaluated.

What is the CDC doing about West Nile virus?

The Centers for Disease Control and Prevention (CDC) is working with state and local health departments, the Food and Drug Administration (FDA) and other government agencies, as well as private industry, to prepare for and prevent new cases of West Nile virus.

Some things CDC is doing include the following:

- Coordinating a nationwide electronic database where states share information about West Nile virus

- Helping states develop and carry out improved mosquito prevention and control programs

- Developing better, faster tests to detect and diagnose West Nile virus

- Creating new education tools and programs for the media, the public, and health professionals

- Opening new testing laboratories for West Nile virus

- Working with partners on the development of vaccines

> **✔ Quick Tip**
> **What else should I know?**
> **If You Find A Dead Bird:** Don't handle the body with your bare hands. Contact your local health department for instructions on reporting and disposing of the body. They may tell you to dispose of the bird after they log your report.

Part Seven

If You Need More Information

Chapter 62

Additional Reading About Skin Concerns

Acne

100 Questions and Answers About Acne. Day, Doris J. Sudbury, MA.: Jones and Bartlett Publishers, 2005.

Acne. American Academy of Dermatology. As of March 20, 2009: http://www.aad.org/public/publications/pamphlets/common_acne.html

Hair Loss

Alopecia Areata. Levy, Janey. New York: Rosen Publishing Group, 2007.

Frequently Asked Questions. National Alopecia Areata Foundation. As of March 20, 2009: http://www.naaf.org/requestinfo/faq.asp

Lupus

The Lupus Book: A Guide for Patients and Their Families. Wallace, Daniel J. New York: Oxford University Press, 2009.

Nail Care

Nail Fungus & Nail Health. American Academy of Dermatology. As of March 20, 2009: http://www.aad.org/public/publications/pamphlets/common_nail.html

---

About This Chapter: Topics in this chapter are listed alphabetically by topic and title. Information in this chapter was compiled from many sources deemed accurate; inclusion does not constitute endorsement.

Skin Cancer

Actinic Keratosis. Skin Cancer Foundation. As of March 25, 2009: http://www.skincancer.org/Actinic-Keratosis/

Facts about Sunburn and Skin Cancer. Skin Cancer Foundation. As of March 25, 2009: http://www.skincancer.org/facts-about-sunburn-and-skin-cancer.html

Quick Facts about Teen Tanning. Skin Cancer Foundation. As of March 25, 2009: http://www.skincancer.org/quick-facts-about-teen-tanning.html

Saving Your Skin: Prevention, Early Detection, and Treatment of Melanoma and other Skin Cancers. Kenet, Barney, and Patricia Lawler. New York: Four Walls Eight Windows, 1994.

Self-Examination. Skin Cancer Foundation. As of March 25, 2009: http://www.skincancer.org/Self-Examination/

Skin Cancer. American Academy of Dermatology. As of March 20, 2009: http://www.aad.org/public/publications/pamphlets/sun_skin.html

Skin Cancer. National Cancer Institute. As of March 25, 2009: http://www.cancer.gov/cancertopics/types/skin

Skin Cancer Information. American Cancer Society. As of March 25, 2009: http://www.cancer.org/docroot/home/index.asp. Click on 'Site Index' at top right-hand corner of page, under 'For Health Information Seekers' select 'Prevention & Early Detection.' Under 'Cancer Prevention' heading, click on 'Sun Safety' then 'Skin Cancer Facts.'

Understanding Basal Cell Carcinoma: What You Need to Know. Robbins, Perry. New York: Skin Cancer Foundation, 2007.

Understanding Melanoma: What You Need to Know. Robbins, Perry, and Maritza Perez. New York: Skin Cancer Foundation, 1996.

Understanding Squamous Cell Carcinoma: What You Need to Know. Robbins, Perry. New York: Skin Cancer Foundation, 2008.

Skin Care And Cosmetic Procedures

The Beauty Bible: From Acne to Wrinkles and Everything in Between. Begoun, Paula. Seattle: Beginning Press, 1997.

Additional Reading About Skin Concerns 391

The Body Art Book: A Complete, Illustrated Guide to Tattoos, Piercings, and Other Body Modifications. Miller, Jean-Chris. New York: Berkley Books, 1997.

Cosmetic Plastic Surgery Procedures At-A-Glance. American Society of Plastic Surgery. As of March 25, 2009: http://www.plasticsurgery.org/Patients_and_Consumers/Procedures/Cosmetic_Procedures.html

Cosmetic Procedures. American Academy of Cosmetic Surgery. As of March 25, 2009: http://www.cosmeticsurgery.org/patients/procedures.cfm

Darker Side of Tanning. American Academy of Dermatology. As of March 20, 2009: http://www.aad.org/public/publications/pamphlets/sun_darker.html

Don't Go to the Cosmetics Counter Without Me. Begoun, Paula, Bryan Barron. Renton, WA.: Beginning Press, 2008.

Encyclopedia of Body Adornment. DeMello, Margo. Westport, CT.: Greenwood Press, 2007.

Facial Rejuvenation: A Total Approach. Goldberg, David J. (ed). New York: Springer-Verlag, 2007.

Ink: The Not-Just-Skin-Deep Guide to Getting a Tattoo. Green, Terisa. New York: New American Library, 2005.

InSPAration: A Teen's Guide to Healthy Living Inspired by Today's Top Spas. Sammons, Mary Beth, and Samantha Moss. New York, N.Y.: Watson-Guptill Publications, 2005.

The New Science of Perfect Skin. Yarosh, Daniel. New York: Broadway Books, 2008.

The Smart Woman's Guide to Plastic Surgery. Loftus, Jean. *Updated Second Edition*. New York: McGraw-Hill, 2008.

Straight Talk About Cosmetic Surgery. Perry, Arthur W. New Haven: Yale University Press, 2007.

Tattoos, Body Piercings, and Other Skin Adornments. American Academy of Dermatology. As of March 20, 2009: http://www.aad.org/public/publications/pamphlets/cosmetic_tattoos.html

Think Before You Ink: Are Tattoos Safe? Food and Drug Administration. As of March 20, 2009: http://www.fda.gov/consumer/features/tattoos120607.html

Skin-Related Diseases and Problems

Coping with Lyme Disease: A Practical Guide to Dealing with Diagnosis and Treatment. Lang, Denise. New York: Henry Holt, 2004.

Directory of Skin Diseases. American Osteopathic College of Dermatology. As of March 25, 2009: http://www.aocd.org/skin/dermatologic_diseases/

Eczema-Free for Life. Nasir, Adnan, and Priscilla Burgess. New York: Harper Collins, 2005.

Infection Common in Patients with Atopic Dermatitis. American Academy of Dermatology. EczemaNet Article. As of March 20, 2009: http://www.skincarephysicians.com/eczemanet/infection.html

Psoriasis: Everything You Need to Know. Langley, Richard G. B. Buffalo, N.Y.: Firefly Books, 2005.

The Scleroderma Book: A Guide for Patients and Families. Mayes, Maureen. New York: Oxford University Press, 2005.

Skin Pictures Slideshow: Adult Skin Problems. MedicineNet.com. As of March 25, 2009: http://www.medicinenet.com/skin_problems_pictures_slideshow/article.htm

Types of Eczema: Atopic Dermatitis. American Academy of Dermatology. EczemaNet Article. As of March 20, 2009: http://www.skincarephysicians.com/eczemanet/atopic_dermatitis.html

Skin—General Information

Andrews' Diseases of the Skin: Clinical Dermatology 10th Edition. James, William D., Timothy G. Berger, and Dirk M. Elston. Philadelphia: Saunders Elsevier, 2006.

Dermatology Guide. About.com. As of March 25, 2009: http://dermatology.about.com/

Fitzpatrick's Color Atlas and Synopsis of Clinical Dermatology. Wolff, Klaus, and Richard A. Johnson. New York: McGraw-Hill, 2009.

The Life of the Skin. Balin, Arthur K., Loretta Pratt Balin, and Marietta Whittlesey. New York: Bantam Books, 1997.

Chapter 63

Resources For More Skin Information

American Academy of Allergy, Asthma and Immunology

555 East Wells Street, Suite 1100
Milwaukee, WI 53202-3823
Phone: 414-272-6071
Website: http://www.aaaai.org
E-mail: info@aaaai.org

American Academy of Dermatology

P.O. Box 4014
Schaumburg, IL 60618-4014
Phone: 847-330-0230
Toll Free: 866-503-SKIN (7546)
Fax: 847-240-1859
Website: http://www.aad.org
E-mail: MRC@aad.org

American Academy of Facial Plastic and Reconstructive Surgery

310 S. Henry Street
Alexandria, VA 22314
Phone: 703-299-9291
Fax: 703-299-8898
Website: http://www.aafprs.org
E-mail: info@aafprs.org

American Academy of Family Physicians

11400 Tomahawk Creek Parkway
Leawood, KS 66211-2680
Phone: 913-906-6000
Toll Free: 800-274-2237
Fax: 913-906-6075
Website: http://www.aafp.org

American College of Allergy, Asthma and Immunology
85 West Algonquin Road, Suite 550
Arlington Heights, IL 60005
Website: http://www.acaai.org

American College of Foot and Ankle Orthopedics and Medicine
5272 River Road, Suite 630
Bethesda, MD 20816
Phone: 301-718-6505
Toll Free: 800-265-8263
Fax: 301-656-0989
Website: http://www.acfaom.org
E-mail: info@acfaom.org

American College of Foot and Ankle Surgeons
8725 West Higgins Road, Suite 555
Chicago, IL 60631-2724
Phone: 773-693-9300
Toll Free: 800-421-2237
Fax: 773-693-9304
Website: http://www.acfas.org
E-mail: info@acfas.org

American Lyme Disease Foundation, Inc.
P.O. Box 466
Lyme, CT 06371
Website: http://www.aldf.com
E-mail: inquire@aldf.com

American Podiatric Medical Association
9312 Old Georgetown Road
Bethesda, MD 20814-1621
Phone: 301-581-9200
Website: http://www.apma.org

American Society for Dermatologic Surgery
5550 Meadowbrook Drive, Suite 120
Rolling Meadows, IL 60008
Phone: 847-956-0900
Fax: 847-956-0999
Website: http://www.asds.net

American Vitiligo Research Foundation
P.O. Box 7540
Clearwater, FL 33758
Phone: 727-461-3899
Fax: 727-461-4796
Website: http://www.avrf.org
E-mail: vitiligo@avrf.org

Center for Young Women's Health
333 Longwood Avenue
Boston, MA 02115
Phone: 617-355-2994
Fax: 617-730-0186
Website: http://www.youngwomenshealth.org

Centers for Disease Control and Prevention

1600 Clifton Road
Atlanta, GA 30333
Toll Free: 800-232-4636
Website: http://www.cdc.gov
E-mail: cdcinfo@cdc.gov

Cleveland Clinic Foundation

9500 Euclid Avenue
Cleveland, OH 44195
Phone: 216-444-2200
Toll Free: 800-223-2273
Website: http://my.clevelandclinic.org

Federal Trade Commission

600 Pennsylvania Avenue, NW
Washington, DC 20580
Phone: 202-326-2222
Website: http://www.ftc.gov

Food and Drug Administration

10903 New Hampshire Ave.
Silver Spring, MD 20903
Toll Free: 888-463-6332
Website: http://www.fda.gov

Healthlink

Medical College of Wisconsin
Office of Clinical Informatics
9200 West Wisconsin Ave., Suite 2975
Milwaukee, WI 53226
Fax: 414-805-7967
Website: http://healthlink.mcw.edu
E-mail: healthlink@mcw.edu

International Hyperhidrosis Society

Suite 6121-A, Kellers Church Road
Pipersville, PA 18947
Website: http://www.sweathelp.org
E-mail: info@SweatHelp.org

Louisiana State University School of Veterinary Medicine

Skip Bertman Drive
Baton Rouge, LA 70803
Phone: 225-578-9900
Fax: 225-578-9916
Website: http://www.vetmed.lsu.edu
E-mail: svmweb@vetmed.lsu.edu

Lyme Disease Foundation

P.O. Box 332
Tolland, CT 06084-0332
Phone: 860-870-0070
Toll Free: 800-886-LYME (5963)
Fax: 860-870-0080
Website: http://www.lyme.org
E-mail: info@lyme.org

Merck & Co., Inc.

One Merck Drive
P.O. Box 100
Whitehouse Station, NJ 08889-0100
Phone: 908-423-1000
Website: http://www.merck.com

National Alopecia Areata Foundation
14 Mitchell Boulevard
San Rafael, CA 94903
Phone: 415-472-3780
Fax: 415-472-5343
Website: http://www.naaf.org
E-mail: info@naaf.org

National Eczema Association
4460 Redwood Highway, Suite 16-D
San Rafael, CA 94903-1953
Phone: 415-499-3474
Toll Free: 800-818-7546
Fax: 415-472-5345
Website: www.nationaleczema.org
E-mail: info@nationaleczema.org

National Cancer Institute
6116 Executive Boulevard
Room 3036A
Bethesda, MD 20892-8322
Toll Free: 800-422-6237
Website: http://www.cancer.gov

National Institute of Allergy and Infectious Diseases
6610 Rockledge Drive MSC 6612
Bethesda, MD 20892-6612
Phone: 301-496-5717
Toll Free: 866-284-4107
Fax: 301-402-3573
Website: http://www3.niaid.nih.gov

National Institute of Arthritis and Musculoskeletal and Skin Diseases
1 AMS Circle
Bethesda, MD 20892-3675
Phone: 301-495-4484
Toll Free: 877-226-4267
Fax: 301-718-6366
Website: http://www.niams.nih.gov
E-mail: NIAMSinfo@mail.nih.gov

National Library of Medicine
8600 Rockville Pike
Bethesda, MD 20894
Phone: 301-594-5983
Toll Free: 888-346-3656
Fax: 301-402-1384
Website: http://www.nlm.nih.gov
E-mail: custserv@nlm.nih.gov

National Psoriasis Foundation
6600 SW 92nd Ave., Suite 300
Portland, OR 97223-7195
Phone: 503-244-7404
Toll Free: 800-723-9166
Fax: 503-245-0626
Website: http://www.psoriasis.org
E-mail: getinfo@psoriasis.org

National Vitiligo Foundation
P.O. Box 23226
Cincinnati, OH 45223
Phone: 513-541-3903
Website: http://www.nvfi.org
E-mail: info@nvfi.org

National Vulvodynia Association
P.O. Box 4491
Silver Spring, MD 20914-4491
Phone: 301-299-0775
Fax: 301-299-3999
Website: http://www.nva.org

Nemours Foundation
10140 Centurion Parkway North
Jacksonville, FL 32256
Phone: 904-697-4100
Fax: 904-697-4125
Website: http://www.nemours.org

Skin Cancer Foundation
149 Madison Avenue, Suite 901
New York, NY 10016
Phone: 212-725-5176
Website: http://www.skincancer.org

Index

Index

Page numbers that appear in *Italics* refer to illustrations. Page numbers that have a small 'n' after the page number refer to information shown as Notes at the beginning of each chapter. Page numbers that appear in **Bold** refer to information contained in boxes on that page (except Notes information at the beginning of each chapter).